Managing Community Growth

Second Edition

D0221915

ERIC DAMIAN KELLY

PRAEGER

Westport, Connecticut
London

Library of Congress Cataloging-in-Publication Data

Kelly, Eric D.
  Managing community growth / Eric Damian Kelly.— 2nd ed.
    p. cm.
  Includes bibliographical references and index.
  ISBN 0–275–97793–5 (alk. paper)—ISBN 0–275–97814–1 (pbk : alk. paper)
  1. City planning—United States. 2. Land use—United States—Planning. 3. Cities and towns—
United States—Growth. 4. Urbanization—United States. 5. Urban policy—United States.
I. Title.
HT167.K44 2004
307.1′216′0973—dc22   2004017544

British Library Cataloguing in Publication Data is available.

Copyright © 2004 by Eric Damian Kelly

Library of Congress Catalog Card Number: 2004017544
ISBN: 0–275–97793–5 (cloth)
       0–275–97814–1 (paper)

First published in 2004

Praeger Publishers, 88 Post Road West, Westport, CT 06881
An Imprint of the Greenwood Publishing Group, Inc.
www.praeger.com

Printed in the United States of America.

The paper used in this book complies with the
Permanent Paper Standard issued by the National
Information Standards Organization (Z39.48–1984).

10 9 8 7 6 5 4 3 2 1

To my parents and grandparents,
who taught me that good citizens can and should
make their communities better places in which to live.

Contents

Tables and Figures

TABLES

FIGURES

Acknowledgments

This book is my work and the opinions (and any errors) are entirely mine. The learning that it represents, however, comes from more than 25 years of work in the field. I have long tried to emulate the late Donald Schön's image of a "reflective practitioner," and I have learned a great deal about managing growth in rapidly growing communities from many clients over the years. I note particularly the opportunity to work with colleagues in growth-managing communities like Westminster, Hilton Head Island, Montgomery County, Rockville, and Lawrence, but I have learned from most of our clients and many of my friends.

It is of course essential to thank those from whom I take the time that I write. Those include my colleagues in the Department of Urban Planning at Ball State University—Profs. Frankel, Parker, Schoen, Segedy, Hill, Keys, Perera, Keuhl and Brown—I appreciate the support. My colleagues at Duncan Associates are also nice enough to recognize the value of my continuing to publish; in addition, other professionals there, including my long-time friend Jim Duncan, and colleagues Clancy Mullen, Kirk Bishop, Lee Einsweiler and Marty Hodgkins, have contributed significantly to my understanding of growth management.

My at-home family is smaller now than it was when I prepared the first edition of this book, but my efforts on this one would not be possible without the patience and support of my wife, Sandra, and the constant comic relief offered by our Polish Lowland Sheepdogs, Warka and Bozo.

I remain indebted to Ann Louise Strong, Jan Krasnowiecki, John Rahenkamp and others who contributed significantly to my education in planning and its implementation, and to the city officials in Westminster who had the confidence to consult with me—and to allow me to learn about growth management with them—when I was a mere lad of 30.

CHAPTER 1

Introduction

Planners in the United States now have more than three decades of experience with growth management programs. During the 1970s and 1980s, planners, public officials, lawyers and others wrote extensively on the subject, but most of that literature addressed the issue from one of three basic perspectives: "how to do growth management"; "how my community did growth management"; or "is growth management legal?" What is largely missing from the literature is a careful consideration of whether growth management is indeed a useful tool and, if so, under what circumstances. The original purpose of this book was to fill that gap. Now, a decade after its first publication, some additional evaluative literature (discussed in Chapter 2) is available but falls primarily into two categories: evaluations of particular programs or critiques of growth management programs from a particular perspective.

GROWTH MANAGEMENT

Growth management is a land and use planning tool. The types of growth management programs discussed in this book are those designed to regulate the location, timing or rate of community growth. Some of those programs directly or indirectly limit the amount of growth that can take place. Others simply control the timing or location of development without attempting to limit the total amount of development or overall population growth. Figure 1.1 compares growth trends in two Colorado communities, Boulder and Westminster. The two cities are about 20 miles apart. Each adopted a growth management program in the 1970s. The increase in population in Boulder from 1970 to 2000 was a little more than 41 percent, while

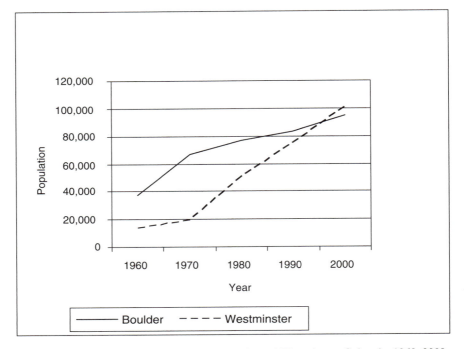

Figure 1.1   Comparative growth trends in Boulder and Westminster, Colorado, 1960–2000.

the growth in Westminster over the same period was 417 percent, although both had growth management programs in place from the 1970s through the year 2000 and beyond. Those differing effects are entirely consistent with the different intentions of the two communities.[1]

Clearly a number of different public policies may *affect* the location, time or rate of community growth—anything from construction of a new highway to a successful (or unsuccessful) economic development program can have such an effect. However, the concern of this book is with those programs that are expressly designed to regulate the location, timing or rate of community growth.

Many citizens and even some public officials may believe that most communities play a direct role in determining the location and timing of growth, if not its rate. That belief is wrong. The system of land use controls in the United States is largely reactive. Local governments review proposals from private developers and approve, disapprove or conditionally approve the projects described in those proposals. Thus, the timing and location of growth are both substantially dependent on initiatives from the private sector. For a variety of reasons discussed in this book, ranging from somewhat intangible "quality of life" issues to the need to plan highway and other infrastructure investment, local governments have a significant stake in the location and timing of growth. A small but significant number of local and state governments have addressed that need by adopting growth management programs.

This book not only traces the history and background of those programs and reviews them, but it tries to provide a context from which a particular community can answer these questions:

- Does growth management work?
- Is it appropriate for our community and the particular problems that we are trying to address?
- Is one type of growth management program more appropriate than another for our community?
- Will it have undesirable (or desirable) side effects?

A NOTE ON THE USE OF TERMS

Cities, towns, townships, villages, boroughs, counties and parishes make land use decisions in various parts of the country. Throughout this book, the term "community" refers to whatever form of local government may interest the reader. In some parts of the book, the distinction between cities and other forms of incorporated municipalities, on the one hand, and the unincorporated areas of counties, on the other, is important; in those sections, the terms "municipality" and "county" refer to those entities.

The structure of these local governments varies, but some group of elected officials makes policy decisions for each of them. That body may be a commission, a board of commissioners, a board of supervisors, a council or a board of freeholders. The principal distinction important to this book is that such a body exercises the legislative authority of the local government (some may also have administrative duties, which is not important here). Throughout this book, the body with such legislative authority is called the "governing body."

The early zoning enabling act, still in effect in many states, created the concept of a "zoning commission" as the adviser to the governing body on zoning matters.[2] Under a separate model law, more frequently modified by the states but still widely adopted, local governments were authorized to create a "planning commission" with broad planning responsibilities and with primary authority for subdivision control. That act also provided that the local government adopting the controls could assign such duties to a zoning commission, making it a "planning and zoning commission," the name still found in many jurisdictions.[3] Thus, the term "planning commission" is used throughout this book to refer to the local body with primary responsibility for planning and land use issues, regardless of the precise local name of that body; where those duties are divided between two bodies, the affected local government must make its own interpretation of how the comments in this book relate to the respective bodies.

Local laws and rules exist under a variety of names. Most municipalities have the power to adopt "ordinances," which constitute the broadest form of local laws. Some states now give ordinance power to some or all counties. However, a number of other states give counties land use control powers without ordinance authority; in those states, zoning and similar enactments are adopted by counties by "resolution." Under the early enabling acts, subdivision controls were adopted by the planning commission, rather than the governing body. Because planning commissions had no authority to adopt laws, the commissions adopted such subdivision controls as subdivision "regulations." Although most (but not all) communities now adopt subdivision controls through the same process as zoning controls, many practitioners still refer to subdivision "regulations." For purposes of this book, these distinctions are insignificant. The term "ordinance" is generally used to refer to local laws, but it is intended to refer to all local controls, regardless of how they are adopted. The terms "regulations" and "controls" are occasionally used interchangeably with "ordinance," and no distinction is intended.

A number of staff members of a local government are involved in the planning and zoning process. Titles vary widely, but for purposes of this book, the following terms are used: "planning director," for the staff person who directs the planning efforts of the community; "zoning officer," for the staff person who directs zoning enforcement and administration; "public works director," for the staff person who directs that department or division of the local government that controls roads, sewer lines, water lines and stormwater systems. In reality, two or more of these jobs may be combined, or a job listed here as one may be divided among several individuals with a variety of titles.

A number of private parties have a stake in the system. The following terms are used in this book to refer to those players: "landowner" refers to someone who owns raw land but who is not a developer; "developer" refers to a person or entity of any sort that turns raw land into a functional part of a community by installing streets and other public improvements and selling or leasing tracts of land (note that a developer may or may not build buildings); "speculator" refers to a person who buys land with the expectation of a rapid, "unearned" gain resulting from some public action such as granting a rezoning or building a new highway (see generally Chapter 5); "homebuilder" refers to one who builds homes; "neighbor" refers to a person residing near a proposed development or public project.

NOTES

1. John M. Snyder, "An Evaluation of Colorado's Attempts to Cope with Rapid Growth" (Ph.D. diss., Colorado State University, 1982), 92. See Chapters 3 and 4 for descriptions of the programs.
2. Edward John Kaiser, David R. Godschalk, and F. Stuart Chapin, *Urban Land Use Planning*, 4th ed. (Urbana: University of Illinois Press, 1995); Eric D. Kelly and Barbara Becker, *Community Planning: An Introduction to the Comprehensive Plan* (Washington, D.C.: Island Press, 2000); Frank So and Judith Getzels, eds., *The Practice of Local Government Planning*, 2nd ed. (Washington, D.C.: International City Management Association, 1988); U.S. Department of Commerce Advisory Committee on City Planning and Zoning, *A Standard State Zoning Enabling Act under Which May Adopt Zoning Regulations*, rev. ed. (Washington, D.C.: Goverment Printing Office, 1926).

3. Kaiser, Godschalk, and Chapin, *Urban Land Use Planning;* Kelly and Becker, *Community Planning: An Introduction to the Comprehensive Plan;* So and Getzels, eds., *The Practice of Local Government Planning;* United States Dept. of Commerce. Advisory Committee on City Planning and Zoning, *A Standard City Planning Enabling Act by the Advisory Committee on City Planning and Zoning Appointed by Secretary Hoover* (Washington, D.C.: U.S. Government Printing Office, 1928).

CHAPTER 2

Growth Management in Context

Growth management as a tool in the U.S. system of land use controls evolved in the third quarter of the twentieth century and developed rapidly through the 1970s and 1980s. Although growth management is itself a useful tool in the appropriate context, it is part of a much larger system. A basic understanding of that larger system is essential to an understanding of growth management and its appropriate uses.

AN OVERVIEW OF THE SYSTEM OF LOCAL PLANNING AND IMPLEMENTATION

Growth management is a tool to implement planning. The system of planning for future growth and land use patterns in the United States is enormously complex, particularly when compared to systems in other nations that have much stronger central planning functions.[1] This complex system provides a relatively complex context for growth management.

Corporations, families, armies and local governments are among the many entities that plan. Plans may address social, environmental, physical, fiscal or other matters. The kind of planning discussed in this book relates to the physical change in communities and regions through development and redevelopment. That activity is generally called "land use planning."[2] Although there is a strong physical emphasis in the field, it also includes related social concerns, such as the affordability of housing and the accessibility of the community to those who may not own automobiles.

At best, a democracy is not an ideal environment in which to implement planning. Reasonable minds can and will differ about what constitutes a desirable future, as well as about what means are best suited to achieve that future. If a community adopts a broadly participatory planning process, the process itself may become paralyzed by conflict or the resulting plan may look like a potluck plan, with conflicting, inconsistent and redundant provisions. The representative system of government, in which a smaller but presumably representative group actually makes decisions, facilitates the development of plans but does not ensure that those plans will be truly representative of community interests or that they will be implemented. The topic of planning in a democracy goes beyond the scope of this book, but it is important to remember that this problem contributes to the complexity of the context for growth management.[3] Regarding the initiative and referendum process lying at the heart of "pure" notions of democratic decision-making, Professor David Callies notes, "The kind of public participation that extends to absolute public decision making erodes, if not destroys, the planning process."[4]

Planning and land use control in the United States take place largely at the local government level (a small number of states are also heavily involved in planning, a subject discussed in Chapter 6). The United States contains more than 3,100 counties[5] and 19,000 municipalities.[6] Not all local governments are active in planning. Many municipalities are too small: 70 percent of the total (about 13,000) serve fewer than 2,500 people; another 19 percent (about 3,700) serve more than 2,500 but fewer than 10,000.[7] Few of the very small local governments are likely to be active in planning, although some certainly are. Virtually all of the 1,000 municipalities with populations greater than 25,000 have some sort of land use controls.

Counties participate in the land use control system in some states. Counties in other states have little or no land use authority, for two different sets of reasons. Some states, particularly in the New England and Middle Atlantic regions, are entirely divided into municipalities for general government purposes, with township governments providing local government services in rural areas. Specifically, in Massachusetts, New Hampshire, New Jersey, Pennsylvania, Rhode Island and Wisconsin every parcel of land in the state falls within an incorporated municipality or a township.[8] Although counties exist in those states and have a variety of duties (most typically social service and law enforcement), there is no land in such states that is located outside municipalities and under exclusive county control. In other states, particularly in the West, large areas of land outside municipalities receive substantial government services from counties; however, some of those states have made a policy judgment that counties should not engage in full-scale land use control. Even among local governments that have the authority to plan and control land use, a number of counties and many smaller municipalities do not exercise their zoning authority. Even allowing for all of those local governments that do not exercise such power, it is safe to estimate that well over 3,000 local governments in the United States are involved in planning decisions and perhaps as many as 10,000.

Several thousand local governments involved in planning over the vast land area of the United States may not seem significant. However, in heavily populated and growing areas, virtually all local governments are likely to be involved in their own separate planning and land use decisions. For example, in the Denver metropolitan area, five counties and more than two dozen municipalities make land use decisions; six of those cities had populations in excess of 90,000 in 2000. In the Des Moines region, a much smaller metropolitan area, there are two counties directly involved in the primary growth area, two other counties affected by (and affecting) it and ten municipalities making land use decisions. Within the Portland urban growth boundary, there are portions of three counties and a total of twenty-four cities; in the Chicago region, there are literally dozens of local governments involved in the system. Similarly, in the New York region, there are dozens of municipalities involved in land use decisions, and those municipalities are located in three different states. Also, in the Washington, D.C., metropolitan area, there are numerous municipalities, plus several counties, and the combination of those is located in three states[9] plus the District of Columbia, with its own jurisdictional complexity.

Including special districts (such as fire districts and water districts), the 2002 Census of Governments found more than 87,000 local government entities in the United States.[10] According to the 1997 governmental census, for which more detailed results were available, some 39,044 of those were general purpose local governments.[11] The 1987 Census of Governments found nearly 32,000 local government entities cluttering the nation's 115 Metropolitan Statistical Areas (MSA).[12] Although in one sense the figure is statistically meaningless, simple division indicates an average of nearly 300 local governments in each MSA; even if not meaningful for any particular MSA, that figure is indicative of the complexity of the planning problem. In 1969, the National Committee on Urban Growth Policy referred to this pattern as a "crazy quilt of political jurisdictions."[13] It has not improved.[14]

Local governments that have adopted growth management programs have largely been located in exactly such complex metropolitan regions. Each of the local governments in such a region has its own territory, its own concerns and its own interests. Further complicating the situation is the fact that not even the territories of these local governments are discreet. Those territories may effectively overlap and conflict. Through "extraterritorial jurisdiction" in some states and through the power to annex additional land in most, municipalities often exercise significant authority over lands not within their limits and thus within the primary control of another local government and possibly within areas of interest to others.

Although there are "regional planning commissions" in a number of metropolitan regions and in other areas, these are largely ineffectual in land use matters.[15] In a few locations, one or more local governments have entered into agreements to plan jointly for land areas of mutual interest and such agreements can work well. However, the fact remains that in virtually every growing metropolitan region, there are many local governments making decisions that do not form part of a logical and comprehensive regional plan.

Even within a particular local government, there are differing and competing interests. Planners may be eager to add more open space to a community, while the parks director, frustrated with recent budget cuts, opposes the addition of any land to the department's maintenance responsibilities. Fiscal and engineering considerations often dominate public works projects. The financial and technical goals driving the process may or may not result in decisions consistent with the more general land use goals of the community. For example, a public agency may choose a highway alignment based on engineering and cost considerations alone; the result of that decision may be to locate a new growth-attracting road-way in an area where the community really does not want growth. The differences among these interests become manifest in a variety of local plans. Most larger local governments have "capital improvements programs" (CIPs) that are often partly or wholly inconsistent with adopted land use plans.[16] Many local governments have separate plans for such substantive interests as parks, circulation (streets and pedestrian systems) and even wetlands plans, all of which may or may not be consistent with one another.

The federal government does nothing to make things better and in some ways confuses the situation further. Despite the reductions in federal spending for local government interests, federal capital expenditure on such public works as highways and sewer plants remain major influences on the timing and location of growth.[17]

Except in Hawaii, Florida, Oregon, California, Washington and Vermont (and now, possibly, Georgia), the state role is very similar to the federal role—little involvement in planning and a number of decisions on funding public projects that may or may not comport with local plans (see, generally, Chapter 6).

As if the system of land use controls itself is not complicated enough, the task assigned to that system poses enormous difficulties. Through the planning process, a local government attempts to plan for the future of land within its jurisdiction. Most of that land is privately owned and many of the landowners involved in a particular community have no idea what they will do with their land in the future. Some are happy farming their land now and have no plans to do anything else, although one or more of those very owners may cheerfully sell out to a developer within the next year or next decade. Other landowners may be holding the land primarily for investment, carefully seeking the best opportunity for sale. Still others may have plans that will never be implemented because of economic or other constraints.

A local government must try to plan for the future of such land, even though its owners, who are more intimately familiar with it, have no plans, impractical plans, impossible plans or plans that simply may change. Although some local planners would resolve that situation by simply dictating future land uses to private owners, residents of the United States relate closely to land, emotionally as well as financially and legally, and they generally resent perceived intrusions on their ownership rights. Most landowners in this country (and perhaps elsewhere) favor land use controls on their neighbors; few actively favor such controls for their own property. Thus, although most responsible owners recognize the need for some system of controls as a part of creating an orderly society, the political burden of proof generally remains on the local government to demonstrate why a particular restriction is necessary and reasonable. The system itself thus remains, in most cases, largely a reactive one.

To provide some basis for order to this potential chaos, the governmental system in this country has given to most local governments certain tools to conduct and implement land use planning. The primary tools are zoning and subdivision controls, both of which are concepts developed early in the last century in large cities and subsequently adapted to broader use. These tools arose from particular needs existing in those cities at the time and still best address those needs. Although in some respects, adaptation of zoning and subdivision controls to other needs has been surprisingly effective, large gaps remain. Because growth management programs attempt to fill two prominent gaps in the regulatory system (the "gaps" are described later in this chapter), it is important to understand the system to understand the gaps.

EARLY TOOLS

The earliest land use controls in this country are beyond the scope of this book, but it is important to remember that land use planning is not just an invention of the twentieth century. The first planning law in the country was a Spanish document called the *Laws of the Indies*. The laws were a series of pronouncements on urban design issued by the Spanish monarchy beginning in the early sixteenth century. Those design standards, which specified the dimensions of the town square, the orientation of major streets and general land use patterns, influenced most early Spanish settlements. The effects of the plans remain clearly visible in the original Spanish settlement areas of San Antonio, Texas; Santa Fe, New Mexico; and St. Augustine, Florida.[18]

Although lacking the monarch's broad authority, many early urban planners in this country owned or controlled the land that they planned, thus making the task a simpler one than is faced by modern planners. The railroad companies, which platted generally rectilinear blocks and lots along the railroad tracks on their grants of land, are prime examples.[19]

However, planning for and managing the patterns of development of contemporary U.S. communities is a far more complex task, involving multiple landowners, divergent interests and the democratic system of government. Contemporary U.S. land use controls themselves evolved from several different efforts in the late nineteenth and early twentieth centuries.

One was the tenement house movement, which was a powerful influence in leading New York to adopt the nation's first comprehensive zoning ordinance in 1916.[20] Responding to concerns about squalid conditions in which families lived in overcrowded rooms without light and air, reformists developed concepts of height limits and setback requirements designed to ensure that most rooms would have direct access to "light and air."[21] Height limits on buildings, now included in most zoning ordinances, were litigated in the courts and ultimately upheld in the U.S. Supreme Court before zoning evolved as a more comprehensive regulatory technique.[22]

At the same time, others were concerned about the impact of uses that many would call "nuisances." Particular uses may or may not have met the legal definition of nuisance, but they were industrial and some types of commercial uses that clearly had adverse external effects on surrounding uses.[23] John Stuart Mill puzzled over the problem of regulating "beer and spirit-houses" in *On Liberty* in 1859, although he concluded that a limitation of the number of them (the kind of approach that zoning or licensing might take today) would be an undue infringement on liberty.[24] Later, dealing with such issues at a practical level, the U.S. Supreme Court upheld the City of Los Angeles in prohibiting the manufacturing of bricks in a residential neighborhood.[25] An interesting aspect of the case is the fact that the industry was in operation before most residents moved into the area. Nevertheless, the high court upheld the city's police power action in closing it down.

Competition among incompatible land uses before the wide adoption of zoning involved more than the obvious ones between residents and polluting industries. Retailers in New York were a major force behind the ultimate adoption of a zoning ordinance there because the retailers wanted such industrial operations as garment-making banned from shopping areas.[26]

In short, zoning did not just appear upon the scene suddenly in the 1910s. Rather, it evolved not only from its European roots[27] but from a variety of efforts already underway in the United States to resolve specific land use and development problems.

ZONING

From the combined efforts of the housing reformers, the retailers seeking purity in their commercial areas and others came the New York City zoning ordinance of 1916.[28] The experience of the committee that drafted that ordinance provided the basis for the Standard Zoning Enabling Act, published by the Department of Commerce in 1924 and in a revised edition in 1926.[29] That Act provided a model that each of the 50 states adopted and that remains the basis for basic land use controls in more than 40 of them. Even those few states that have substantially amended (or, in a half-dozen cases, even replaced) the model Act, have retained zoning as the basis of land use controls.[30] Thus, the New York City ordinance, which was developed in response to turn-of-the-century big-city problems, became the model for land use control in the entire nation.

Zoning is a very simple concept. It provides for the division of the community into districts, or zones, that are most typically called "zoning districts." Within each district the community provides regulations that address three general sets of issues:

Use. The use of land and buildings falls into four general categories: agricultural, industrial (or manufacturing), commercial (or business) and residential. Larger communities may have a number of subcategories of each general category, providing for such special districts as neighborhood business, office, light industrial, warehouse and downtown.

Intensity. Zoning regulations limit the amount of a particular use that can take place on a designated piece of land. A community may regulate residential density indirectly through the specification of a minimum lot size (for example, a minimum lot size of 9,000 square feet generally allows about four dwelling units per acre, after allowing for streets) or directly, through a limitation on the number of dwelling units per acre. Communities typically express intensity limits in commercial and industrial areas by "floor-area ratio" ("FAR"), a number specifying the number of square feet of floor area of building permitted for each square foot of land (for example, an FAR of .5 would allow a 5,000 square foot building on a 10,000 square foot lot). Height restrictions affect the intensity of use, as well as the bulk of a building.

Bulk. Bulk regulations address such matters as building setbacks from lot lines or streets (sometimes expressed as requirements to preserve front, rear and side yards), and maximum building coverage (the amount of land that can be covered by buildings on it). Height regulations also affect building bulk. Although height regulations are perhaps most important as restrictions on intensity in downtowns and other commercial areas, they are important as determinants of building size in residential neighborhoods where intensity is established at one or two dwellings per specified lot.[31]

The use, intensity and bulk regulations vary from district to district within the community, although they must be uniform throughout a particular district. As indicated above, the major differences among categories of districts depend on use types. Residential subcategories typically differ by the intensities allowed in various districts, whereas commercial and industrial subcategories may differ as to both the lists of permitted uses and the intensities at which such uses may be conducted.

A recurring theme in U.S. zoning law and practice is the primacy of the single-family residence. Early zoning ordinances were based on the concept of a pyramid, with the zone at the top being the most restrictive and each zone permitting all uses permitted in the zones above it on the pyramid, plus some additional ones. A residential zone permitting one-family and two-family residences typically appeared at the top of the pyramid, with industrial or manufacturing zones at the bottom. Later, communities restricted the zone at the top to single-family dwellings. The pyramid has largely disappeared from current practice for a variety of reasons,[32] including the fact that, in today's litigious and environmentally conscious climate, industries are as eager to avoid incompatible (or complaining) neighbors as residents have always been.

Norman Williams cited three periods of regulation in residential zones.[33] In the early period, from the adoption of the New York City ordinance in 1916 until the early 1920s, he found that the emphasis of zoning was on providing light and air to residential units; in a second period, from the 1920s to the present, there has been a distinction among residential building types, differentiating single-family homes from duplexes, duplexes from townhouses and townhouses from apartments; and, in the current third period, the emphasis is on regulating total residential density.[34]

That was a logical step in the evolution to growth management. Residential density is a better measure of development impact than residential building type, because it addresses with reasonable accuracy the number of probable residents. The number of residents, in turn, determines the probable demand on everything from schools to the street system. The substance of Williams's third period thus coincides with the current interest in growth management.

The Zoning Map

The key to zoning is the zoning map, which identifies the boundaries of the various zones or districts in the community. Because the regulations vary by district, the boundaries on the map are boundaries at which regulations change, becoming relatively more, or less, restrictive. The map works well to preserve established areas in their present character, but it does not work well in undeveloped areas; in such areas, it legally institutionalizes public planners' best guesses as to what undecided property owners may want to do with their property at some point in the future. The politics of zoning—and the resulting litigation—focus heavily on the frequent local decisions to grant (or deny) property owners "rezonings," or map changes. Clearly such changes are necessary, because it is impossible for public planners to predict accurately how each undeveloped piece of property within the community will (or even should) be used in the future. Despite the importance of such changes, those who drafted the original act clearly were not too concerned with changes in it. In a book written a decade after the Act was written, the principal author of the Act mentioned map amendments only in a brief paragraph on the notices required for such amendment.[35] The book included no discussion whatsoever of the difficulties involved in making the substantive decision to amend this legal document.[36]

Although in a general way, the zoning map should influence the location of growth, it has relatively little impact for two reasons. First, the map is so frequently changed that it is often not taken very seriously.[37] Second, most communities "over-zone" by designating excessive areas of land for some uses. The latter phenomenon is a simple function of the fact that in most communities there is far more vacant land than development is likely to consume in the foreseeable future. It must be designated for something and communities typically designate it for agricultural (a designation which serves essentially as a "holding" zone), residential (a designation that is generally considered acceptable in most locations), or industrial (a designation that may encourage uses that help the economic base). However, because the zoning map does nothing to set development priorities among the various tracts of land in each category, private sector initiatives still determine which of those tracts develop in what order.

Clearly, this problem with zoning springs directly and logically from its roots. The creators of zoning designed it to solve problems of established neighborhoods, not of undeveloped areas. Within an established neighborhood, the problem of determining the correct zone for a particular piece of property is a simpler one than with a large, undeveloped area.

Despite these problems, zoning remains the dominant form of land use control in the United States. There is no survey indicating how many of the 39,000 general local governments in the United States have zoning, but most larger local governments in all 50 states have adopted zoning; Houston remains the major exception. Zoning is the most widely used local land use control, the one that evokes the greatest emotion and resulting local political interest, and the one that generates the most litigation, with tens of thousands of appellate court cases.[38] Despite the apparently dominant role of zoning in the system of development control in the United States, it is important to remember that it regulates only three things—use, intensity and bulk—and that it really does not address the critical issues of the timing and location of growth.

SUBDIVISION CONTROL

Clearly, there is more to land development than simply the use or intensity of the use of land. New development requires new streets, parks, sewers and schools, all of which should form a logical part of a larger system.

Many local governments use subdivision controls to address some of those issues. Although the definition varies slightly from state to state, a typical definition of subdivision is, "all divisions of a tract or parcel of land into two or more lots, building sites, or other divisions. . . ."[39]

Scott identified efforts in Los Angeles and Cincinnati in 1922–1924 as early major efforts at subdivision regulation.[40] According to Scott, the Los Angeles effort required that new subdivisions conform to a general gridiron pattern of principal streets, and Cincinnati based its subdivision controls on a state law that permitted cities that had adopted a long-range plan of streets and parks the right to regulate subdivisions.[41]

In those early days the focus was on roads and highways. Land developers created roads in the process of developing their respective properties. If the roads in one development had no relation to the roads in the next development or to the general road system of the community, the result became a maze, which is not only inconvenient to the public but can pose a hazard by limiting access for public safety vehicles.

Although it is not documented in the literature, early concerns with subdivisions were clearly broader than just planning concerns. Before subdivision regulations, a developer could simply grade in a "road" of whatever width he might choose and with few if any improvements. Eventually the unimproved road would become a rutted or muddy mess, leading to requests (or demands) from residents to improve it. The local government then might find that the roadway was too narrow or too steep or otherwise not easily suited to improvement, thus requiring the acquisition of additional land. Affected landowners, who were typically also residents and voters, undoubtedly greeted less than warmly any public acquisition of additional land. Furthermore, public officials faced the difficult choice of having to pay for the road improvements either from general revenues or from a special assessment of the property in the neighborhood. Using general revenues to make major repairs in one neighborhood was not likely to be popular among taxpayers in general. On the other hand, property owners in the neighborhood would be likely to protest the special assessment. Public officials who played no part in creating the problem faced the frustration of having to bear the practical and political burdens of solving it. Through advance public regulation they could require a developer to develop the roads to reasonable public standards, thus avoiding this unattractive choice later.

Although one major treatise cited early subdivision acts, including an 1833 law in Michigan,[42] later commentators noted that such laws before 1928 simply addressed the issues related to land titles, requiring an orderly process of recording plats with a consistent method of identifying blocks and lots.[43] Professor Robert Freilich identifies four periods of subdivision regulation, beginning with the "title" period just described and then entering a period, from 1928 through World War II, focused on subdivision arrangement and the completion of internal improvements. He identifies the post–World War II period as a third phase, during which communities began to look at the adequacy of public facilities and to address the availability of park lands and open space. Freilich's fourth period of subdivision regulation coincides with the growth management period addressed in this book and focuses on the same issues.[44]

Early subdivision regulations focused on road issues, but subdivision regulations have evolved easily to include requirements for many other public improvements. Although early subdivision controls regulated only the layout of streets, modern controls include construction and paving requirements, as well as the developer providing curbs and gutters, sidewalks, internal sewer and water lines, and streetlights and street signs. Some local ordinances also include requirements for trees along streets, bus stop benches or kiosks and other items, but the hard infrastructure items form the core of most subdivision controls.[45]

The use of "subdivision" of land as the trigger for the dominant form of development regulation, which is really a quirk of history, leaves modern planners with occasional problems. A large shopping center or apartment complex may be built on a single parcel of land and thus not be a "subdivision" in the ordinary sense of the word. If such a development is not a subdivision, then how does the community regulate the installation of infrastructure and its coordination with the larger infrastructure system of the community? Communities have developed a variety of solutions to this question (including a strained interpretation by one state legislature that such developments are to be construed as "subdivisions").[46] At the same time that this problem arises, increasingly restrictive "subdivision" control Acts can bring within their scope land divisions by farmers and others that have no development intent whatsoever and no real impact on the communities. The Arkansas legislature has taken a more rational approach, revising its subdivision Act to regulate "development."[47]

Subdivision regulations have been adapted effectively to contemporary problems. It has not been a significant conceptual or legal leap to go from requiring the improvement of subdivision roads that link the community's road network to mandating that developers similarly provide sewer and water lines that are part of a larger network. Yet, as the discussion below indicates, the issues of public facilities go far beyond what is built by the subdivider on the site.

HOW GROWTH MANAGEMENT FITS INTO THE SYSTEM

This chapter provides an introduction for growth management. It describes an existing and relatively complex system of planning and land use controls. Many developers and landowners believe that land is already over-regulated—without such a thing as growth management. With that system of controls in place, why is growth management necessary? As the Montgomery County (Maryland) Planning Board noted in its *First Annual Growth Policy Report* in 1974, "Comprehensive planning, at least in theory, has always sought to manage growth."[48] That same report noted that an effective management policy must address three key parameters of growth: location, timing, and cost. It further noted that the traditional model (zoning and subdivision controls) was "strong on location, but weak on timing and cost."[49]

Zoning was not designed to deal with change. As one commentator has noted in comparing growth management programs to zoning:

And, in contrast to zoning, which is passive and static, growth management is active and dynamic. While zoning defines the desired fully built town, the ultimate equilibrium, growth management seeks to maintain an ongoing equilibrium between development and conservation, between various forms of development and the concurrent provision of infrastructure, between the demands for public services generated by growth and the supply of revenues to finance those demands, and between progress and equity.[50]

Most local involvement with zoning occurs through the process of "rezoning," or changing the zoning map. However, the system is not well suited to such changes. Zoning evolved in New York City to preserve and enhance neighborhoods that were already largely built. Because of these historical roots, zoning maps are prepared as though the community is static. It would be more realistic to view a zoning map as simply a snapshot of the community and its zoning at a particular moment, because it will almost certainly change. A static map of an already-developed area (as much of New York City was when zoning evolved there) works reasonably well and serves the purpose of providing stability in those areas, which is indeed one of the principal purposes of zoning. In many cases, there is also political support of existing residents to support the status quo, offsetting the political pressure of those who may want changes in the map. Such support generally does not exist for preservation of what may be entirely arbitrary zoning designations in undeveloped areas.[51]

In contrast, a static map of undeveloped areas poses a number of problems. If the undeveloped portion of the city is small and it is surrounded by only one kind of land use, then there may be a particular use that is logical for that tract and there may be little difficulty in ensuring that such use ultimately occurs. However, where there are large undeveloped areas of land within a community, as there are in most communities, two types of problems arise. First, it is very difficult to project exactly what will take place where. A zoning map of undeveloped land may be viewed by some as a mandate, but considering the frequent zoning changes in most communities, it should realistically be treated as a "best guess." Further, whether the map represents a mandate or a guess, the community itself may want to change it in the future. Community plans prepared in the 1960s often included vast areas of vacant land along railroad tracks as future locations for industry. Today, the type of industry sought by most communities occupies smaller parcels and wants highway access, often in locations similar to those sought by retailers. This change of circumstance requires both that communities identify some areas formerly designated for other purposes as suitable for industry and that some other use be designated for lands formerly designated as industrial.

Through the process of updating their master plans, some communities actually change the zoning of raw land as needs change. However, there are political difficulties in accomplishing this. Landowners typically view any zoning change not initiated by them as disadvantageous and thus oppose such changes, sometimes in court. Thus, it is more common for such changes to take place in reaction to rezoning petitions from landowners and developers.

All of this means that the zoning map is not a very useful tool for planning capital improvements such as new highways, parks and schools. Few communities are rich enough to build major roads and trunk sewer and water lines into all undeveloped areas of the community. Thus, to the extent that a community wants to invest in infrastructure for future needs, public officials would like to know where and when growth will occur. Because the zoning map does not guarantee what development will take place in what location, many communities simply wait to see where and what development will occur before making such improvements. However, the result of that very practical policy is that such improvements are not available before development takes place.

Furthermore, simply providing such facilities where they are most convenient for developers may be beneficial to those developers but may be bad public policy. In most communities, it is easier to provide such improvements in some locations than in others. For example, it is easier to provide road and utility extensions to land directly adjacent to the developed parts of the community than to provide such extensions to land located further from the urban center. The substantial costs involved in extending improvements to more remote, or "leapfrog," development were well-documented in a 1974 study entitled *The Costs of Sprawl*.[52] Although other aspects of the report have been criticized, there is no serious question about the basic premise that it is more expensive to provide services to development that is located farther away (see discussion of the report and some critiques of it in Chapter 7). For several reasons, however, some sites contiguous to the existing community may be easier to serve than other sites that are equally close to the community. Possible reasons for such circumstances may include: topography, because sewer lines generally flow by gravity to the plant and it is thus difficult to serve land that is lower than the plant or that is lower than some point intervening between the site and the plant; elevation, because water pressure is a direct function of elevation and adequate pressure cannot be provided above some elevation; and the availability of existing improvements, such as trunk sewer lines, with substantial excess capacity in some locations but not others.

All of this is, in part, a function of time. If the state highway department expects to build a new loop freeway around the northwestern part of a community five years from now, land lying along that route will be far more accessible in five years than it is today. If the community is currently building a new sewage treatment plant expected to open in two years, large areas of land that do not currently have public sewer service now will have easy access to it when the plant opens.

Zoning addresses neither of these issues. It designates the future use of land, without regard to when, if ever, that will take place. A zone designating land as suitable for single-family homes on $1/4$-acre lots makes no distinction between land already developed for such purposes in 1963 and undeveloped land that may not be easily accessible or practically serviceable for many years. What the map does is to permit someone who wishes to develop the land for that purpose (subject to other local regulations). However, zoning does not offer the basis for a reasonable prediction as to when a particular parcel will develop.

Zoning may not even predict accurately *how* the parcel will develop. For the many reasons outlined above, the initial zoning selected for a parcel may be proved by later events to be "wrong" or at least no better than some other use. Even if it is not wrong, it may well change. Marion Clawson notes:

In the developing suburbs . . . zoning has proven largely ineffective. Where land is yet to be developed, land use zones, based upon a general plan or on some other grounds, have generally had little popular support when initially adopted or when changes are proposed. Such zoning may even have had negative results; it may be easier and cheaper to break the existing zoning than to conform to it.[53]

Although subdivision controls deal with public improvements, typical subdivision regulations only require that the developer provide such facilities on the site being developed. Nothing in typical subdivision regulations requires that adequate services leading up to the site be available for the development.

The availability of infrastructure in the larger community to support new development has become of increasing concern since about 1970, which is about the time that local officials in many communities became interested in the timing and location of growth. A relatively early survey of communities using some form of growth management found that officials in those communities were far more concerned about development timing than they had been in the previous decade.[54]

This increased concern came in the period in which Congress adopted the Federal Water Pollution Control Act Amendments of 1972 and the Federal Safe Drinking Water Act. These Acts, essentially for the first time, imposed serious penalties on local governments that allowed overloaded systems to deliver inadequately treated sewage to the public waters or inadequately treated drinking water to their residents.[55]

Local officials may have had other concerns. Most communities have piping and pumping capacity to deliver and receive far more water and wastewater, respectively, than they can effectively treat. Thus, the treatment plant capacity is the limiting factor for a community. However, the capacity of a treatment plant is not like the capacity of a pipe or a bowl, in which it is obvious when the plant exceeds its capacity. Treatment plants can physically allow excess water to flow through; the plant simply discharges the excess, or it may allow the excess flow to dilute the total output of the plant, so that nothing coming out of the plant is treated fully. Thus, before the passage of these new laws, it was possible for local officials to allow a plant to exceed its design capacity by a little or by a lot. Further, many plants installed before the passage of those laws used simpler (and less adequate) treatment techniques than modern plants and thus could be expanded more cost-effectively.

Under the federal scheme for environmental regulation, states, with pressure from the federal government, took an increasing interest in the quality of drinking water delivered to residents of a community and sewage received from them through the local sewage treatment plant. The result of this increased scrutiny was, in some areas, a significant number of moratorium orders, under which federal or state agencies prohibited local governments from connecting additional units to public sewer systems in particular. The broader result was clearly a greater interest of local officials in whether their systems could absorb additional capacity.[56]

Some of the pressure, of course, came from citizens. Many communities had excess capacities in their roads, parks and schools, in particular as a result of federal public works projects during the Depression and during World War II. These excess capacities served the initial spurts of growth in most communities. Most communities continued to expand their infrastructure systems, but many clearly did not expand those systems at the same rate at which the community was expanding in size. Overloading conditions on roads and in school buildings occur gradually and may not at first be of great concern to residents. However, as delays at traffic lights stretch from seconds to minutes and as school hallways become classrooms, the crowding takes its toll on citizen patience. Two well-known growth management programs adopted in the early 1970s—in Boulder, Colorado, and Livermore, California—were adopted by citizen initiative, reflecting citizen frustration both with problems resulting from the rates of growth in the communities and with apparent government inaction to address the problems.[57] Public officials adopted growth management programs to address directly these problems of development location and timing. Typical growth management programs, described in more depth in subsequent chapters, include:

Adequate Public Facilities standards prohibit development except where adequate (defined) public facilities are available. Such controls may not directly address the issue of the location or timing of growth. However, they indirectly regulate both, because in most communities adequate public facilities are not available immediately in all parts of the community.

Phased Growth programs regulate the location *and* timing of new development based on community plans. Although such programs typically regulate growth based in part on the availability of facilities, such programs may also weigh environmental, economic and general land use factors in establishing the phasing programs. Further, although adequate public facilities ordinances most frequently address the capacity of roads and of sewer, water and stormwater systems, phased growth programs often account for plans for schools, libraries and other non-infrastructure services in determining preferred phasing of growth.

Urban Growth Boundaries limit the long-term location of growth to land within a designated boundary. Although many communities have short-range boundaries beyond which they are unlikely to encourage or permit expansion, relatively rigid long-term boundaries are not common. Hawaii has used a form of statewide zoning to establish such boundaries around all of its cities. The state planning law in Oregon requires that local governments there include long-range urban growth boundaries in their plans and implementation programs. Boulder has created a boundary by purchasing an open-space greenbelt around the city.

Rate-of-Growth programs establish specified rates of growth for the communities using them. Although the ability of the community to serve development may be a factor in developing such rates, the controlling factor in such programs is usually a local perception of what is an "acceptable" growth rate. Although phased growth programs are likely to allow more development in some years than in others, because there is simply more capacity to absorb growth at some times than others, rate-of-growth programs impose a continuing standard on the rate of growth. Typically that standard is a percentage increase in the housing stock, such as those in Boulder and Livermore. Petaluma, California, has used a limit of 500 new dwelling units as the basis for its program for many years, although that number represented a decreasing percentage of the community's housing base.

Regulating the timing and location of growth may seem like common sense to a reader today. However, few communities were doing it even by the early 1990s, and when the first such efforts began they ran entirely counter to the trend. In 1969, University of Pennsylvania's Professor Jan Krasnowiecki noted:

With the exception of a lower New York court, *Josephs v. Town Board of Town of Clark-stown* [citation omitted; case discussed in Chapter 3], the courts have taken a skeptical view of the idea that inadequacy of school or other facilities, or the added tax burden of providing adequate facilities, is a legitimate reason for preventing development. . . . Accordingly, the principle that comes out of the cases is that a local government cannot justify delaying or limiting development because certain basic services and improvements are inadequate or unavailable, unless it also establishes a justification for the inadequacy or unavailability of the service.[58]

In short, the early efforts at growth management represented a significant change in the practical operation of land use controls and required a significant change in the legal climate for such controls.

Communities implementing growth management programs may adopt them separately from their zoning and subdivision ordinances or may combine them as part of a unified development ordinance. One of the frustrations of the development industry is that so many communities have added requirements to an already-complex system, rather than adopting well-designed and comprehensive programs, including all requirements as part of a unified regulatory scheme and integrated process.[59] However, as one study of the issue suggested, the procedural issue is really somewhat separate from the substantive one; it is possible for a community to implement a very comprehensive but also efficient system of land use controls or a less comprehensive one that also happens to be inefficient.[60] The management of approval procedures will be left to other authors and other times.

NOTES

1. H.W.E. Davies et al., *Planning Control in Western Europe* (London: Her Majesty's Stationery Office, 1989); Richard Wakeford, *American Development Control: Parallels and Paradoxes from an English Perspective* (London: Her Majesty's Stationery Office, 1990).

2. Edward John Kaiser, David R. Godschalk, and F. Stuart Chapin, *Urban Land Use Planning,* 4th ed. (Urbana: University of Illinois Press, 1995); Eric Damian Kelly and Barbara Becker, *Community Planning: An Introduction to the Comprehensive Plan* (Washington, D.C.: Island Press, 2000); Frank So and Judith Getzels, eds., *The Practice of Local Government Planning,* 2nd ed. (Washington, D.C.: International City Management Association, 1988).

3. For more discussion of the issue of planning in a democracy, see Eric Damian Kelly, "Planning v. Democracy," *Land Use Law & Zoning Digest* 38, no. 7 (1986); David L. Callies, Nancy C. Neuffer, and Carlito Caliboso, "Ballot Box Zoning: Initiative, Referendum and the Law," *Washington University Journal of Urban and Contemporary Law* 39 (1991); and Roger W. Caves, *Land Use Planning: The Ballot Box Revolution, Sage Library of Social Research; V. 187* (Newbury Park, Calif.: Sage Publications, 1992).

4. Callies, Neuffer, and Caliboso, "Ballot Box Zoning: Initiative, Referendum and the Law," 92.

5. United States Bureau of the Census, "Government Organization," in *2002 Census of Governments* (Washington, D.C.: U.S. Department of Commerce, 2002), Table 2. Counting Louisiana's parishes, some census divisions in Alaska, two new counties footnoted in the census but not included in the table and jurisdictions in some states where a city essentially covers the territory equivalent to a county (Virginia accounts for most of these), the actual total is 3,136.

6. Ibid. The actual number in the 2002 report is 19,429.

7. Ibid., Table 7.

8. Ibid.

9. Virginia, Maryland and West Virginia.

10. United States Bureau of the Census, *Census of Governments* (U.S. Department of Commerce, December 2002 [cited November 2003]); available from www.census.gov/govs/www/cog2002.html.

11. "Government Organization" (Washington, D.C.: U.S. Bureau of the Census, 1999).

12. United States Bureau of the Census, "Government Organization," in *1987 Census of Governments* (Washington, D.C.: U.S. Department of Commerce, 1987).

13. Donald Canty, Urban America (Organization), and National Committee on Urban Growth Policy, *The New City* (New York: Published for Urban America Inc., 1969).

14. United States Bureau of the Census, "Government Organization," Table 1. Although this report shows a substantial decline in the number of local governments between 1942 and 1972, there has been a steady increase in the number of local governments since 1972.

15. See discussions in Jonathan Barnett, *The Fractured Metropolis: Improving the New City, Restoring the Old City, Reshaping the Region*, 1st ed. (New York: IconEds., HarperCollins, 1995); Myron Orfield, *Metropolitics: A Regional Agenda for Community and Stability* (Washington, D.C., and Cambridge, Mass.: Brookings Institution Press and Lincoln Institute of Land Policy, 1997); Donald N. Rothblatt and Andrew Sancton, *Metropolitan Governance: American/Canadian Intergovernmental Perspectives, North American Federalism Project; vol. 1* (Berkeley, Calif.: Institute of Governmental Studies Press, University of California, 1993).

16. See Eric Damian Kelly, *Planning, Growth, and Public Facilities: A Primer for Local Officials*, *Planning Advisory Service Report No. 447* (Chicago, Ill.: American Planning Association, Planning Advisory Service, 1993), and additional sources cited there; see also, regarding more general capital planning and budgeting issues, Joseph H. Brevard, *Capital Facilities Planning* (Chicago: American Planning Association, 1985).

17. Mark E. Hanson and Harvey M. Jacobs, "Private Sewage System Impacts in Wisconsin: Implications for Planning and Policy," *Journal of the American Planning Association* 55 (1989); Peter Newman and Jeffrey R. Kenworthy, *Cities and Automobile Dependence: A Sourcebook* (Aldershot, Hants., England; Brookfield, Vt.: Gower Technical, 1989); "Transportation, Urban Form and the Environment: Proceedings of a Conference," in *Special Report Series* (Washington, D.C.: Transportation Research Board, 1991); Urban Systems Research & Engineering, "The Growth Shapers: The Land Use Impacts of Infrastructure Investments" (Washington, D.C.: U.S. Council on Environmental Quality, 1976). For further discussion, see Chapter 5.

18. Francois-August de Montequin, "The Planning of Spanish Cities in America: Characteristics, Classification, and Main Urban Features," in *Society for American City and Regional Planning History: Working Paper Series* (Hilliard, Ohio: 1990); John William Reps, *Town Planning in Frontier America* (Princeton, N.J.: Princeton University Press, 1969).

19. Reps, *Town Planning in Frontier America*; Stephen E. Ambrose, *Nothing Like It in the World: The Men Who Built the Transcontinental Railroad 1863–1869* (New York: Simon & Schuster, 2000).

20. Richard F. Babcock, *The Zoning Game: Municipal Practices and Policies* (Madison: University of Wisconsin Press, 1966); Edward M. Bassett et al., *Zoning: The Laws,*

    Administration, and Court Decisions During the First Twenty Years (New York: Russell Sage Foundation, 1936); Mel Scott, *American City Planning since 1890: A History Commemorating the Fiftieth Anniversary of the American Institute of Planners* (Berkeley: University of California Press, 1969).

21. Scott, *American City Planning since 1890: A History Commemorating the Fiftieth Anniversary of the American Institute of Planners.*

22. *Welch v. Swasey*, 214 U.S. 91 (1909).

23. See, generally, discussion in Daniel R. Mandelker, *The Zoning Dilemma: A Legal Strategy for Urban Change* (Indianapolis, Ind.: Bobbs-Merrill, 1971).

24. John Stuart Mill, *On Liberty*, 1986 trade paperback ed. (Buffalo, N.Y.: Prometheus Books, 1859).

25. *Hadacheck v. Sebastian*, 239 U.S. 394 (1915).

26. Babcock, *The Zoning Game: Municipal Practices and Policies*; Bassett et al., *Zoning: the Laws, Administration, and Court Decisions During the First Twenty Years.*

27. Babcock, *The Zoning Game: Municipal Practices and Policies*; Bassett et al., *Zoning: The Laws, Administration, and Court Decisions During the First Twenty Years*; Scott, *American City Planning since 1890: A History Commemorating the Fiftieth Anniversary of the American Institute of Planners.*

28. Bassett et al., *Zoning: The Laws, Administration, and Court Decisions During the First Twenty Years.*

29. United States Department of Commerce, Advisory Committee on City Planning and Zoning, *A Standard State Zoning Enabling Act under Which Municipalities May Adopt Zoning Regulations.* The process is described by the principal author of the act in Bassett et al., *Zoning: The Laws, Administration, and Court Decisions During the First Twenty Years*, and by a subsequent historian and commentator in Babcock, *The Zoning Game: Municipal Practices and Policies.*

30. Denny Johnson, Patricia E. Salkin, and Jason Jordan, "State of the States: A Survey of State Planning Reforms and Smart Growth Measures in Order to Manage Growth and Development," ed. Denny Johnson (Chicago: American Planning Association, 2002).

31. Eric Damian Kelly, "Zoning," in *The Practice of Local Government Planning,* 2nd ed., eds. Frank So and Judith Getzels (Washington, D.C.: International City Management Association, 1988).

32. Ibid.

33. Norman Williams, *American Land Planning Law: Cases and Materials* (New Brunswick, N.J.: Center for Urban Policy Research, Rutgers University, 1978), vol. 3A (1985).

34. Ibid., 856.

35. Bassett et al., *Zoning: The Laws, Administration, and Court Decisions During the First Twenty Years.*

36. Ibid. For a more detailed discussion, see Kelly, "Zoning."

37. See, for example, Marion Clawson, *Suburban Land Conversion in the United States: An Economic and Governmental Process* (Baltimore, Md.: Published for Resources for the Future by the Johns Hopkins University Press, 1971).

38. Babcock, *The Zoning Game: Municipal Practices and Policies*; Williams, *American Land Planning Law: Cases and Materials.*

39. N. C. Genl. Stats. Sect. 160A-376.

40. Scott, *American City Planning since 1890: A History Commemorating the Fiftieth Anniversary of the American Institute of Planners*, 207–08.

41. Ibid.

42. E. C. Yokley, *The Law of Subdivisions* (Charlottesville, Va.: Michie Co., 1963), 1.
43. Robert H. Freilich and Michael M. Schultz, *Model Subdivision Regulations: Planning and Law—A Complete Ordinance and Annotated Guide to Planning Practice and Legal Requirements*, 2nd ed. (Chicago, Ill.: Planners Press, 1995), 1–3.
44. Ibid., 3–6.
45. Richard Ducker, "Land Subdivision Regulation," in *The Practice of Local Government Planning,* 2nd ed., ed. Frank So and Judith Getzels (Washington: International City Management Association, 1988).
46. Colo. Rev. Stats. Sect. 30-28-101(10)(A).
47. Ark. Rev. Stats. Sect. 14-56-417.
48. Montgomery County Planning Board, "First Annual Growth Policy Report: Framework for Action" (Silver Spring: Maryland-National Capital Park and Planning Commission, 1974), 6.
49. Ibid., 35.
50. Benjamin Chinitz, *City and Suburb: The Economics of Metropolitan Growth, Modern Economic Issues* (Englewood Cliffs, N.J.: Prentice-Hall, 1965), 6.
51. Clawson, *Suburban Land Conversion in the United States: An Economic and Governmental Process*, 7.
52. Real Estate Research Corp., "The Costs of Sprawl: Environmental and Economic Costs of Alternative Residential Development Patterns at the Urban Fringe" (Washington, D.C.: U.S. Council on Environmental Quality, 1974).
53. Clawson, *Suburban Land Conversion in the United States: An Economic and Governmental Process*, 7; Tom Daniels, *When City and Country Collide: Managing Growth on the Urban Fringe* (Washington, D.C.: Island Press, 1999), 57–58.
54. David J. Brower, *Urban Growth Management through Development Timing* (New York: Praeger, 1976).
55. Clark Binkley, *Interceptor Sewers and Urban Sprawl* (Lexington, Mass.: Lexington Books, 1975); some of the consequences are discussed in Michael R. Greenberg, "A Commentary on the Sewer Moratorium as a Piecemeal Remedy for Controlling Development," in *Growth Controls*, ed. James W. Hughes (New Brunswick, N.J.: Center for Urban Policy Research, 1974).
56. Richard D. Tabors, Michael H. Shapiro, and Peter P. Rogers, *Land Use and the Pipe: Planning for Sewerage* (Lexington, Mass.: Lexington Books, 1976), 16; see further discussion of consequences in Greenberg, "A Commentary on the Sewer Moratorium as a Piecemeal Remedy for Controlling Development."
57. James Duncan and Associates, Inc. and Eric Damian Kelly, "Adequate Public Facilities Study for Montgomery County, Maryland" (Austin: James Duncan and Associates, Inc., 1991).
58. Jan Krasnowiecki, "Model Land Use and Development Planning Code," in *Final Report: Legislative Recommendations*, ed. Maryland. Planning and Zoning Law Study Commission (Baltimore, Md.: Colony Press, 1969), 82.
59. Fred P. Bosselman, Duane A. Feurer, and Charles L. Siemon, *The Permit Explosion: Coordination of the Proliferation, Management & Control of Growth Series* (Washington, D.C.: Urban Land Institute, 1976).
60. Ibid.

CHAPTER 3

Early Growth Management Activity

Although growth management became a topic in the literature beginning in the 1970s, and the best-known early programs were adopted in the late 1960s and early 1970s, three early efforts should not be ignored.

THREE EARLY PROGRAMS

Milford, Connecticut, provides one little-noted example of an early growth management program; that community adopted a growth phasing ordinance in the early 1950s. Under the Milford program, the community adopted a phasing map, establishing high- and low-priority areas for subdivisions. The community required that a developer in a low-priority area demonstrate that roads, schools and sewer, water and stormwater systems were adequate to serve the proposed development. The community limited the impact of the program on developers by allowing the phased development of even low-priority subdivisions, at the rate of 20 percent of the project per year.[1]

Perhaps more significant was the early effort of Clarkstown, New York, because it clearly influenced the efforts of neighboring Ramapo fifteen years later; those efforts in turn were well-publicized and influenced the trend toward growth management in a number of communities in the United States. Like Milford, Clarkstown adopted its ordinance in the mid-1950s. The planning and legal issues are well-documented by one of the authors of the original program, Norman Williams, Jr., in his treatise on land planning, although he modestly (and characteristically) does not take credit for his part in the ordinance.[2]

Clarkstown is in Rockland County, New York, just north of the New Jersey state line. For the first time, the town was easily accessible from the metropolitan area by way of the newly constructed Tappan Zee Bridge across the Hudson River. According to Williams, the intent of the plan was to:

concentrate new residential development in the area around New City [the county seat], and along a corridor extending south from New City to the intersection of the two expressways. . . . [A] roughly circular area around New City (together with an extension south towards the interchange) was zoned for immediate suburban development with 15,000-square-foot lots. An outer ring was zoned for one-acre development. . . . However, the most important planning principles were involved in the intermediate district, the second ring. . . . [That] area was zoned in a special district where residential development could proceed as of right at any time on one-acre lots, but the town board was authorized to issue a special permit for development on 15,000-square-foot lots, in any situation where that board could make a series of special findings, including a finding that school facilities would not be overcrowded.[3]

The only court to consider the Clarkstown program upheld it.[4] In evaluating the program after ten years in operation, Williams concluded:

In the ten years under the ordinance, 1955 to 1965, the predominant development in Clarkstown was in fact concentrated in the area around New City and in the corridor extending south towards the interchange. . . . An analysis of the subdivisions approved in successive two-year periods makes it clear that, speaking generally, the subdivisions approved (particularly in the [intermediate] district) in the earlier years were closer in, nearer the older settlement in New City, and that the location of such subdivisions tended to move farther out as time went on.[5]

One interesting aspect of the Clarkstown program is that, unlike some later programs, it preserved the opportunity for development of lower-cost housing types. Williams noted that "in the original Clarkstown ordinance, substantial areas of vacant land were zoned for apartments and relatively small-lot single-family development. . . ."[6]

Another program adopted in the 1950s was the urban growth boundary around Lexington, Kentucky, implemented jointly in 1958 by Lexington and Fayette Counties to protect the bluegrass country and horse farms around the city.[7] That boundary was not a regulatory tool but an intergovernmental agreement limiting the geographic area to which urban services would be extended, a topic discussed further in Chapter 5.

THE MARYLAND PROPOSAL

One of the most foresighted of the early growth management efforts was never adopted. Dissatisfied with the operation of traditional zoning and subdivision controls in addressing the growth issues in the Washington and Baltimore suburbs, the Maryland general assembly created a "Planning and Zoning Law Study Commission" in the mid-1960s. That commission took a broad look at the problems facing local governments in addressing growth issues and proposed a new program. Included in its final report is a proposed "Model Land Use and Development Planning Code" prepared for the commission by Jan Krasnowiecki, then on the faculty at the University of Pennsylvania Law School.[8]

That code, among other things:

- expressly authorized local governments to regulate the timing and location of growth, based in part on the availability of public services;
- addressed the problem of funding "off-site" improvements, such as roads and parks that serve multiple subdivisions, and required a "fair allocation" of the costs of such improvements;
- prohibited the imposition of development costs on developers to such an extent that it would preclude affordable housing;
- clarified the relationship between the comprehensive plan and zoning decisions; and,
- bound developers to plans approved by the community.

Had it been adopted, the proposed code would have placed Maryland nearly two decades ahead of most of the country. Many of the later growth management efforts described in this book involve attempts to grapple with the issues that the Maryland proposal addressed so clearly. Montgomery County, Maryland (see Chapter 4, under "Comprehensive Programs"), has addressed more of those issues than any other local government, and the state of Florida has tackled many of them in its state planning and growth management laws (see Chapter 6). Since 1992, however, no operating growth management program is as comprehensive as the 1969 Maryland proposal. Although the emphasis of this book is on the national experience with programs that have been adopted and implemented, Krasnowiecki's proposal for Maryland was so far-sighted that this brief history would be incomplete without it.

THE RAMAPO PROGRAM

[handwritten margin note: — timing of devo program via a points for infra. program — upheld by Court.]

The first implementation of a growth management program after the one in Clarkstown did not come for a dozen years. At that time, Ramapo, Clarkstown's immediate neighbor to the west, adopted a program that would become far more famous than the Clarkstown program on which it was modeled.

The Ramapo program was elegantly simple. Like many growth management programs, it was added to a local regulatory structure that already included zoning and subdivision controls. The new program required one more step in the public approval process, a step designed to ensure that some public facilities would be available to serve the development. Public facilities providing a basis for project review under the program included sewers, drainage, public park or recreation facility, school site, major public road and firehouse.

The ordinance allocated five points to each category (except firehouse, which received three points) based on how well the proposal met the intent of the requirement. For example, a project for which 100 percent of the necessary drainage capacity was available received 5 points, while a project with only 50 percent of the required capacity received only 1; similarly, a project with direct access to a park or major road received 5 points in that category, while one at a greater distance received correspondingly fewer points. In addition to receiving typical zoning and subdivision approvals, a project had to earn 15 of the 23 points under the growth management ordinance. The owner or prospective developer of land that did not meet the basic criterion had one of two choices: to await the construction of additional public improvements; or to construct, at her or his own expense, sufficient public improvements to bring the point total up to 15.

A key element in the Ramapo program, and an important consideration of New York's highest court in upholding the program,[9] was the fact that the community had adopted an elaborate plan, including an 18-year capital facilities program. The plan and the program together called for the complete development of Ramapo over that 18-year-period. The existence of the plan was clearly important to New York's high court decision to uphold the program; the court expressed grave concern about the potentially exclusionary effects of such a program but seemed satisfied that Ramapo had committed itself to a process of orderly development, rather than to one of exclusion.

Note that the Ramapo program did not actually ensure the availability of all necessary services. With enough points in other categories, it was possible for a development to qualify for approval with no fire protection or no drainage capacity whatsoever available to it.

Neither the Ramapo plan nor the program itself worked exactly as intended, and the community repealed the growth management program in 1983, after thirteen years of operation. The problems with the program were well-documented in a 1977 study.[10] Two of the findings were particularly important. Of the facilities used by the town as the basis for the program, the town of Ramapo controlled only parks, sewage collection (not treatment), drainage and some roads. Many roads, the proposed regional sewer system, schools and fire protection were the responsibilities of other entities, meaning that Ramapo's "plans" for construction of such facilities were more like wish lists than plans. The second problem was that the town never really followed the system, awarding unearned points because of a planning problem and approving nearly as many lots that did *not* meet the standards of the ordinance as were approved through compliance with it. In addition, the impact of the program was probably just to reduce Ramapo's share of regional growth, not to change the growth patterns. Like most economic trends, the growth pressures that temporarily overwhelmed Clarkstown, Ramapo and Rockland County had waned by the 1980s.

Despite its limitations, the Ramapo program was significant for several reasons. First, it was innovative for its time. Second, as Williams noted, the court decision upholding it was the "first opinion by a major appellate court approving

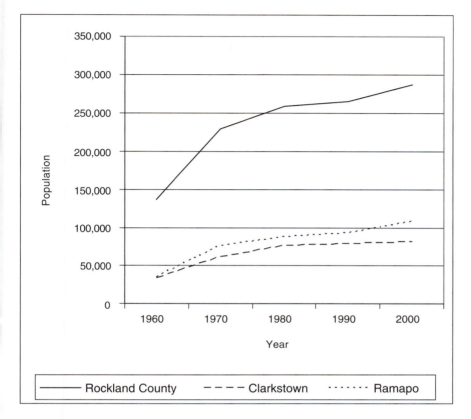

Figure 3.1   Growth trends in Rockland County, New York, and two of its towns.

an elaborate timing-of-development scheme."[11] Third, the program was well-documented in the literature, in significant part through the efforts of Robert Freilich, a land use attorney involved in its development.[12] Fourth, even if it was somewhat derivative of the Clarkstown program, that program never became well-enough known to influence widely the practice of planning,[13] whereas the Ramapo program became widely known, as the diverse citations in this section suggest.

- limit growth to 500 houses/yr.
- then a UGB.

THE PETALUMA PROGRAM

The other major growth management program that became well known in the early 1970s was that of Petaluma, California. That community's rate-of-growth program was also well-publicized and the subject of a well-known court decision under which it was eventually upheld.

Petaluma, like Ramapo, was far enough from a major city that it missed early waves of metropolitan growth. Located in Sonoma County, generally east of San Francisco, the city grew from a population of about 10,000 in 1950 to 25,000 in

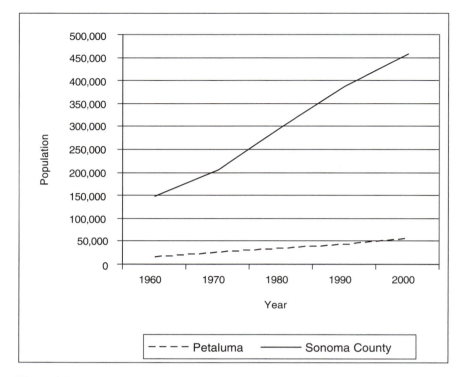

Figure 3.2   Growth trends of Petaluma, California, compared to Sonoma County, 1960–2000.

1970, after which it endured two years in which its estimated population grew by 5,000 (20 percent) per year. It adopted an initial moratorium and its first "residential development control system" toward the end of that growth spurt.[14]

The Petaluma program was simpler and far less interesting than the Ramapo program. All that it did was to establish a limit of 500 new residential dwelling units per year for the community. That limit was suballocated between single-family residences and apartments and between the eastern and western halves of the community. There were a number of exceptions for individually owned lots and other unusual circumstances. On a population base of approximately 35,000, it permitted an annual increase of approximately 5 percent in the housing stock. The program remains in effect, based on an updated plan but still using the original number of 500 dwelling units per year, a number that represents a smaller percentage of a housing base now serving 45,000 people.[15] Note, however, that in most years applications for new development have not approached the limit established under the program; construction of 500 dwelling units in each year since 1972 would result in a 2000 population substantially greater than 45,000.

Although the Ninth Circuit Court of Appeals and the U.S. Supreme Court ultimately determined to allow the Petaluma program to stand, in part because of procedural problems with a case challenging it, the only court that considered it in depth, the U.S. District Court, struck the program down, finding that Petaluma had "purposefully" limited its public facilities, including a delivery limit requested by the city in a water supply contract under which a water district delivered water to the city. The court found that the city did not have any significant or unresolvable capacity problems but rather that it was manipulating public facility capacity to limit growth.[16] In a footnote to its opinion, the appellate court indicated that it would also be likely to uphold the program on substantive legal grounds; however, there is no analysis in its short opinion to support that assertion and no response to the many problems that the lower court found with the program.

Like the Court of Appeals in the Ramapo case, the federal judge who considered the Petaluma program expressed concern about the potentially exclusionary effects of the Petaluma program; however, unlike the New York court, he concluded that the program was indeed exclusionary, finding, among other things, that the population goal selected by the community was arbitrary and unrelated to regional needs.[17] The Ninth Circuit Court of Appeals reversed the lower court, in part because it found problems with the use of the "right to travel" as the jurisdictional basis for much of the claim. The "right to travel" was a tenuous basis on which a number of early exclusionary zoning cases were brought into federal court.[18]

Petaluma's program, although less sophisticated than Ramapo's, had an equal impact on planning practice. It and the Ramapo program were the two featured programs in the second volume of what began as a three-volume *Management & Control of Growth* series published by the Urban Land Institute in 1975.[19] Like Ramapo, Petaluma had a professional who was dedicated to the program and who told its story widely—Frank Gray, who was planning director in the city during important years in the development of the program.[20] Gray and Petaluma's mayor, Helen Putnam, were frequent conference speakers in the 1970s.[21] Not coincidentally, Gray subsequently became director of planning in Boulder, Colorado, which modeled its rate-of-growth program on Petaluma's.

The Petaluma program has been a greater success than the Ramapo program in certain respects. Five years after its adoption, a doctoral candidate writing a dissertation found that the program had succeeded in reducing the growth rate of the community and helped mitigate some of the growth-related problems identified by the community, including double sessions in the schools.[22] Williams concluded that in its early years the Petaluma plan had significantly slowed the rate of growth in the community.[23] The program remained in effect in 2003, two decades after the repeal of the Ramapo program.[24] In 1998, when Petaluma had reached a population of 50,000,[25] voters in the city approved an urban growth boundary.[26] According to a 2002 planning document, the urban growth boundary included 10,300 undeveloped acres, with designated "expansion" areas totaling another 330 acres; with minor exceptions, the boundary can only be amended before December 31, 2018, by referendum to the voters.[27]

THE EARLY LITERATURE

A significant body of widely available growth management literature published in the early 1970s contributed to the spread of the concept. The Urban Land Institute and the American Society of Planning Officials (now the American Planning Association [APA]) both published reports on growth management in the early 1970s. Certainly, the publication of these reports in part reflected an already-spreading interest in the subject, but the publication also made information about the new techniques available to public officials around the country. Before 1969, there appears to have been only one lonely cry for any sort of growth management: a short article by Henry Fagin, then planning director of the Regional Plan Association in the metropolitan New York region.[28]

Thus, to understand the evolution of growth management techniques in the United States, it is important to examine some of the early literature in the field. In 1969, the American Society of Planning Officials published *Toward a More Effective Land-Use Guidance System: A Summary and Analysis of Five Major Reports* as part of its Planning Advisory Service series.[29] APA circulates publications in that series to subscribers automatically, thus guaranteeing initial distribution. The organization also sells the PAS reports to others through its direct-mail "Planners Book Service."[30] Although the report did not expressly use the term "growth management" and did not refer specifically to evolving growth management efforts in New York, California and elsewhere, it did provide summaries of five other reports that, at least in part, addressed concerns of planners in urban areas. Those reports, some of which are separately discussed, included:

- a *Model Land Development Code* proposed by the American Law Institute to replace existing zoning and subdivision enabling acts and to provide broader authority for more diverse and comprehensive planning and land use control;
- *Building the American City*, the report of the National Commission on Urban Problems, a commission appointed by President Johnson and commonly identified by the name of its chair, former Senator Paul H. Douglas;
- *Urban and Rural America: Policies for Future Growth*, a 1968 report of the Advisory Commission on Intergovernmental Relations, addressing the complexity of the governmental structure that attempts to manage growth, as well as the urban–rural relationship in a changing economy;
- a 1969 Canadian report entitled *Report of the Task Force on Housing and Urban Development;* and
- a 1967 report actually prepared by ASPO, *New Directions in Connecticut Planning Legislation.*

Each of those reports addressed a number of issues and topics going beyond the scope of the current inquiry, but Heeter's synthesis of the recommendations of the reports for a future land use control system was both interesting and helpful. Among the conclusions he synthesized from the report were that: a future land use control system should involve a dynamic concept of "land-use guidance" rather than a "static, end-state concept," as in zoning; it would involve the creative use of incentives and restraints; it would involve public land acquisition; it would recognize the difference between developed areas and undeveloped ones; it would be controlled by state goals and policies and monitored by a state agency; and the use of land use controls for exclusionary purposes would be prohibited.[31] As the descriptions of contemporary local and state programs in the next two chapters suggest, some communities and states have developed programs entirely consistent with Heeter's vision.

Earl Finkler prepared two reports published by the American Planning Association in the early 1970s, *Nongrowth as a Planning Alternative*[32] and *Nongrowth: A Review of the Literature*.[33] The titles suggested contemporary concerns with growth, reflected in the publication of two major population growth studies in 1972. One, *The Limits to Growth*, sometimes called "The Club of Rome Report," because of its origins from a group meeting in Rome, explored the implications of exponential world population growth.[34] It used a systems approach to explore the carrying capacity of the earth, with particular emphasis on the environment's ability to absorb pollutants and on the land's ability to produce crops to feed a growing population. The report proposed a model of "global equilibrium" through stabilized world population. The second study, of population growth in the United States, contained this expression of contemporary thinking:

In the brief history of this nation, we have always assumed that the progress and "the good life" are connected with population growth. In fact, population growth has frequently been regarded as a measure of our progress. If that were ever the case, it is not now. There is hardly any social problem confronting this nation whose solution would be easier if our population were larger. Even now, the dreams of too many Americans are not being realized; others are being fulfilled at too high a cost. Accordingly, this Commission has concluded that our country can no longer afford the uncritical acceptance of the population growth ethic that "more is better." And, beyond that, after two years of concentrated effort, we have concluded that no substantial benefits would result from continued growth in the nation's population.[35]

The U.S. report, often called "the Rockefeller Commission Report" after the Commission chairman, John D. Rockefeller III, dealt not only with the side effects of growth, but it challenged the very premise that "growth is good," or, more specifically, that growth brings economic prosperity. The report concluded with seven pages of recommendations, ranging from population research to recommendations that remained appropriate twenty years later—sex education, management of immigration, availability of abortion and sterilization in government-funded programs.[36]

Finkler's reports provided a local perspective on these national and world concerns about population growth. Drawing on both the Club of Rome Report and the Rockefeller Commission Report, Finkler explored the policy implications of population growth, at local, national, and global levels. He extended the logic of the Rockefeller Commission argument that "growth is not good" to the local level. In the first report, he identified four "alternative orientations" toward growth:

1. Growth is inevitable.
2. Growth equals progress.
3. Stop all population growth.
4. Growth is a variable to be influenced in pursuit of a desirable quality of life.[37]

✓ In the report, Finkler urged that planners should play a leadership role in establishing local efforts to limit or manage growth. "Nongrowth (in addition to logical, limited, planned, and other forms of growth) should be studied by planners and blended into planning considerations. The topic should be relevant in most communities facing growth, regardless of size or type of jurisdiction. It can be a mistake to deal only with the results of growth, while automatically eliminating growth as a factor in itself."[38]

Finkler and David Peterson prepared another work on the subject. Entitled *Nongrowth Planning Strategies: The Developing Power of Towns, Cities and Regions*, it was published by a commercial publisher in 1974.[39] It expressed a stronger editorial position against growth and expressed disappointment at Boulder, Colorado's failure to fulfill completely Finkler's hopes for it. He lamented, "Ever since I first visited Boulder on nongrowth field research in April 1972, I felt that this might really be the community to send a strong, well-formulated antigrowth message to the nation."[40]

Two other aspects of the book are interesting. First, Boulder was the only community case study included in the book, although Ramapo and Petaluma were probably more famous at the time. Second, in this book, not published by the American Society of Planning Officials (ASPO), which had published his earlier works, Finkler criticized his former associates at ASPO for being slow to include growth management as a topic on national conference programs and in its publications. He also took ASPO officials to task for changing the name of the first such program from one containing the word "nongrowth" to one describing "growth controls."[41]

James Hughes collected a set of essays for the Center for Urban Policy Research, which published them under the title *New Dimensions of Urban Planning: Growth Controls*.[42] However, despite the title, the focus of the book was on exclusionary suburban zoning and housing opportunity in New Jersey (see discussion of this topic in Chapter 9). The book presented a balanced view of the issues, discussing the pressures that led to such exclusion as well as the problems resulting from it. However, it added nothing to the real growth management literature.

In 1975, the Urban Land Institute, with funding from the Department of Housing and Urban Development, published the first three volumes in a series entitled *Management & Control of Growth*. The first three volumes all bore the same title, *Management & Control of Growth: Issues, Techniques, Problems, Trends*.[43] The eighteen hundred pages in these initial volumes from ULI provided the first broad and comprehensive look at growth management. The series made that information widely available to planners, local officials and others interested in the issues. In its introduction, it echoed the concerns of the Club of Rome Report and the Rockefeller Commission Report, as well as Finkler's restating of those concerns at a local level:

The ethic of growth in America is increasingly being challenged; no longer is it being accepted unquestioningly as a premise of progress. Its effects on the quality of life are widely debated, and its management and control are seen by many as essential elements of modern land use policy. In more and more communities across the country, the costs and benefits of continued growth are emerging as major public issues. There is hesitation over accommodating further development with its attendant consequences of greater numbers of residents and higher densities, economic expansion, rapid consumption of land, and alteration of environment.[44]

However, the ULI report also recognized that the issue was a complex one, with multiple interests affected and multiple points of view. The introduction continued, in the next paragraph, "At the same time, this trend has not been without vigorous opposition; dissent over implications of unwise growth restrictions has been heard from various business interests, property owners, builders, and advocates for the disenfranchised: the poor, minorities, the underemployed, and the aged."[45]

Volume I of the series examined land policy and environmental policy, presented the national and international debate over population growth, discussed land use controls and provided an initial look at growth management and one of its possible side effects—exclusion.[46] Volume II provided in-depth looks at and multiple perspectives on the programs in Ramapo and Petaluma. It examined one of the legal issues raised in some of the cases (the right to travel), provided a brief look at a variety of regulatory techniques for managing growth, discussed the impacts of growth on local government finance and examined the influence on growth of such policies as interim zoning and utility extension policies.[47] Volume III examined other regulatory techniques, including transferable development rights, planned unit developments and efforts to preserve agricultural lands. It also examined the respective state and federal roles in growth management, as well as the regional implications of such programs. Finally, it provided a broad look at the issues from the perspective of developers.[48]

Also in 1975, ASPO published *Urban Growth Management Systems,*[49] which provided brief descriptions of thirteen operating growth management programs, including those in Boulder, Petaluma and Ramapo. It also included an introduction to the legal issues involved in growth management and some discussion of the apparent effects of these still-fledgling programs. It included an extensive bibliography, much of it consisting of literature drawn from closely related fields and topics.[50]

Is "Non-growth" a Local Choice?

The early literature raised this basic question, which has largely disappeared from the growth management dialogue. However, it is worthy of brief consideration here, because it dominated so much of the early literature in the field.

Although Finkler was an advocate of "non-growth," he failed to address the question of how a community can stop growing.[51] The examples included in the 1972 report were all examples of managed growth rather than "non-growth." Many current residents of two of Finkler's examples, Los Angeles and Orange County, California, would probably question whether their communities were even valid examples of managed growth.

A 1975 study entitled *No Growth: Impacts on Metropolitan Areas* studied the effects of non-growth, but each of the examples was a former boomtown suffering from economic decline and substantial out-migration; none of the communities had consciously decided not to grow.[52] Whether a community can realistically choose not to grow is a question that is largely beyond the scope of this book. As a practical matter, despite Finkler's early efforts, few communities have attempted to stop growth entirely through growth management tools. The most publicized such effort, one in Boca Raton, Florida, would have imposed a limit on the number of dwelling units in the city, but the proposed cap was roughly triple the population level at the time that it was proposed. Thus, it was, at least over the short-run, anything but a non-growth plan. Although a Florida court struck down the population cap,[53] related zoning limitations remained in effect. St. Petersburg, Florida, briefly considered an actual population cap, but the city council defeated the measure on second reading.[54] The nature of the proposal, which included a cap that was lower than the current population, and its sponsorship, a council member opposed to growth controls, suggested that it was more a political statement than a serious proposal; however, it garnered four votes of seven on first reading. St. Petersburg politicians apparently then abandoned extreme efforts. The city's plan adopted in 2000 showed substantial growth since the 1970s and projected significant continued growth through the planning horizon of 2020.[55] Zoning changes resulting from early 1970s growth studies, however, led to a reduction of the theoretical zoning capacity of the city from a build-out population of 700,000 to 400,000.[56]

The Montgomery County (Maryland) Planning Board addressed the issue of non-growth directly in its *First Annual Growth Policy Report* in 1974. It stated in part, "In this report, the Board does not recommend a specific limit on the total number of people the County might ultimately house or the number that should be 'admitted' each year. The County is not sovereign; people have a right to move; and we are persuaded that such population 'caps' are both unwise and of dubious constitutionality."[57]

CONCLUSION

Clearly, these significant pieces of early literature were both a cause and a symptom of growing interest in growth management. In a 1974 survey of members of the International City Managers Association, 253 communities responded "Yes" to the question, "Has your community adopted policies to limit the growth of its population?"[58] The Urban Land Institute, American Planning Association and other organizations and publishers were in part responding to market demand, but the wide availability of these publications provided information about growth management to more communities. Thus, the experience with growth management from the early 1970s into the 1990s has been quite different from the lonely pioneering effort of Clarkstown in the 1950s.

NOTES

1. Lawrence B. Burrows, *Growth Management: Issues, Techniques, and Policy Implications* (New Brunswick, N.J.: Center for Urban Policy Research, Rutgers University, 1977).
2. Williams, *American Land Planning Law: Cases and Materials*, vol. 3A (1985), 185–86.
3. Ibid., vol. 3A (1985), 106–07; two footnotes and some parenthetical material omitted from original.
4. In *re Josephs v. Town Board of Clarkstown*, 24 Misc.2d 366, 198 N.Y.S.2d 695 (Sup. Ct. Rockland County, 1960).
5. Williams, *American Land Planning Law: Cases and Materials*, vol. 3A (1985), 108–09.
6. Ibid., 106, n. 34.
7. Heidi A. Anderson, "Use and Implementation of Urban Growth Boundaries" (Denver: University of Colorado, Center for Regional and Neighborhood Action, 1999), 4.
8. Maryland Planning and Zoning Law Study Commission, "Legislative Recommendations: Final Report" (Baltimore, Md.: Colony Press, Inc., 1969).
9. *Golden v. Board Planning of Town of Ramapo*, 30 N.Y.2d 359, 334 N.Y.S.2d 138, 285 N.E.2d 291 (1972); *app. dism.*, 409 U.S. 1003 (1972).
10. Hammer, Siler George Associates, "Impact on Ramapo Fiscal and Economic Conditions of the Town's Growth Control Ordinance" (Washington, D.C.: Hammer, Siler George Associates, 1977).
11. Williams, *American Land Planning Law: Cases and Materials*, vol. 3A (1985), 120.
12. Freilich and Schultz, *Model Subdivision Regulations: Planning and Law: A Complete Ordinance and Annotated Guide to Planning Practice and Legal Requirements*, 5–8; Michael E. Gleeson, "Effects of an Urban Growth Management System on Land Values," *Land Economics* 55 (1979); see additional discussion by several authors in Randall W. Scott et al., *Management & Control of Growth: Issues, Techniques, Problems, Trends* (Washington, D.C.: Urban Land Institute, 1975), vol. 2, 1–120.
13. This author has found only four references to it in the literature: Burrows, *Growth Management: Issues, Techniques, and Policy Implications*; Henry Fagin, "Regulating the Timing of Urban Development," *Law and Contemporary Problems* 20, no. 2 (1955); Krasnowiecki, "Model Land Use and Development Planning Code"; Williams, *American Land Planning Law: Cases and Materials*. Burrows cited an earlier edition of the Williams work as his source.
14. Michael E. Gleeson et al., "Urban Growth Management Systems," in *Planning Advisory Service* (Chicago, Ill.: American Society of Planning Officials, 1975); Scott et al., *Management & Control of Growth: Issues, Techniques, Problems, Trends*, vol. 2.
15. James Duncan & Associates, Inc. and Eric Damian Kelly, "Technical Appendix to Adequate Public Facilities Study for Montgomery County, Maryland" (Austin, Tx.: James Duncan & Associates, Inc., 1991); City of Petaluma, "Residential Growth Management System User's Guide" (Petaluma, Calif.: City of Petaluma, 1991 [est.] and 1987).

16. *Construction Industry of Sonoma County v. Petaluma,* 375 F.Supp. 574 (1974); *rev.* 522 F.2d 897 (C.A. 9, 1975), *cert. den.* 424 U.S. 934.

17. Williams, *American Land Planning Law: Cases and Materials,* vol. 3A (1985), 151–59.

18. There is a brief but clear discussion of the issue in Gleeson et al., "Urban Growth Management Systems," 70–72, and a more detailed discussion in David R. Godschalk, *Constitutional Issues of Growth Management,* rev. ed. (Washington, D.C.: Planners Press, 1979), 73–94.

19. Scott et al., *Management & Control of Growth: Issues, Techniques, Problems, Trends,* vol. 2, 121–210.

20. See, for example, Frank B. Gray, "The City of Petaluma: Residential Development Control," in *Management & Control of Growth,* ed. Randall W. Scott, David J. Brower, and Dallas D. Miner (Washington, D.C.: Urban Land Institute, 1975).

21. See a brief description of her activities at "50 Who Shaped Our Century: Helen Putnam, 1909–1984," *Press Democrat* 2003.

22. Mary Morgan Abe, "Urban Growth Management: Trends, Issues and Responsibilities" (Ph.D. diss., Claremont Graduate School, 1977).

23. Williams, *American Land Planning Law: Cases and Materials,* vol. 3A (1985), 158.

24. Dyett & Bhatia, "City of Petaluma General Plan 2025: Existing Conditions, Opportunities and Challenges Report" (Petaluma, Calif.: City of Petaluma, 2002), Chapter 6, 58. According to the cited study, prepared as background for a new planning effort, "the Residential Growth Management System is designed solely to limit the construction of new dwelling units to a maximum average of 500 allotments per year. The system manages the inventory of housing units but allows the market to dictate location and density."

25. Tobias Young, "Infill Likely as Petaluma Growth Confined," *Press Democrat,* June 13 1999.

26. Dyett & Bhatia, "Existing Conditions 2002," Chapter 6, 58; Young, "Infill Likely as Petaluma Growth Confined."

27. Dyett & Bhatia, "Existing Conditions 2002," Chapter 6, 58.

28. Fagin, "Regulating the Timing of Urban Development."

29. David Heeter and American Society of Planning Officials, *Toward a More Effective Land-Use Guidance System: A Summary and Analysis of Five Major Reports* (Chicago, Ill.: American Society of Planning Officials, 1969).

30. Found at www.planning.org/bookservice/.

31. Heeter and American Society of Planning Officials, *Toward a More Effective Land-Use Guidance System: A Summary and Analysis of Five Major Reports,* 7, 8.

32. Earl Finkler, "Nongrowth as a Planning Alternative: A Preliminary Examination of an Emerging Issue," in *Planning Advisory Service* (Chicago: American Society of Planning Officials, 1972).

33. Earl Finkler, "Nongrowth: A Review of the Literature," in *Planning Advisory Service* (Chicago: American Society of Planning Officials, 1973).

34. Donella H. Meadows and Club of Rome, *The Limits to Growth: A Report for the Club of Rome's Project on the Predicament of Mankind* (New York: Universe Books, 1972).

35. Commission on Population Growth and the American Future, "Population and the American Future" (Washington, D.C.: Commission on Population Growth and the American Future, 1972).

36. Ibid.

37. Finkler, "Nongrowth as a Planning Alternative: A Preliminary Examination of an Emerging Issue," 2.
38. Ibid.
39. Earl Finkler and David Lee Peterson, *Nongrowth Planning Strategies: The Developing Power of Towns, Cities, and Regions* (New York: Praeger, 1974).
40. Ibid., 33.
41. Ibid., 62–70.
42. James W. Hughes, *New Dimensions of Urban Planning: Growth Controls, New Dimensions of Urban Planning Series*, vol. 1 (New Brunswick, N.J.: Center for Urban Policy Research, Rutgers, The State University of New Jersey, 1974).
43. Scott et al., *Management & Control of Growth: Issues, Techniques, Problems, Trends*.
44. Ibid., vol. 1, 2 (footnote omitted).
45. Ibid., vol. 1, 2.
46. Ibid., vol. 1.
47. Ibid., vol. 2.
48. Ibid., vol. 3.
49. Gleeson et al., "Urban Growth Management Systems."
50. Ibid., 115–38.
51. Finkler, "Nongrowth as a Planning Alternative: A Preliminary Examination of an Emerging Issue"; Finkler, "Nongrowth: A Review of the Literature"; Finkler and Peterson, *Nongrowth Planning Strategies: The Developing Power of Towns, Cities, and Regions*.
52. Edgar Rust, *No Growth: Impacts on Metropolitan Areas* (Lexington, Mass.: Lexington Books, 1975).
53. *City of Boca Raton v. Boca Villas Corp.*, 371 So.2d 154 (Fla. App. 1979). For a related discussion of growth strategies in Boca Raton in that period, see Charles E. Cobb, Jr., "A Developer's View of Boca Raton"; ECO Northwest Inc., "Growth Management Study of Boca Raton"; and Marie L. York, "Boca Raton's Changing Approach"—all in *Growth Management: Keeping on Target?* ed. Douglas R. Porter (Washington, D.C.: Urban Land Institute, 1986).
54. "25,000 in St. Petersburg, Florida, to Be Deported? To Kuwait?" *Planning*, April–May 1974.
55. City of St. Petersburg. Development Services Department. St. Petersburg, "St. Petersburg Comprehensive Plan" (St. Petersburg, Fla.: Development Services Department, 2000).
56. Ibid., Chapter 1, GID-8.
57. Montgomery County Planning Board, "First Annual Growth Policy Report: Framework for Action," 6.
58. Cited in David E. Dowall, "An Examination of Population-Growth-Managing Communities," *Policy Studies Journal* 9 (1980).

CHAPTER 4

Types of Contemporary Growth Management Regulations

This chapter describes contemporary growth management programs in operation. Fifteen years elapsed between the conclusion of the events in the previous chapter's history and the date when the first edition of this book was prepared, but the history of that period is best told by describing the contemporary programs that grew out of it, rather than by presenting a continuing historical narrative. The decade between the two editions of this book (1993 to 2004) saw continued refinement of growth management programs at the local levels, but the major innovations were in state legislation and are discussed in Chapter 6. The descriptions of the programs provided in this chapter provide the context for the analysis contained in the last part of the book.

PROGRAM TYPES

There are four basic types of regulatory growth management programs in effect today:

- Adequate public facilities (concurrency) requirements
- Growth phasing programs, including urban service limits
- Urban growth boundaries
- Rate-of-growth programs

The programs are quite different in philosophy, operation and effect. Some communities have adopted more comprehensive regulatory structures that include aspects of more than one of these programs, but the programs themselves are quite distinct.

ADEQUATE PUBLIC FACILITIES REQUIREMENTS

Subdivision regulations, described in Chapter 2, require that public improvements, such as roads, drainage facilities, utility lines and even streetlights and street signs, be provided within the subdivision. Some communities use the subdivision process to require developers to provide fringe facilities such as a turning lane or a traffic light at the entrance to a new development.

Nothing in a typical set of local subdivision regulations, however, addresses the larger community issues:

- Can the street outside the development, or the street or highway into which it in turn connects, absorb more traffic?
- Does the sewer line in the area have additional capacity, or is there even a sewer line in the area?
- Can the drainage channels downstream from the site handle additional run-off?
- Does the water system have enough raw water, enough flow and enough pressure to serve the site?
- Do the central sewer and water treatment plants have enough additional capacity to serve this development?

These are all questions to which there are readily ascertainable engineering answers. A sewer line is either full or it is not. Similarly, a water treatment plant and a drainage system have determinable capacities. The traffic capacity of a road involves some judgment calls, all revolving around the question of how much congestion the public is willing to tolerate at rush hour; however, once that judgment has been made, the determination of whether the road can handle additional traffic within those parameters can be objectively answered.

Some communities may also want to ask questions that are somewhat more difficult to answer:

- Can the schools hold additional students? If there is excess capacity in the schools, is it located near the area where the proposed development will occur?
- Can the police department serve the area?
- Will there be adequate fire protection?
- Can the public library serve the new development?

Although there are cases in which the answer to one of these questions is an unequivocal "No," in many cases the judgment is more complex. Driving down another mile or so of streets in a suburban area will probably not greatly tax a busy police department. Assuming that an additional 100 miles of street to patrol would indeed tax most departments, the question becomes, "where is the breaking point?" Although a school may be "at capacity," it is always possible to squeeze in a few more rows of desks; when does the capacity really become a problem? Montgomery County, Maryland, has for a number of years measured capacity for "clusters" of schools in a geographic area, recognizing that shifting attendance boundaries is a method that, in some cases, may address capacity problems.

Typical subdivision regulations simply do not address these very basic community issues. Some might argue that zoning should be tailored to the development capacity of a site, as determined by public facility capacities. That argument misses a fundamental point, which is that, although most of the zoning map is relatively static, the capacity of public facilities changes constantly as new facilities are built and new development absorbs existing capacity. If the community prepared a zoning map designating permitted uses and intensities based on available capacities in 1999, it was almost certain to be wrong by the time this book is published. Certainly most communities change small parts of the zoning map each year, but most of the map remains basically the same from year to year; these public facility capacities change literally on a daily basis. Thus, attempting to map the capacities with anything other than a dynamic, automated system makes little sense; to run such a constantly changing map through the rigors of official adoption involved in approving a zoning map, often requiring several weeks in the process, makes no sense. Even with the increasing implementation of geographic information systems (GIS) to track local data, by 2003 the author had seen no systems that combined the dynamic capacity data of large infrastructure systems with automated, area-specific capacity computations. In other words, it was still necessary—and probably will be for the foreseeable future—to have human intervention to recalculate area capacities, area by area, based on data available from automated systems containing infrastructure data. The only exception is in traffic, in which complex modeling systems track capacity by "Traffic Analysis Zones."[1]

Thus, many communities now adopt ordinances requiring that developments not be approved unless adequate public facilities are currently available, or will be available by the time demand from the new development requires that capacity. In Florida the concept is called "concurrency" and is mandatory under state law there.[2] For example, Broward County, Florida (Ft. Lauderdale is the county seat), requires that development proposals meet adequate public facility requirements for ten different types of facilities: regional roadway network; road rights-of-way; access to major and collector roads; surface water (stormwater) management; water supply; sewage treatment; solid waste collection and disposal; regional and local parks; school sites and buildings; and police and fire protection.[3] Vermont's Act 250 (see Chapter 6) contained a very similar list.[4] Colorado has long required that counties make findings as to the adequacy of water supply and wastewater treatment arrangements before approving subdivisions.[5]

One without a great deal of experience in planning matters might reasonably ask how communities have survived without having such basic requirements in their local ordinances. The answer is, "Often rather poorly."

If community growth is moderate, excess capacity in existing systems may be adequate to absorb additional growth. Furthermore, to some extent, local residents may tolerate increased traffic congestion and crowding in the schools as necessary results of growth. In a growing community, however, eventually some system is likely to fail. The result in such circumstances is typically a building "moratorium," in which the community refuses to issue building permits for new development.[6] In Livermore, California, a moratorium was adopted by citizen initiative, resulting from obvious frustration with the impacts of growth. The initiative imposed a moratorium on the issuance of building permits until double sessions in the school were eliminated, water rationing was eliminated and sewage treatment was brought into full compliance with applicable regulations.[7] The California Supreme Court upheld the program.[8] Livermore subsequently replaced the moratorium with a rate-of-growth program.[9] A proposed new General Plan in 2003 actually projected annexation of additional territory by the city, particularly to the north and northwest.[10] Projected growth under the plan, however, was limited by growth boundaries adopted before the planning process for the 2003 proposal and then incorporated into the plan; the southern growth boundary was adopted by another citizen initiative in 2000; and the northern growth boundary was adopted by city council in 2002.[11] Growth remained an issue, however, with council candidates in 2003 debating the merits of a separate, northern growth boundary adopted by the city council in 2002.[12]

The Livermore case raises an additional issue that should be mentioned briefly, although a detailed analysis of it is beyond the scope of this work. Since the first planning and zoning enabling acts were written in the 1920s, there has been an underlying notion that planning should provide guidelines for zoning and land use decisions, as well as capital investments and other community decisions. Although that notion has at times been lost in practice, the opportunity for planning remains and local procedures that involve the planning commission in all or most such decisions are designed to enhance that opportunity. When the system fails to the point that the governing body delegates control of the policy issue to the citizens of the community through referendum, the community loses the opportunity for planning. There is no logical way for the voters as a body politic to engage in rational planning.[13]

A moratorium is a worst-case result for all parties. Because the moratorium generally takes effect at the building permit stage, it comes after the community has granted development approval. That often occurs at both the zoning and subdivision stage, and sometimes after developers have made significant investments in site improvements. A developer fares better under a program that denies a development proposal early in the process due to a lack of public facilities than with one that allows the development to proceed, with a substantial investment in the project, and then stops the project before it reaches the last step before generating sales and a recovery of investment. The problem can be large. For example, when Westminster, Colorado, prepared a detailed study of its development capacities and demands prior to adopting the second phase of a growth management plan in 1978, it found that its governing body and planning commission had approved far more development than the city could serve in the reasonable future. Developments (and parts of developments) approved by the city but not yet containing buildings included: 3,630 "permit-ready" platted lots, for which all city requirements had been completed; more than 1,000 additional lots that were platted but unimproved and thus not "permit-ready"; more than 2,000 acres (not lots) of potential residential development in approved, active development; and an additional 2,500 acres of potential residential development in approved but currently inactive projects. To place those figures in perspective, the city by that time had enough capacity to serve only 2,600 additional dwelling units (fewer than the number that could be placed on "permit-ready" lots) over the subsequent two- to three-year period.[14] Westminster's problem was compounded by the fact that it needed the "tap fees" (connection fees imposed on new development, now often called "impact fees") from new development to amortize substantial debt incurred in the early 1970s to extend major utility lines into undeveloped and developing areas.[15]

The circumstances of a Westminster or a Livermore reflect a lack of planning and, in the face of significant demand (which both Livermore and Westminster encountered), a very real community crisis. With a significant investment held in abeyance, perhaps indefinitely, a rational developer may see little choice but to sue. However, public officials in such a community are likely to be little happier with the moratorium than the development community. A community often adopts a moratorium because political pressure or their duties as public officials preclude their allowing continuing overloads on public systems. For example, Westminster needed the revenue from new development to amortize bonded indebtedness on an extensive network of sewer and water lines constructed into developing areas. The city council there adopted an initial brief moratorium and a subsequent growth management program in spite of that need, because the city lacked the treatment plant capacity and raw water necessary to serve the demand.[16]

Just understanding the problem is not enough; a community needs adequate public facilities standards in its local ordinances. Chester, Connecticut, denied subdivision approval to a project for which the local planning commission found that the road leading to the subdivision was "inadequate to provide safe access and egress to the proposed lots for either residents or emergency vehicles." The Connecticut Supreme Court reversed the town's decision, because there was nothing in the subdivision ordinance requiring adequate access to the site, and the developer had apparently agreed to meet all the requirements that were in the ordinance.[17]

How do adequate public facilities standards manage growth? There are two answers to that question. First, one of the dominant concerns in rapidly growing communities is the availability of public services; adequate public facilities standards address that concern directly, by insuring that new development does not take place unless the facilities are available to support it. Second, an adequate public facilities ordinance directly affects the location of growth, by providing additional "incentives" to ensure that growth locates near existing public facilities (see more detailed discussion in Chapter 5).

The goal of Adequate Public Facility (APF) regulations is to ensure that new development occurs only when and where there is actual facility capacity to serve that development. The leading efforts in implementing APF controls are in Florida, which has mandated "concurrency" through state law.[18] Concurrency is a comprehensive program intended to ensure that adequacy of public facilities for new development exists; APF regulations are one part of such a program. One commentator provides this description of Florida's concurrency law and regulations:

Concurrency is a legislatively enacted growth management tool for ensuring the availability of adequate public facilities and services to accommodate development. The foundation for a legally viable concurrency system is the formulation and implementation of a capital improvements plan for delivering essential public facilities in a timely manner by linking the approval of new development to the current and future availability of adequate public facilities. Ideally, concurrency regulations should seek to avoid the necessity for any moratoria on development by ensuring that both existing and planned public facilities are available as needed in light of a community's growth. . . . A capital improvements program must be set forth in the local government's comprehensive plan and establish both LOS standards for the facilities subject to concurrency and present the means for meeting the LOS standards. Development impacts that result in service levels below the adopted LOS standards will not be allowed.[19]

Note that APF regulations are only one part of concurrency—and, as the placement of the reference at the end of the quoted material suggests, it is not necessarily the most important. An effective program to ensure the adequacy of public facilities for new development must include multiple elements:

- A **comprehensive plan** for the area in which concurrency is an issue.
- **Functional plans for affected systems,** including water, wastewater, roads and other public facilities.
- A **capital improvements program** based on the comprehensive plan and showing what facilities will be built to accommodate the growth and development patterns shown in the comprehensive plan.
- A **means of financing** the capital improvements program; most communities today include some means of ensuring developer participation in financing the growth-related infrastructure costs.
- **Design-** or **performance-based regulations** drafted to ensure that new development will be served by adequate public facilities.
- An optional element, which is some form of **capacity allocation** when there is a shortage in a critical facility—normally water or sewer.

GROWTH PHASING PROGRAMS

A growth phasing program regulates the location and/or timing of new development, generally based on the availability, or presumed availability, of public facilities. In principle such a program is thus somewhat like an adequate public facilities program; however, in practice it is quite different. The most effective such programs are coordinated with capital improvements planning, which ensures that new facilities will be made available in the areas planned for growth (see Chapter 5).

The Ramapo program, described in Chapter 3, is an early example of a growth phasing program. It focused primarily on the timing of growth by allocating points to a proposed development based on the availability of public improvements; it was coupled with a plan that called for the installation of necessary public improvements throughout the community over an 18-year period (see, generally, Chapter 3 and sources cited there). The concept of the program was that development would take place generally where public facilities were readily available, enabling developers to earn the "points" necessary under the program, before it took place in areas with few or no public facilities. The timing of development would thus generally follow the timing of public improvements, as described in the plan.

The Clarkstown program, also described in Chapter 3, was a growth phasing program more clearly directed at locational phasing. To quote again from Norman Williams, the intent of the Clarkstown plan was to "concentrate new residential development in the area around New City, and along a corridor extending south from New City to the intersection of the two expressways."[20]

Although both programs were more effective in ensuring the availability of at least some public facilities than a traditional program, neither guaranteed that all public facilities would be available. Recall, for example, that in Ramapo a total of 23 points signified the immediate availability of all designated public facilities, but the program required only 15 points. It would have been theoretically possible under the Ramapo program to obtain development approval for a project with no road access or completely inadequate off-site drainage capacity. Such an extreme case might have been unlikely to occur, but it is not at all improbable that, even under such a program, a community may approve a development without the full availability of public facilities.

Growth phasing remains a popular type of growth management program. For example, four out of eight programs included in a national study of large-scale growth management programs were classified by the authors as "growth phasing" programs.[21] Those included a comprehensive growth management package in Montgomery County, Maryland, described in more depth below, and the Westminster program, that also includes adequate public facilities requirements. However, it also included programs in San Jose and Livermore, California, which are based entirely on the concept of growth phasing.

The Livermore program, since abandoned, was largely based on timing.[22]

San Jose, California, phases growth in several specific geographic areas of the city.[23] The city's plan has evolved into a comprehensive program of growth management, including:

- **Urban Growth Boundary**: Establishes the ultimate limit of urbanization in San Jose.

- **Urban Service Area Boundary**: Defines the area in the city where urban services are, or will be, available to serve urban development.

- **Infill Development**: Controls a variety of services costs through increased efficiency.[24]

Like the growth phasing program in Livermore, the San Jose program was adopted by the city council after an initial moratorium adopted by citizen initiative in 1973.[25]

As with the Clarkstown and Ramapo programs, there was nothing in the intermediate growth phasing programs in Livermore and San Jose that ensured that actual capacity would be available to serve new development, or that the community would permit new development to the extent of available capacity. In those programs, the growth phasing began with a concept of adequate public facilities that the community translated into a simpler allocation of new dwelling units to be permitted. Today, both communities have moved toward more comprehensive strategies, designed to guide growth geographically and ensure that facility capacity will be available concurrently with the development creating a demand for it.

Why would a community adopt a growth phasing program, rather than a set of adequate public facilities standards, if both accomplish the same thing? Although it is not possible to document here the thought processes of those who have made all of the decisions, there are two probable answers to that question. One possibility is that the growth phasing program may appear simpler than adequate public facilities standards.

First, growth phasing programs are generally simpler for the public and for many developers to understand than adequate public facilities requirements. With an adequate public facilities ordinance, it may not be possible to determine whether any development, or how much development, can take place at a particular location without making a reasonably detailed analysis of each affected public facility or service. Under a growth phasing program like those in San Jose and Livermore, a citizen or a developer can easily determine that the community will permit 100 more units or 1,000 more units, or no more units, in a particular area in a particular period. A performance-based program for concurrency or adequate public facilities does not lend itself to easy metrics or to sound bites in political campaigns.

The other, equally valid, answer to the question of why a community might choose a growth phasing program over an adequate public facilities one is that growth phasing addresses a different issue than the adequate public facilities program. One author cited a survey of citizens in Livermore early in the growth management period in which 74 percent of those surveyed agreed with the statement that "Livermore should grow at a controlled rate, provided services to the residents do not suffer."[26] Note the two parts to that response: 1) protect service levels; 2) control the rate of growth. Adequate public facilities standards would ensure the adequacy of services, but in a year in which systems enjoyed adequate capacities, such controls might not slow the rate of growth. A phased growth system addresses both of those issues.

The perceived simplicity of the growth phasing programs does not necessarily translate into simplicity in operation. Most growth phasing programs, including all of those described here, have been added to the development review process as additional permitting steps.[27] Developers and some observers view the proliferation of permitting requirements as a major impediment to the provision of affordable housing.[28] A community can easily integrate adequate public facilities standards into existing development review processes, thus making the operation of such a program often simpler than the operation of a growth phasing program.

There is a political side to all of this. In communities that have experienced a recent crisis, the concern over growth may focus on traffic or the availability of water. However, a sewage treatment plant at 99 percent of capacity or a water system nearing the point of overload simply do not engender much casual conversation within a community. The crisis at the sewage treatment plant is likely to be noticed only downstream, if flow through the plant exceeds the design capacity and either overwhelms its treatment capacity or partly bypasses the plant, with either event resulting in increased water pollution. Similarly, the first evidence of shortage in a water system is typically noticed by firefighters, who discover that they cannot draw the hundreds of gallons of water they need from two or three hydrants at the same time. Even as firefighters notice such changes, there is typically adequate water in the system for people to shower, run their dishwashers and wash their cars.

In contrast to these critical but hidden system overloads, other perceptions of growth do generate discussion and concern. One of the primary perceptions of growth relates to suburban "sprawl." A 1974 publication documented *The Costs of Sprawl* in fiscal terms and provided a documented financial incentive for communities to attempt to limit sprawl, regardless of whether public facilities are generally available.[29] Although not all analysts agree that the economic impacts of sprawl are entirely negative (see, generally, Chapter 9), there are other problems with sprawl. Those include the consumption of a finite land resource and some intangible perceptions about desirable urban form (see Chapter 7).

The fact is that adequate public facilities may be available in a relatively remote location. It is not unusual for a community to extend major public facilities to a remote industrial plant or to a public facility, such as an airport, often making those same public facilities available to a strip of intervening land (see general discussion in Chapter 5). Some of that land may be relatively remote from the community, and its development may be perceived as contributing to sprawl. A requirement for adequate public facilities for new development would not preclude the development of such property, but a phased development scheme would.

Thus, a critical difference between the two types of programs is often the purpose of the program. Those drafting the language for adopting a program may prepare a purpose statement with recitations of the limited availability of public facilities. That may be the real purpose of the program, but the city may just include such language because the city attorney believes (probably correctly) that tying the proposal as closely as possible to concepts of the "public health and safety" will improve its defensibility.[30]

However, the real purpose of a growth phasing program may be to prevent "sprawl" and the changes of urban form and negative perceptions that go with it. In one survey of communities with development timing controls (loosely defined there to include subdivision regulations and capital investment strategies),

78 percent of the respondents mentioned "reduction of urban sprawl" as an objective of the development timing strategy. That purpose tied with "environmental protection" for second place, trailing only "provision of adequate urban services," which was mentioned by 84 percent of the respondents.[31] The prevention of sprawl may be just as valid a goal as the protection of capacity in public facilities, but it is quite a different one.

The next section of this chapter deals with "urban growth boundaries." Such growth boundaries are quite different from "urban service area boundaries" and "urban service limits," which are a form of growth phasing. Whereas urban growth boundaries are regulatory programs directed at controlling private development, urban service area boundaries or limits are typically adopted policies intended to guide the local government's own decisions in making capital expenditures and in allowing others to make expenditures to extend critical public facilities—typically sewer and water systems. Chapter 5 includes a discussion of the use of infrastructure investments as a growth management tool. The urban service area boundary or limit programs enhance the use of that tool in two ways: first, the boundaries make the policy visually explicit, thus making it very clear to developers what land will be easily developable and what land will not; second, the boundary policies limit the ability of city staff and elected officials to authorize extensions that may seem fiscally attractive because a developer, or a group of homeowners with a crisis, has agreed to pay for the extension and its operating costs.

Perhaps the first example of such a program was the service boundary around Lexington, Kentucky, adopted on the recommendation of a planning consultant and a joint city–county planning commission.[32] Its pioneer status was recognized with a "National Historic Planning Landmark" award from the American Institute of Certified Planners. The boundary remained in effect in the 2001 Comprehensive Plan for the city and county. Its purpose, according to the plan, is:

This concept delineates the location of urban growth by dividing the county into an Urban Service Area, where development is encouraged, and a Rural Service Area, where urban-oriented activities are not permitted. Areas of future growth within the Urban Service Area were identified so that "complex urban services and facilities, public and private, could be developed logically and economically."[33]

Another early example of such a boundary was the first effort to control growth in Boulder—the adoption of its "Blue Line" by referendum. The policy really amounted to a "brown line," because it constituted a charter amendment prohibiting the city from providing water service to any property above a specified elevation (5,750 feet) on the city's spectacular mountain backdrop, the Flatirons.[34] In an arid state like Colorado, the lack of availability of water service is typically a major impediment to development, although in theory the property beyond the boundary could have developed under county regulations. Note that the City of Boulder subsequently adopted an open-space purchase program and included that area in land that was acquired for a greenbelt.[35]

The Twin Cities of Minneapolis–St. Paul, Minnesota, has a long history of managing regional growth within its Metropolitan Urban Service Area, the designation of the area within which the regional cooperative agency will permit connections to the regional sewer system.[36] The regional wastewater disposal system is one part of a cooperative regional system that leaves most land use decisions with local governments.[37]

As the Montgomery County program, described later in this chapter, demonstrates, it is also possible to combine more than one type of program.

This section has distinguished between growth phasing programs that attempt to phase the location of growth and those that, like the Petaluma Housing Implementation Program, control the timing of growth through imposing specific numerical permit limits. Obviously, such a distinction is most significant over the short-run; over the long-run, the issues are interrelated. The practical question in most cases, and one that contains both issues of timing and location, is when a particular piece of land will develop. Although the Ramapo program, with its 18-year plan, was based on timing, some land was immediately available and some was not; thus, at every stage it included location as well as timing controls. In the final analysis, the issues of timing and location are in one sense separate but in many other ways very closely related.

The effect of a growth phasing program on growth is not complex, if the community implements the program as planned. As an analyst who reviewed growth management efforts throughout Colorado noted in commenting on the Westminster requirements for adequate public facilities, "[A]lthough the location of development is never predetermined by the city, it is economically advantageous to the developer to locate either contiguous to the city or within the city in the role of an infill development."[38]

Growth patterns and timing may not be entirely predictable with an adequate public facilities program, but they should be reasonably predictable (or at least the maximums should be reasonably predictable) with a growth phasing program.

URBAN GROWTH BOUNDARIES

As the name suggests, an urban growth boundary is a line drawn around the city that defines the limits of urban growth; it is a type of growth phasing program. Some phasing programs, such as the early one in Clarkstown, attempt to phase growth by limiting all growth, or more intense growth, to a particular area of the community at a particular time.

However, an urban growth boundary, as the term is used here, is more rigid than a simple phasing program. Boulder later created another form of urban growth boundary, through its acquisition of a publicly owned greenbelt that almost completely surrounded the city by 1992[39] (see discussion in Chapter 5). Because the Boulder charter makes it very difficult for the city to sell the open space, the boundary is likely to be very permanent.

The primary source of most of the more rigid urban growth boundaries is the state. In Hawaii, the state has created a form of statewide zoning, under which it designated urban, rural, conservation and agricultural districts (described in Chapter 6). Although the boundaries have been subject to surprisingly frequent change, they are still far more rigid than any locally drawn lines on a zoning or growth management map have proved to be. Even after the changes, the program has served its purpose by restricting 95 percent of the state's land to agricultural and conservation uses.[40]

Oregon took another approach in its state law. It required that local governments prepare local plans and implementation strategies that included 20-year growth boundaries. Thus, since the mid-1970s, communities in Oregon have had urban growth boundaries (see Chapter 6 for more discussion about the Oregon program). Two thoughtful commentators have noted that the wide adoption of a strong regional growth boundary like the one in Portland is unlikely, "In most regions, the tradition of home rule is too strong, and a centralized policy does not acknowledge the different character of a constellation of urban, suburban, and rural communities."[41]

Establishing an urban growth boundary requires either a very self-centered attitude for a community or an enormous amount of foresight. Because population growth trends change so much over time, it is difficult to imagine accurately projecting the land area needed for growth over a 20-year period.[42] Knaap has noted the significant effects of the rigidity of the Portland boundary on the land market[43] (see discussion in Chapter 10).

An urban growth boundary establishes a clearer "urban edge" than other forms of growth management. Nelson has suggested that the Oregon program will produce an "ultimate urban form."[44] In doing so, it puts a limit to continuous urban sprawl. On the other hand, it seems more likely than other forms of growth management to spur leapfrog, or discontinuous, development beyond the boundary (see description and map of such effects from the Boulder program in Chapter 7).

Note that an urban growth boundary addresses urban form and does not directly address the issues of adequacy of public facilities or even the fiscal impacts of growth. Presumably, constraining development within a limited boundary will lead to reduced capital and operating costs, thus minimizing negative fiscal impact on the community, but recent studies do not wholly support that conclusion. Further, urban growth boundaries do not necessarily regulate the timing of growth within that boundary. A phased growth system may suggest a series of concentric boundaries, with growth gradually moving out through them, thus facilitating the gradual expansion of public facilities. The establishment of a long-term growth boundary, such as those in Boulder and Portland, does not provide a basis for planning the orderly expansion of public facilities in the early years, because there is then far more undeveloped land within the boundary than the community can or should serve with major roads and public utilities. As two experienced planners note, "A large UGB will require planners to manage growth in a concerted way *within* the boundary."[45]

In short, urban growth boundaries address exactly what they appear to address. They limit the long-range boundaries of urban growth and do little else. They can, of course, be used in conjunction with other techniques. However, it is important to remember that these boundaries do not directly address issues such as heavy traffic, overcrowded schools and overloaded public services that typically lead to the adoption of growth management programs.

There are those who take a far more positive view of urban growth boundaries than this author. In particular, see the work of Chris Nelson and Gail Easley.[46]

RATE-OF-GROWTH PROGRAMS

An adequate public facilities requirement may effectively regulate the rate of community growth, based on the actual capacity of public facilities at any given time. Some growth phasing programs, such as the San Jose program described earlier in this chapter, may translate the availability of public facilities into a maximum permissible growth rate in any given year. However, a few communities regulate the rate of growth directly.

The two primary examples are programs in Petaluma, California, described in Chapter 3, and Boulder, Colorado, which based its program on the Petaluma program. Petaluma had experienced constant growth that surged to an annual rate of 10 percent by 1971. In the face of this last spurt of growth, Petaluma adopted the first stage in its growth control program—a moratorium on rezonings, followed by a moratorium on annexations. In August 1972, the city adopted a "Residential Development Control System" that was the predecessor of the "Residential Growth Management Program" that remained in place in 2003.[47]

The Petaluma program is relatively simple. It originally provided an allocation of 500 new residential units per year, with suballocations between two sides of town and between single-family and multi-family housing. It is noteworthy that, based on the population at the time of the program's original adoption, the 500 units represented a maximum annual growth rate of more than 5 percent; by 1991, the effective rate limit was closer to 3.5 percent. That computation is of more theoretical than practical significance, however, because Petaluma's growth did not approach the maximum permissible growth in the 1980s. In 1990, the city had 16,546 dwelling units, and by 2000, it had 20,204, compared to 12,540 in 1980[48] (see Table 4-1). Without regard to several exemptions that would have permitted more units, the basic program would have permitted growth to 22,540 dwelling units by 2000. By 2000, the city had adopted a more comprehensive growth management program, so it is unclear whether the market simply fell short of the worst-case scenario imagined in the growth limit or whether the other implementation tools held growth below the 500-unit annual limit. By 2000, some 30 years after the program was adopted, its limit of 500 dwelling units per year would have allowed an annual growth rate of about 2.5 percent.[49]

In considering the Petaluma program, it is important to recall that, in a suit filed by homebuilders, the Federal District Court examining the program found

Table 4-1
Permitted Growth in Petaluma at 500 Dwelling Units per Year Compared to Actual Growth, 1970–2000

	1970	1980	1990	2000
Cumulative units allowed by program	N.A.	13,175	18,175	23,175
Actual total units	8,175	12,540	16,546	20,304
Cumulative difference	N.A.	635	1,729	2,871

Sources: Actual number of units from Bureau of the Census, 2000, *American Fact Finder, Quick Tables,* http://www.census.gov; Bureau of the Census, 1991, *Census of Population and Housing: Summary Population and Housing Characteristics,* Part 6, Table 18; Bureau of the Census, 1982, *Summary Characteristics by Governmental Units and Standard Metropolitan Statistical Areas,* Part 6, Table 2; Bureau of the Census, 1972, *City and County Data Book,* Table B-2; other lines computed by author.

that the city generally had adequate public facilities capacity and that it had "purposefully" limited its water supply. Although the city raised the issue of public facilities in defending its program, clearly the city has never based the program limits on the adequacy of public facilities. Even without the detailed analysis by the federal court, one could easily deduce that it is very unlikely that the combination of roads, sewer, water and schools in a community would be able to absorb exactly 500 new residential units each year for nearly 20 years. Clearly, the remaining capacity of such systems is "lumpy," becoming extremely limited at times and then increasing dramatically as a new plant or major trunk line or road is added to the system.[50]

The Boulder program was a second-generation version of the Petaluma one. Boulder adopted its first program in 1976, four years after adoption of the program in Petaluma. The original version of the plan resulted from a citizen initiative and was named the "Danish plan" after citizen–activist and, later, city council member Paul Danish. The original plan imposed a 1.5 percent annual limit on the increase in the number of dwelling units in the city; the current plan allows a growth rate of 2 percent. During the early years of the growth management program, Boulder even hired the Petaluma planning director as its own.

As in Petaluma, public facility capacity is not the basis for the Boulder growth limit. In fact, the Boulder Valley Comprehensive Plan, adopted in 2001, echoes some of the antigrowth literature concerns from the 1970s literature (discussed in Chapter 3). The plan's policy basis includes:

Residents of the Boulder Valley, and a growing number of fellow Americans, are increasingly challenging the ethic that all growth is good growth. No longer is unconditional growth being accepted unquestioningly as a necessary premise of progress and an enhanced standard of living. Growing environmental concerns, a recent and renewed awareness of the energy crisis confronting us at the national and local levels, together with a growing loss of sense of community, have combined with increased significance to make us realize that we do not have unlimited room or resources. . . . The spreading patterns of settlement and development that characterize our urban areas are the legacy of the old illusion that we had endless acres of land to build on and unlimited energy to burn. The Citizen's Advisory Committee on Environmental Quality and the Task Force on Land Use and Urban Quality issued a report, *The Use of Land: A Citizen's Policy Guide to Urban Growth,* which begins with the finding that Americans must begin to view land as a resource, as limited as minerals, water and clean air, and indicates that there is a new mood in America. Increasingly, people are asking what urban growth will add to the quality of their lives; they are questioning the way relatively unconstrained, piecemeal urbanization is changing their communities, and are rebelling against the traditional processes of government and the marketplace, which, they believe, have inadequately guided development in the past.[51]

In a court challenge to a related city policy (but not to the growth management program itself), the Colorado Supreme Court sustained a lower court ruling that required that the city provide sewer and water service to land outside the city limits for which the city had denied service based on its growth policy.[52] There was in the findings in the case no indication that the city was unable to serve the developer. The Boulder program remained in effect and a centerpiece of joint city–county planning in 2003. As in Petaluma, actual growth in the city has remained below that permitted by the program (see Table 4-2).

Presumably, a program in which public officials adjust the growth limit annually, based on actual capacity, should be tied more closely to actual service capacities. In observing a similar system in operation in San Juan Capistrano, however, one commentator noted that a technical report prepared by the staff seemed to be largely irrelevant to the actual decision about the growth allocation for the year.[53] "My impression was that the technical findings of the report had long been eclipsed by the hours of public hearings associated with setting San Juan's yearly growth quota. This seemed to be an essentially political event where the unrest of the protectionists was balanced against the unrest of those with land to develop and the costs of extending services was balanced against the cost of litigation for withholding them."[54]

It is interesting that Boulder and Petaluma have taken separate but similar steps to simplify their programs. Both originally included "merit" reviews, in which development projects competed for scarce permits through complex and comprehensive reviews that awarded "points" for quality of architectural design, site planning, energy conservation and a multitude of other issues, with building opportunities in tight years allocated to those projects achieving the most points.[55] Both Boulder and Petaluma amended their programs in the 1980s to simple proration programs, requiring very little administration and greatly reducing the burden on private developers. Under the simplified programs, each city simply divides the available permits in a particular period pro-rata among the competing developers.

Table 4-2
Permitted Growth in Boulder at 2 Percent per Annum, Compared to Actual Growth, with Boulder County as Reference, 1970–2000

	1970	1980	1990	2000
CITY OF BOULDER				
Actual population	66,870	76,685	83,312	94,673
Projected population with 2 percent annual increase (1970 base)	N.A.	81,514	99,365	121,126
Projected population with 2 percent annual increase (1980 base)	N.A.	N.A.	93,479	113,950
BOULDER COUNTY				
Actual population	131,899	189,625	225,339	291,288
Projected population with 2 percent annual increase (1970 base)	N.A.	160,784	195,995	238,917
Projected population with 2 percent annual increase (1980 base)	N.A.	N.A.	231,153	281,773

Sources: Actual number of units from Bureau of the Census, 2000, *American Fact Finder, Quick Tables,* http://www.census.gov; Bureau of the Census, 1991, *Census of Population and Housing: Summary Population and Housing Characteristics,* Part 6, Table 18; Bureau of the Census, 1982, *Summary Characteristics by Governmental Units and Standard Metropolitan Statistical Areas,* Part 6, Table 2; Bureau of the Census, 1972, *City and County Data Book,* Table B-2; other lines computed by author.

In a question-and-answer format in a 1991 Residential Growth Management System: User's Guide, Petaluma noted succinctly that: "The biggest difference between the present system and its predecessor is the elimination of the point system used to rate projects to determine whether or not they qualified for allotments. That process had become a burden for both staff and the developer, and had been regularly criticized for being too subjective in its scoring procedure."[56]

A background memorandum prepared by the Boulder planning director, explaining the revised program to the Boulder City Council, similarly noted that the pro-rated allocation method was a change "made at Planning Board, based upon the almost unanimous support for the sole use of the prorated method by the building community."[57] A Boulder builder, complaining of the "hassle involved," "the time to process a development" and "the complexity of the ordinances," helps to explain the support for the simpler program in comments about the old program:

[T]he growth control ordinance tries to deal with issues of quality in a quantitative way—by putting numbers on things and saying, "You can only do this and that at this or that rate." It is impossible to deal with qualitative issues in a quantitative way; this practice, quite simply, detracts from good planning. The experience in Boulder has been that the planning department has deteriorated in quality because it has had to concentrate on counting numbers and on administering a highly bureaucratic system. Boulder's is not a lousy planning department—its staff members are good planners. Perhaps under the newest system, they will even be able to get back to planning.[58]

Clearly the political and philosophical basis for a rate-of-growth program is quite different from the pragmatic ones that lead to adoption of adequate public facilities controls. The author of the original Boulder program noted in an article that:

[T]he first attempt to pass a growth control ordinance in Boulder came about in 1971, when the Boulder chapter of Zero Population Growth (ZPG) put a proposed dwelling-unit cap of 40,000 to a vote by the initiative process. This move sufficiently frightened the prevailing local establishment that the latter persuaded the city council to put an alternative advisory question on the ballot, urging the city government to keep the growth rate "substantially below the rates experienced during the 1960s."[59]

It is interesting, but not particularly surprising, to note that this proposal from Zero Population Growth in Boulder came at a time when the studies for the Club of Rome Report[60] and the Rockefeller Commission Report[61] were underway and just a year before Finkler's publications on "non-growth" planning options appeared.[62] The timing of this early proposal, as well as the ultimate program itself, illustrates the significant difference in apparent motivations behind "rate-of-growth" programs and other growth management programs that are more clearly based on community growth capacity. Although Boulder voters did not pass "the Danish plan," as it was often called, until 1976, and although it sprang from the roots of the city's own advisory question on the 1971 ballot and not from the ZPG proposal, the concerns addressed were clearly the same: the actual rate of growth, or change, in the community. Even if there was plenty of water and a substantial excess of sewage treatment capacity, the majority of people in Boulder simply felt that a 5 percent annual growth rate represented too much change (note that the 5 percent rate used as a benchmark in Boulder was half the annual growth rate that preceded the adoption of the Petaluma program). Although any growth management program is likely to slow the rate of growth at certain times, an analyst who studied several programs in Colorado illustrated the difference between the types of programs.[63] In contrasting Westminster and Boulder, a mere 20 miles north, he found continuing acceleration in the rate of growth during the early years of the Westminster program and a dramatic slowing of the rate of growth in the early years of the Boulder program.[64]

COMPREHENSIVE PROGRAMS

Most of the programs cited so far, and most of the programs in effect, are not comprehensive programs of managing community change, but rather single regulatory tools directed at particular local issues. The Boulder and Petaluma programs address the rate-of-growth issue without particular regard to the availability of public facilities, while adequate public facilities controls simply address the public facilities issues. The programs in San Jose, Boulder, Livermore and Petaluma regulate only residential growth.

Although some of these programs operate as part of a larger plan, many do not. A 1991 national survey of seventeen communities (an eighteenth was the control) regarded as "growth management communities" found that:

- only three of them had both development timing requirements and adequate public facilities ordinances (Boulder, Livermore and Westminster);
- three of the communities had neither;
- two had only development timing controls, and nine had only adequate public facilities controls;
- the control community, Montgomery County, Maryland, had both.[65]

Note that the response of Livermore to the question was somewhat deceptive, because its development timing control was its adequate public facilities ordinance. Thus, from the surveyed group, a group identified as communities with some sort of active growth management program, only Westminster, Boulder and Montgomery County clearly had programs with both adequate public facilities and development timing elements in 1991; in Boulder, the timing requirements applied only to residential uses, although in Westminster and Montgomery County they applied to most land uses.

Boulder provides a useful illustration. The city council adopted its adequate public facilities requirements separately from the growth management program, in 1977, and they remain separate from the growth management program.[66] The city has engaged in joint planning with Boulder County for more than two decades. It has actively used its control of crucial public facilities in fringe areas as a control tool.[67] It has also invested millions of dollars in dedicated sales tax revenues in the acquisition of a large greenbelt around the community, to halt urban sprawl and to limit the encroachment of other communities into the area.[68]

The Westminster program is the simpler of the two comprehensive growth management programs. It measures the capacity of the community to provide service at a given time in "service commitments," with one service commitment being equal to the system demand imposed by a single-family, detached home. The city council, based on staff recommendations, annually determines the capacity of the city to provide service for the following year and then allocates that capacity among six categories of potentially competing users: A, active residential projects; B, other residential projects; C, non-residential projects; D, service contracts with users outside the city; E, senior housing; F, two later-added categories dealt with reclaimed water and one specific project.[69]

The city created the two categories of residential uses in the original program in 1977 to give preference to partially built but still-active projects, for three reasons: first, developers of such projects clearly had the most current commitment to their projects and thus would suffer the greatest harm if stopped; second, such developers were the most certain to use the allocations promptly, thus providing needed "tap fee" revenues to the city; and, third, the city wanted to reduce as rapidly as possible the backlog of approved but partially built projects.[70] Categories E and F included in the program a reserve for the types of allocations that are the subject of exemptions in other programs such as those in Boulder and Petaluma. If the program is truly based on capacity limitations, exemptions are virtually inexcusable— every ounce of water or other unit of service must be considered in accounting for the demands of growth on that limited capacity. Within Category C, economic base industries received a high priority. One commentator found just 5 years later that Westminster had achieved significant success in attracting new jobs.[71]

In Westminster, as in Petaluma and Boulder, growth pressures from the mid-1980s into the early 1990s fell far below past growth rates and thus below the growth permitted under the programs; thus, the program was not subject to significant pressure during that time; in the 1990s, growth accelerated and tested the system; the city demonstrated its confidence in the system by adopting a 10-year extension of it, effective from 2000 to 2010.[72] The Westminster program, like the programs in Petaluma, Ramapo and elsewhere, was initially challenged in court. The city won in each of the challenges.[73]

Unlike many of the other communities involved in growth management, Montgomery County, containing a number of northwestern suburbs of Washington, D.C., continued to grow rapidly through the 1980s and the 1990s. The county thus continued to test the limits of its growth management program.

The "annual growth policy" is the key to the growth management program in Montgomery County. The county's planning board adopted the first such policy in 1974.[74] That policy document noted that it followed by 10 years the adoption of a general plan intended "to provide for consolidated development with the least amount of sprawl, the most coordinated form of transportation, and the most accessible open space."[75] It also noted that an adequate public facilities ordinance already applied to the subdivision process and that a limited "staging" (phasing) concept applied to plans for individual communities.[76] However, the 1974 document represented the first comprehensive approach to addressing growth in the booming suburban area. Serious limitations on sewage treatment capacity were a major concern in Montgomery County then, with additional capacity not expected to come on line for 4 years or more.[77] It noted the existence of separate sewer capacity allocation policies and commented, "In summary, it seems reasonable to conclude that much of the growth rate of the suburban ring nodes in the next six years will be dependent upon whatever sewer allocation policy is established for the Rock Creek interim plant."[78]

Although the later growth policy documents served as regulatory tools, the original one really updated the general plan. It reaffirmed the three goals of the plan:

1. To channel the bulk of long-range growth in the county to the I-270 corridor in the form of satellite cities which have both jobs and housing in a balanced ratio and which reduce travel demands. . . .
2. To focus a more limited amount of growth in "nodal" areas, or activity centers, within the suburban ring. . . .
3. To build a network of bus and rail transit lines to serve movements through this area and, in so doing, to reduce traffic congestion and air pollution.[79]

To implement those policies, it outlined a series of recommendations for both regulation and capital investment by the county. It specifically recommended construction of major highways and the Rockville treatment plant because, "Improving access to the corridor is the prime requisite to make it attractive to new jobs, and job increases there are the key to achievement of a balanced growth pattern in the corridor that can lessen auto travel needs and take the pressure off the suburban ring nodes."[80]

The growth policy again acknowledged that most growth in the near future would take place in the area in which the county was allocating sewer capacity and thus recommended transit and other improvements in that area, in order to accommodate the inevitable growth in ways compatible with the plan.[81] Finally, the policy recommended increased coordination among governmental agencies influencing and serving growth, including multiple county agencies.[82]

From that early planning document, Montgomery County has developed its annual growth policy into a sophisticated and complex regulatory tool. Simply adopting the policy is a relatively complex process that begins months before the new policy will become effective. The county bases its capital investments on the growth policies, but the capital improvements program itself also affects the allocation of growth within the county.[83]

The growth management program divides the county into thirty policy areas (that number had grown by 2003 from seventeen 12 years earlier), and the annual policies phase growth differently for each area, based on its capacity to absorb growth and other policy considerations. A key element in the program is the "staging ceiling" for each policy area, defined by the county as "the maximum amount of land development that can be accommodated by the existing and programmed public facilities serving the area, at an assigned level of service standard."[84] Simply put, in computing public facilities capacity under its adequate public facilities policies, the county considers not only existing facilities but also those that the county has included in its adopted capital improvements program. That is a realistic policy approach, because development of most proposed projects will occur over a period of months or years after the approval date and such projects thus do not immediately require all facility capacities.

Sewer service was the most scarce resource and thus the critical determinant of the location of new growth in the original 1974 program, but by 1991 transportation had become the key element countywide, and it became a critical issue again around the turn of the century, when growth in the county accelerated and outpaced the provision of new transportation capacity.[85]

Another major element of the annual growth policy is a section establishing policies for the administration of the adequate public facilities requirements. Although such guidelines may not be necessary for sewer and water facilities, for which engineering computations can determine capacities, they are essential for other facilities for which the determination of capacity involves policy judgments. For example, a traffic level that is totally unacceptable in one community may be entirely acceptable in another, because the second community is willing to tolerate stop-and-go traffic at rush hour and the first is not. One of the policy determinations that Montgomery County has made is that it is willing to accept heavier projected traffic loads on roads near transit stations.[86] Such a policy serves two purposes: it acknowledges that people driving to the train create local traffic, although they help to reduce regional traffic; second, and perhaps more important, it creates a situation in which road conditions make the use of mass transit more attractive.

Although raising some concerns about a new requirement for traffic impact projections for some developments, a developer termed the Montgomery County program "strict but reasonable, and a known quantity."[87]

There is more to the Montgomery County program than just the pieces described here. The county implements its planning program, of which the growth policy is a major part, through a series of sector plans (for geographic sectors of the county) and local master plans within the separate cities in the county. The 1992 growth policy itself identified interrelationships among a total of eight different sets of county policies: land use policy; economic policy; housing policy; transportation policy; community facilities policy; natural resources policy; social policy; and fiscal policy.[88]

The county also has a program of traditional planning in established communities and an aggressive program to protect agricultural land. In Montgomery County, as in Boulder, the growth management program is simply one piece of a complex array of planning and development controls.[89]

No single growth management or other land use control technique can address all of the concerns of a rapidly growing community. Thus, a few communities with serious commitments to managed growth have adopted comprehensive programs consisting of multiple, coordinated techniques addressing all types of new development.

THE ROLE OF EXACTIONS

"Make growth pay its own way" is a call heard perhaps more often than "manage growth" among citizens concerned with rising taxes and, in many cases, declining levels of service. In response to that call from citizens and to a variety of local fiscal pressures, by the early 1990s, most local governments in growing areas had adopted broad policies for "exactions" through which developers are required to pay for the infrastructure improvements required by new growth.

Growth, of course, is an abstract concept and not one with a checkbook. Thus, it cannot "pay its own way." Although one effect of exactions may be to increase the cost of new housing, thus requiring residents of new housing (who may or may not be new residents of the community) to help pay for the costs of growth, there is evidence that a significant portion of the cost is borne by the developer, with some of it back-charged to the land seller.[90] Although most local governments have long required developers to pay for such on-site improvements as street paving and utility lines within a subdivision, exaction requirements go farther. They may require that a developer improve a road leading up to a site or a drainage way leading away from it. Traffic impact analyses may lead to requests (or demands) that a developer install a traffic light at an intersection near the development project or construct adjacent turning lanes to improve access into and out of the development. Through "impact fees" (the most common term, although there are many others), a community may assess a developer for a share of the cost of a larger facility such as a major arterial roadway or a new sewer plant.

Clearly, the subjects of exactions and growth management overlap in principle, in politics and in practice. A comprehensive growth management program can and should include rational policies on exactions. However, there are far more communities that have exaction policies than communities that have growth management policies, and the two are typically adopted and administered separately.

Exactions, of course, have their own effects on urban form, the fiscal position of the municipality and the availability of public facilities. Operationally those are quite separate from, and sometimes quite different from, the effects of growth management. For example, a community may have an impact fee policy related to roads and an adequate public facilities standard related to roads. Simply paying the impact fee may not guarantee the developer that there is sufficient road capacity to permit the proposed project, because financing of the project may depend on the payment of such fees by several developers.

The literature on exactions is broad.[91] Not everyone accepts exactions enthusiastically, in significant part because of the tendency for them to increase housing costs.[92]

OTHER REGULATORY TECHNIQUES

This chapter describes four majors regulatory types of growth controls: adequate public facilities requirements, rate-of-growth controls, urban growth boundaries and growth phasing regulations, along with examples of more comprehensive programs that include elements of more than one of those techniques.

Some analysts include more techniques under the general heading of "growth management." An author producing a slim volume in California in 1990 listed twenty-six, including a number of zoning techniques, some non-regulatory techniques, such as those discussed in the next chapter, and some other regulatory techniques that are not included here.[93] This book is limited to actions intended to direct the timing or location of growth or both, and the author has thus consciously omitted some of the techniques included by other authors under a more general definition of "growth management." Other sources provide a thorough treatment of zoning and other regulatory techniques that can affect the quality of growth.[94]

LATER LITERATURE ON LOCAL GROWTH MANAGEMENT

The later (post-1975) literature is in some ways not as interesting as the early literature. There were several dissertations, two dozen or so books and a large volume of articles. Several provided useful case studies. Others updated the early literature. A few contained some interesting evaluative material (discussed separately in Chapters 7 through 11). What has been surprisingly missing from the later literature is any sort of comprehensive policy examination at growth management programs in general and how those programs affect the communities that adopt them. That deficiency was noted repeatedly in papers offered at a conference on research needs in the field.[95]

The Urban Land Institute (ULI) continued its series of publications on the subject. It included in the series a 1976 publication on the complexities of the regulatory process,[96] although, for reasons that are not clear, it reserved the next volume number in the series for a later publication. The Institute published Volume IV in the *Management & Control of Growth* series in 1978 with the subtitle, *Techniques in Application.*[97] That book, like the earlier ones in the series, contained a series of useful essays on various aspects of growth management. Innovative approaches to land use management, many of them quite separate from growth management, were the subject of the first section of the book. Other sections covered practical aspects of administering growth management, fiscal impact analysis, environmental issues and, in a brief section, the implications of growth management for housing.

In 1979, ULI published *Growth and Change in Rural America*, a thoughtful analysis of the demographic, economic and other changes taking place in non-metropolitan areas.[98] It included some recommendations for improvement under the general heading of "growth management."[99] However, as in some later studies, the authors used the phrase broadly and included within that chapter tax incentives, infrastructure investment policies, land purchases, innovative zoning tools and, interestingly, mobile home regulation.[100]

Although ULI discontinued the designation of books as being in the *Management & Control of Growth* series after 1979, it published additions to the collection in 1986 and 1989. The 1986 book, entitled *Growth Management: Keeping on Target?* was clearly an update of the earlier studies.[101] It revisited several of the communities included in the earlier studies—Petaluma, Boulder, Boca Raton, Montgomery County—and added some new ones. It included a broader look at the social and equity issues involved in growth management than any of the earlier reports. One of the most interesting parts of the book is a short but very thoughtful essay by Paul Niebanck,[102] in which he assesses the benefits and "byproducts" of growth management. He notes great concern about one particular byproduct: "Most dramatically, the decline in residential opportunity for poor people, for people of color, and, yes, for middle-class people, resulting from the decidedly negative effects of growth management on housing prices."[103]

Three years later, ULI published *Understanding Growth Management: Critical Issues and a Research Agenda,* based on papers from a September 1988 conference sponsored by ULI and the Center for Urban and Regional Studies at the University of North Carolina, Chapel Hill.[104] As the title suggests, the focus of the book is on what society does not know about growth management and the need for further research. Most striking perhaps is the fundamental question left open, as stated by one of the participants. "Moreover, despite the plethora of Boulder studies, there has been no research analyzing whether Boulder is a better place to live as a result of its growth management program."[105]

In the same publication, in a concluding chapter outlining a proposed research agenda, Porter notes that quality of life as an area of research "has hardly been touched."[106] He goes on to note that the field even lacks measurable standards for quality of life, in order to provide the basis of a study. In a chapter entitled, "The Ecology of 'Quality of Life' and Urban Growth," Myers notes that "the poor state of knowledge about quality of life has hampered negotiations about growth management. . . . few can agree on its definition . . . it is very difficult to measure quality of life in any comprehensive fashion."[107]

The first post-1975 contribution of the American Society of Planning Officials and its successor, the American Planning Association, to the library of books on growth management was an excellent introductory legal work entitled *Constitutional Issues of Growth Management.*[108] It was developed as a teaching tool and included a dozen illustrative case studies, with clear and careful discussions of the law related to each. It also included a good discussion of the policy issues involved in growth management, noting that, "In the final analysis, growth management plans will be judged by the people of the region and, in some cases, by the courts. Each plan will be looked at in terms of its impact on a particular local and regional situation and in terms of its internal logic and consistency."[109] The author provided three guidelines for effective growth management plans:

- Methods employed for benchmark technical studies, impact analyses and plan making should be systematic, rigorous and replicable.

- Internal consistency of growth management approaches is as important as accuracy. There must be a clear relationship between the findings of the basic studies, the public purposes to be served, the plan adopted and the regulations used to carry out the plan.

- Explicitness is a third fundamental for growth management plans. . . . such plans cannot afford to be broad-brush, general collections of possible futures.[110]

A second and more practical contribution from that organization was a summary of growth management techniques, developed from a study performed for the Puget Sound Region by James Duncan and Associates.[111] It offered the broadest and most comprehensive examination of techniques in application since ULI's *Management & Control of Growth* series 20 years earlier.

The International City Management Association published another collection of essays, edited by John DeGrove, who played a key role in the development of growth management and concurrency in Florida.[112] That book consisted almost entirely of short articles on major programs, most of them originally published in popular and trade journals such as *Planning* and *Governing*. Although the collection included no new analytical material, it did include a useful, if somewhat disjointed, collection of articles on current issues in the field.

This period saw the publication of a number of significant works on the state role in growth management, including those that advanced the concept of "smart growth." Chapter 6 includes its own literature review and citations to works on that subject; those are not repeated here. However, two are worthy of particular note. Robert Healy wrote an in-depth analysis of the state role in land use that was first published in and updated by Healy and John Rosenberg in 1979.[113] The two overlap considerably. Both provide a broad examination of the role of the state in land use and in-depth analyses of the statewide programs in Vermont and Florida and the coastal zone program in California.

Popper also contributed an interesting work to the literature on the state role in planning and growth management in 1981.[114] It contained the broadest policy analysis since Bosselman and Callies' work a decade earlier.[115] Popper's book also included a short section on the politics of state land use control.

Two important works came out of the University of California–Berkeley. Teitz provided policy analysis in support of his plea for a "growth policy for California."[116] Innes examined the importance of state-level programs in achieving coordination among multiple levels of government and in involving citizens in important planning decisions.[117] It is unfortunate that the only broad look at state growth management and land use activity with information dating later than the very early 1980s was DeGrove's twenty-page essay on the subject in ULI's publication on a future research agenda for the field.[118] Although the "quiet revolution" failed to spread across the United States as some had anticipated, the implementation of evolutionary techniques continued in Vermont, Oregon, Florida and elsewhere, and a more recent look at the subject would be useful addition to the literature. Chapter 6 of this book makes a small contribution to that effort.

Several dissertations examined particular growth management programs in depth. Abe provided a rather cursory review of the state of growth management and a very brief look at the Petaluma program in her 1977 dissertation at the Claremont Graduate School.[119] Snyder's 1982 dissertation at Colorado State University suggested an evaluation of state efforts but actually contained an interesting and useful comparison of the growth management programs in Boulder and Westminster.[120] He examined both the political and the practical aspects of the programs and examined data on their effectiveness after approximately 5 years of experience in Westminster and nearly 10 years in Boulder.

Knaap made a careful analysis of the effects of the Portland urban growth boundary on land prices and subsequently adapted the material into article form.[121]

Others have cited his work extensively,[122] and it provides the basis for some of the analysis in Chapter 9.

Dubbink first encountered growth management as a regional environmental planner for the California Coastal Commission.[123] He later completed doctoral work and prepared a dissertation on growth management in one of the communities with which he had previously worked, Bolinas, and one with which he had no prior experience, San Juan Capistrano. He based the dissertation largely on personal interviews, attempting to find the motives of those implementing growth management programs, as well as some of the results. His analysis balances empathy for the subjects of his study with a critical view of the results of their efforts. He concluded that growth management largely represented futile preservation efforts of newcomers to semirural communities. He characterized the results as "anti-suburb suburbs." Because of the broad perspective contained in it, it is a particularly important contribution to the literature.

For a 1986 dissertation for the University of California–Berkeley, Greenberg conducted an extremely thorough analysis of the growth management programs of Livermore and other communities in the Amador valley.[124] It provided a detailed history of the ups-and-downs of growth management politics in several communities that share a geographical location but that differ greatly in their politics. The comparative political histories are particularly interesting.

A later academic contribution to the field came in the form of a working paper prepared for the Public Research Institute at San Francisco State University.[125] It provided a review of eleven different growth management programs in effect in cities and counties in the Bay Area. All fall within the definition of growth management used in this book. The authors also provided one of the few attempts prior to this book to place the programs in categories. The categories there ("flexible systems, point systems, first come first served systems, and flexible criteria systems") seem less descriptive and thus less useful than those proposed in this book, but the effort of the authors to compare particular programs to similar programs in other communities is very useful.

The Lincoln Institute of Land Policy sponsored a statistical analysis of the demographic and other characteristics of communities adopting growth management programs in California.[126] Although their definition of "growth management" included standard zoning techniques, such as building height limits, the study provides useful demographic data on growth managing communities.

An important addition to the literature in 2001 was a work edited by Gerrit Knaap, dealing with *Land Market Monitoring for Smart Urban Growth.*[127] Knaap and a colleague contributed a chapter on monitoring residential land markets; that chapter, together with a separate one on monitoring housing affordability, offer the planner concerned with the possible adverse affects of growth management programs on housing prices (see Chapter 10) with tools to address that issue while managing growth.[128]

Researchers at the University of California–Berkeley contributed a number of working papers on growth management issues to the literature in the late 1980s and early 1990s. Particularly notable is a 1991 contribution of Landis.[129] A problem with his work in using it to analyze programs in other jurisdictions is that his working definition of growth management is one that this author would apply to "land use controls." It included zoning and subdivision controls, fees, annexation policies and infrastructure policies.

A number of articles and books on particular aspects of land use control, such as housing policy, joined the literature in this period. The topical chapters that follow include appropriate references to significant literature on those topics. Although there has been surprisingly little literature that attempts to provide any sort of broad evaluation of growth management efforts, the last chapter cites a substantial portion of what exists. Short reports by Landis[130] and Fischel[131] are particularly noteworthy, as is a brief article by Benjamin Chinitz.[132]

CONCLUSION

Each of the four types of growth management techniques addresses somewhat different community concerns and has somewhat different effects. Adequate public facilities requirements directly control the impacts of development on public facilities and ensure that capacity will be available to serve new development as it occurs. Such requirements indirectly phase growth, because they make development most feasible in areas that already have most urban services, which are generally areas contiguous to existing development; for that reason, such requirements help to reduce sprawl. However, in many communities, there are some (or many) public facilities available in locations that are relatively remote from the community or in areas that, for other reasons, may be low on the list of the community's priorities for development. Adequate public facilities requirements will not prevent development in such locations, nor will they halt development in a high growth market in any location to which developers can afford to pay most of the costs of extending facilities.

Growth phasing programs directly control the timing of growth in particular locations, generally based on the availability of public facilities. Such a program can be used to reduce sprawl and is more likely to be effective in reducing sprawl than are adequate public facilities standards. However, as the examples illustrate, growth phasing programs, used alone, may result in the approval of projects for which most facilities are available but for which some are not.

Urban growth boundaries most effectively define the limits of urban growth and thus create a clear delineation between developed and undeveloped lands. Although such boundaries reduce contiguous sprawl, they may, if too tightly drawn, promote leapfrog development.

Rate-of-growth programs, which are the least common of the types discussed here, directly regulate the community's growth rate without particular regard to capacity. Development under such a program may occur more slowly, or more quickly, than public facility capacities would otherwise permit. Such a program does not necessarily control the location of development and may or may not affect the pattern of urban growth.

These regulatory techniques are analyzed in subsequent chapters of the book, together with the non-regulatory techniques presented in Chapter 5.

NOTES

1. Avijit Mukherjee, Eugene R. Russell, and E. Dean Landman, "Building a Travel Demand Model for a Small City," *Transportation Quarterly* 55, no. 4 (2001); for some innovative work in the field, see G. Arampatzis et al., "A GIS-Based Decision Support System for Planning Urban Transportation Policies," *European Journal of Operations Research* 152, no. 2 (2004).
2. Fla. Stat. §163.3180; discussed in James C. Nicholas, "Growth Management and Smart Growth in Florida," *Wake Forest Law Review* 35, no. 3 (2000), and in Eric Damian Kelly, ed., *Zoning and Land Use Controls*, Supplemented to date. ed., 10 vols. (New York: Matthew Bender & Company, 2003), vol. 1, sect. 4.06.
3. Broward Co. Code, §5-182 (available at www.municode.com); discussed in James Duncan and Associates Inc. and Kelly, "Adequate Public Facilities Study for Montgomery County, Maryland."
4. Codified as Vt. Stat. Ann. tit. 10, § 6021.
5. Colo. Rev. Stat. Sec. 30-s28-133(6).
6. Greenberg, "A Commentary on the Sewer Moratorium as a Piecemeal Remedy for Controlling Development." For a discussion of the legal implications of a moratorium, see Eric Damian Kelly, "Piping Growth, the Law, Equity and Economics of Sewer & Water Connection Policies," *Land Use Law & Zoning Digest* 36, no. 7 (1984); Kelly, ed., *Zoning and Land Use Controls*, vol. 2, Chapter 22.
7. Richard T. Le Gates and Sean Nikas, "Growth Control through Residential Tempo Controls in the San Francisco Bay Area," in *San Francisco State University Public Research Institute Working Paper Series* (San Francisco: 1989), 20; Williams, *American Land Planning Law: Cases and Materials*, vol. 3A (1988), 164–67.
8. *Associated Homebuilders of Greater Eastbay, Inc., v. City of Livermore*, 18 Cal3d 582, 135 Cal Rptr 41, 557 P2d 473 (1976).
9. James Duncan and Associates Inc. and Kelly, "Adequate Public Facilities Study for Montgomery County, Maryland."
10. City of Livermore, "City of Livermore General Plan: 2003–2025 [Draft]," (Livermore, Calif.: City of Livermore, 2003), I-2.
11. Ibid., Chapter 3, Land Use Element, 3–7, 3–8.
12. Bonita Brewer, "Livermore Candidates Divided on Growth," *Contra Costa Times*, October 1, 2003.
13. Callies, Neuffer, and Caliboso, "Ballot Box Zoning: Initiative, Referendum and the Law"; Thomas Cronin, "The Pros and Cons of Popular Initiatives," in *Management & Control of Growth: Updating the Law*, ed. Frank Schnidman and Jane Silverman (Washington, D.C.: Urban Land Institute, 1980); Daniel J. Curtin, Jr. and Thomas C. Wood, "Ballot Box Planning, Growth Control" (San Francisco: McCutchen, Doyle, Brown & Enersen, 1989). See additional articles in Frank Schnidman and Jane Silverman, *Management & Control of Growth: Updating the Law*, vol. 5 (Washington, D.C.: Urban Land Institute, 1980).
14. City of Westminster, "[Untitled Working Documents on Growth Management] A, B, C and D" (Westminster, Colo.: City of Westminster, 1978), charts 78C(1) through 78C(4) and Report B, 13.

15. City of Westminster, "Growth Management Plan: Phase II Report" (Westminster, Colo.: City of Westminster, 1978). The Westminster situation in 1977 and 1978 is described in somewhat more detail in Eric Damian Kelly, "Comment on Westminster Growth Control Cases," *Land Use Law & Zoning Digest* 34, no. 3 (1982), and in depth in Snyder, "An Evaluation of Colorado's Attempts to Cope with Rapid Growth."
16. Kelly, "Comment on Westminster Growth Control Cases"; Snyder, "An Evaluation of Colorado's Attempts to Cope with Rapid Growth"; Westminster, "Growth Management Plan: Phase II Report."
17. *Reed v. Planning and Zoning Commission of Chester*, 208 Conn 431, 544 A2d 1213 (1988).
18. Fla. Stats. §163.3180.
19. Ronald L. Weaver, "Concurrency, Concurrency Alternatives, Infrastructure, Planning and Regional Solution Issues," an article included in "Nelson Symposium on Florida's Growth Management Legislation," 12 *Florida Journal of Law and Public Policy*, 251–52 (Spring 2001); citation to statute, cited immediately above, and other notes omitted.
20. Williams, *American Land Planning Law: Cases and Materials*, vol. 3a (1985), 106.
21. James Duncan and Associates Inc. and Kelly, "Adequate Public Facilities Study for Montgomery County, Maryland."
22. Ibid.; James Duncan and Associates Inc. and Kelly, "Technical Appendix to Adequate Public Facilities Study for Montgomery County, Maryland"; Le Gates and Nikas, "Growth Control through Residential Tempo Controls in the San Francisco Bay Area."
23. City of San Jose (San Jose, Calif.: City of San Jose, San Jose 2020 General Plan).
24. Ibid., 1 (summary, under "Major Strategies").
25. James Duncan and Associates Inc. and Kelly, "Adequate Public Facilities Study for Montgomery County, Maryland."
26. Douglas Andrew Greenberg, "Growth and Conflict at the Suburban Fringe: The Case of the Livermore-Amador Valley" (Ph.D. diss., University of California, 1986), 321.
27. James Duncan and Associates Inc. and Kelly, "Adequate Public Facilities Study for Montgomery County, Maryland."
28. See several chapters in Bosselman, Feurer, and Siemon, *The Permit Explosion: Coordination of the Proliferation*; for a later discussion based on the work of a federally appointed study commission, see Advisory Commission on Regulatory Barriers to Affordable Housing, "'Not in My Backyard': Removing Barriers to Affordable Housing" (Washington, D.C.: U.S. Department of Housing and Urban Development, 1991).
29. Real Estate Research Corp., "The Costs of Sprawl: Environmental and Economic Costs of Alternative Residential Development Patterns at the Urban Fringe."
30. See, for example, Staff of the U.S. General Accounting Office, "Land Use Issues" (Washington, D.C.: U.S. General Accounting Office, 1978).
31. Brower, *Urban Growth Management through Development Timing*, 109.
32. Anderson, "Use and Implementation of Urban Growth Boundaries"; Lexington-Fayette Urban County Planning Commission, "2001 Comprehensive Plan" (Lexington, Ky.: Lexington-Fayette Urban County Planning Commission, 2001).
33. Lexington-Fayette Urban County Planning Commission, "2001 Comprehensive Plan," I-4.
34. Albert A. Bartlett, *Recollections of the Origins of Boulder's Blue Line City Charter Amendment* (Boulder Community Network, September 26, 2000 [cited November 2003]); Snyder, "An Evaluation of Colorado's Attempts to Cope with Rapid Growth."

35. City of Boulder, "Boulder Open Space, Parks and Trails Map" (Boulder: Zia Maps/City of Boulder, 1991); City of Boulder, "Boulder's Open Space: Then and Now" (Boulder: City of Boulder, 1992); City of Boulder, Planning and Development Services Department and Boulder County Land Use Department, "Boulder Valley Comprehensive Plan" (2001).

36. William Fulton and Ted Mondale, "Managing Metropolitan Growth: Reflections on the Twin Cities Experience," in *Case Study* (Washington, D.C.: Brookings Institution, 2003); see also, Orfield, *Metropolitics: A Regional Agenda for Community and Stability.*

37. Orfield, *Metropolitics: A Regional Agenda for Community and Stability.*

38. Snyder, "An Evaluation of Colorado's Attempts to Cope with Rapid Growth," 248.

39. Boulder, "Boulder Open Space, Parks and Trails Map."

40. David L. Callies, "Dealing with Scarcity: Land Use and Planning," in *Politics and Public Policy in Hawaii*, ed. Zachary A. Smith and Richard C. Pratt (Albany: State University of New York Press, 1992).

41. Fulton and Mondale, "Managing Metropolitan Growth: Reflections on the Twin Cities Experience," 3.

42. Uri Avin and Michael Bayer, "Right-Sizing Urban Growth Boundaries," *Planning*, February 2003.

43. Gerrit Knaap, "The Price Effects of Urban Growth Boundaries in Metropolitan Portland, Oregon," *Land Economics* 61 (1985).

44. Arthur C. Nelson, "Oregon's Urban Growth Boundary Policy as a Landmark Planning Tool," in *Planning the Oregon Way: A Twenty-Year Evaluation*, ed. Carl Abbott, Deborah A. Howe, and Sy Adler (Corvallis: Oregon State University Press, 1994).

45. Avin and Bayer, "Right-Sizing Urban Growth Boundaries," 26.

46. V. Gail Easley, "Staying Inside the Lines: Urban Growth Boundaries," in *Planning Advisory Service* (Chicago: American Planning Association, 1992); Nelson, "Oregon's Urban Growth Boundary Policy as a Landmark Planning Tool"; see also, Arthur C. Nelson and James B. Duncan, *Growth Management Principles and Practices* (Chicago and Washington, D.C.: Planners Press, American Planning Association, 1995).

47. Dyett & Bhatia, "Existing Conditions 2002."

48. United States Bureau of the Census, *Quick Tables* (U.S. Department of Commerce, 2000 [cited November 2003]); available from http://factfinder.census.gov/.

49. 2000 population was 54,548, and household size was 2.70. Ibid. (cited).

50. See discussion of this concept in David [Theodore] Dubbink, "Cosmopolitan Villages: Growth Management Planning and the Vision of Small Town Society" (University of California, Los Angeles, 1983), 176–79.

51. Boulder and Department, "Boulder Valley Comprehensive Plan," 119–20.

52. *Robinson v. City of Boulder*, 190 Colo 357, 547 P2d 228 (1976); the lower court opinion, which rejected a challenge to the original, "interim" growth policy, is reproduced at pp. 237–252 in Scott, Brower, and Miner 1975b. The case is also discussed in Eric Damian Kelly, "*Robinson v. Boulder,* a Balance to *Ramapo* and *Petaluma,*" *Real Estate Law Journal* 5 (1976).

53. Dubbink, "Cosmopolitan Villages: Growth Management Planning and the Vision of Small Town Society."

54. Ibid., 129.

55. See, generally, James Duncan and Associates Inc. and Kelly, "Adequate Public Facilities Study for Montgomery County, Maryland"; the Boulder point program is

described in Sandra Cooper, "Growth Control Evolves in Boulder," in *Growth Management: Keeping on Target*, ed. Douglas R. Porter (Washington, D.C.: Urban Land Institute, 1986).

56. Petaluma, "Residential Growth Management System User's Guide," Chapter 3, answer to question 2.

57. Ed Gawf, January 15, 1985.

58. James Leach, "A Homebuilder Looks at Boulder's Growth Controls," in *Growth Management: Keeping on Target?* ed. Douglas R. Porter (Washington, D.C.: Urban Land Institute, 1986), 35. The publication date is deceptive; the article was based on remarks at a 1985 conference. The context of the article, including the last sentence included in the quotation, make it clear that the quoted remarks are about the old system, which had been replaced by the pro-rated system some months before the conference.

59. Paul Danish, "Boulder's Self Examination," in *Growth Management: Keeping on Target?* ed. Douglas R. Porter (Washington, D.C.: Urban Land Institute, 1986), 27.

60. Meadows and Club of Rome, *The Limits to Growth; a Report for the Club of Rome's Project on the Predicament of Mankind*.

61. Commission on Population Growth and the American Future, "Population and the American Future."

62. Finkler, "Nongrowth as a Planning Alternative: A Preliminary Examination of an Emerging Issue"; Finkler, "Nongrowth: A Review of the Literature."

63. Snyder, "An Evaluation of Colorado's Attempts to Cope with Rapid Growth."

64. Ibid., 286–88.

65. James Duncan and Associates Inc. and Kelly, "Technical Appendix to Adequate Public Facilities Study for Montgomery County, Maryland," unpublished screening survey.

66. Ibid.

67. See, generally, discussion of Robinson, above, and Chapter 5; as well as specific discussions of Boulder in Cooper, "Growth Control Evolves in Boulder"; Gleeson et al., "Urban Growth Management Systems," 10–11; Sylvia Lewis, "The Town That Said No to Sprawl," in *Balance Growth: A Planning Guide for Local Government*, ed. John Melvin De Grove (Washington, D.C.: International City Management Association, 1990).

68. Boulder and Department, "Boulder Valley Comprehensive Plan"; Cooper, "Growth Control Evolves in Boulder."

69. City of Westminster Code §11-3-4, available at www.ci.westminster.co.us/Code/title11/T11C3.htm.

70. Kelly, "Comment on Westminster Growth Control Cases"; Westminster, "[Untitled Working Documents on Growth Management] A, B, C and D."

71. Snyder, "An Evaluation of Colorado's Attempts to Cope with Rapid Growth," 219–22.

72. City of Westminster Code §11-3-4, available at www.ci.westminster.co.us/Code/title11/T11C3.HTM.

73. See Kelly, "Comment on Westminster Growth Control Cases"; the most important of the court decisions was *P.W. Investments v. City of Westminster*, 655 P2d 1365 (Colo 1982).

74. Montgomery County Planning Board, "First Annual Growth Policy Report: Framework for Action."

75. Ibid., 34.

76. Ibid., 38.

77. Ibid., 52–53, 107–12.
78. Ibid., 111.
79. Ibid., 117.
80. Ibid., 125.
81. Ibid., 125–26.
82. Ibid., 127–35.
83. Montgomery County Planning Board, "FY. 1991" (Silver Spring: Maryland-National Capital Park and Planning Commission, 1990), 13–20.
84. Ibid., 4.; Montgomery County Planning Board, "Annual Growth Policy for Montgomery County, 2003" (Silver Spring: Maryland National Capital Park and Planning Commission, 2002), 14.
85. Joseph Clancy, "Montgomery County's Development Hurdles," in *Growth Management: Keeping on Target?* ed. Douglas R. Porter (Washington, D.C.: Urban Land Institute, 1986); Montgomery County Planning Board, "Annual Growth Policy for Montgomery County, 2003," 8.
86. See Montgomery County Planning Board, "Annual Growth Policy for Montgomery County, 2003," 16, 17, but note that the policy itself has been included in the annual policies for many years.
87. Clancy, "Montgomery County's Development Hurdles," 97.
88. Montgomery County Planning Board, "FY. 92 Annual Growth Policy" (Silver Spring: Maryland-National Capital Park and Planning Board, 1991). Although the 2003 policy did not reiterate this list, there is no indication that it has changed substantially.
89. Matt Hamblen, "Montgomery County at the Crossroads," *Planning*, June 1991.
90. Andrew R. Watkins, "Impacts of Land Development Charges," *Land Economics* 75, no. 3 (1999).
91. See, for example, Connie B. Cooper, Eric D. Kelly, and American Planning Association, *Transportation Impact Fees and Excise Taxes: A Survey of 16 Jurisdictions, Planning Advisory Service Report No. 493* (Chicago: American Planning Association, 2000); James E. Frank and Robert M. Rhodes, eds., *Development Exactions* (Chicago: Planners Press, 1987); Arthur C. Nelson, *System Development Charges for Water, Wastewater, and Stormwater Facilities* (Boca Raton, Fla.: CRC Press, 1995); Arthur C. Nelson and American Planning Association, *Development Impact Fees: Policy Rationale, Practice, Theory, and Issues* (Chicago: Planners Press, American Planning Association, 1988); Susan G. Robinson, ed., *Financing Growth: Who Benefits? Who Pays? And How Much?* (Washington, D.C.: Government Finance Research Center, 1990).
92. Richard F. Babcock, ed., "Symposium: Exactions: A Controversial New Source for Municipal Funds," *Law and Contemporary Problems* 50 (1987).
93. Irving Schiffman, *Alternative Techniques for Managing Growth* (Berkeley: Institute of Governmental Studies, University of California at Berkeley, 1990).
94. See Kelly and Becker, *Community Planning: An Introduction to the Comprehensive Plan,* So and Getzels, eds., *The Practice of Local Government Planning* and sources cited in both.
95. David J. Brower, David R. Godschalk, and Douglas R. Porter, eds., *Understanding Growth Management: Critical Issues and a Research Agenda* (Washington, D.C.: Urban Land Institute, 1989).
96. Bosselman, Feurer, and Siemon, *The Permit Explosion: Coordination of the Proliferation.*

97. Frank Schnidman, Jane A. Silverman, and Rufus D. Young, Jr., eds., *Management & Control of Growth: Techniques in Application*, 4 vols., vol. 4, *Management & Control of Growth* (Washington, D.C.: Urban Land Institute, 1978).

98. Glenn V. Fuguitt, Paul R. Voss, and J. C. Doherty, *Growth and Change in Rural America*, 7 vols., vol. 7, *Management and Control of Growth* (Washington, D.C.: Urban Land Institute, 1979).

99. Ibid., 75–90.

100. Ibid., 88–89.

101. Douglas R. Porter, *Growth Management: Keeping on Target? Lincoln Institute Monograph; #86-1* (Washington, D.C.: Urban Land Institute, in association with Lincoln Institute of Land Policy, 1986).

102. Paul L. Niebanck, "Conclusion: The Second Generation of Growth Management," in *Growth Management: Keeping on Target?* ed. Douglas R. Porter (Washington, D.C.: Urban Land Institute, 1986), 215–16.

103. Ibid., 216.

104. Brower, Godschalk, and Porter, eds., *Understanding Growth Management: Critical Issues and a Research Agenda*.

105. Ibid., 162.

106. Douglas R. Porter, "Significant Research Needs in the Policy and Practice of Growth Management," in *Understanding Growth Management: Critical Issues and a Research Agenda*, eds. David J. Brower, David R. Godschalk, and Douglas R. Porter (Washington. D.C.: Urban Land Institute, 1989), 189.

107. Dowell Myers, "The Ecology of 'Quality of Life' and Urban Growth," in *Understanding Growth Management: Critical Issues and a Research Agenda*, eds. David J. Brower, David R. Godschalk, and Douglas R. Porter (Washington, D.C.: Urban Land Institute, 1989), 87.

108. Godschalk, *Constitutional Issues of Growth Management*.

109. Ibid.

110. Ibid., 218–19.

111. Nelson and Duncan, *Growth Management Principles and Practices*.

112. John DeGrove, ed., *Balanced Growth: A Planning Guide for Local Government* (Washington, D.C.: International City Management Association, 1991).

113. Robert G. Healy and Resources for the Future, *Land Use and the States* (Baltimore, Md.: Published for Resources for the Future by Johns Hopkins University Press, 1976); Robert G. Healy, John S. Rosenberg, and Resources for the Future, *Land Use and the States*, 2nd ed. (Baltimore, Md.: Published for Resources for the Future by Johns Hopkins University Press, 1979).

114. Frank Popper, *The Politics of Land-Use Reform* (Madison, Wis.: University of Wisconsin Press, 1981).

115. Fred P. Bosselman, David L. Callies, and Council on Environmental Quality (U.S.), *The Quiet Revolution in Land Use Control* (Washington, D.C.: For sale by the Supt. of Docs., U.S. Government Printing Office, 1972).

116. Michael Teitz, "California Growth: Hard Questions, Few Answers," in *California Policy Choices*, eds. John J. Kirlin and Donald R. Winkler (Los Angeles: University of Southern California, 1991).

117. Judith Innes, "Implementing State Growth Management in the U.S.: Strategies for Coordination," in *Institute of Urban and Regional Development Working Paper Series* (Berkeley, Calif.: Institute of Urban and Regional Development, 1991).

118. John DeGrove, "Growth Management and Governance," in *Understanding Growth Management: Critical Issues and a Research Agenda*, eds. David J. Brower, David R. Godschalk, and Douglas R. Porter (Washington, D.C.: Urban Land Institute, 1989).

119. Abe, "Urban Growth Management: Trends, Issues and Responsibilities."

120. Snyder, "An Evaluation of Colorado's Attempts to Cope with Rapid Growth."

121. Gerrit Knaap, "The Price Effects of an Urban Growth Boundary: A Test for the Effects of Timing" (Ph.D. diss., University of Oregon, 1982); Knaap, "The Price Effects of Urban Growth Boundaries in Metropolitan Portland, Oregon."

122. William A. Fischel and Lincoln Institute of Land Policy, *Do Growth Controls Matter?: A Review of Empirical Evidence on the Effectiveness and Efficiency of Local Government Land Use Regulation* (Cambridge, Mass.: Lincoln Institute of Land Policy, 1989), 23–24.

123. Dubbink, "Cosmopolitan Villages: Growth Management Planning and the Vision of Small Town Society," 26.

124. Greenberg, "Growth and Conflict at the Surburban Fringe: The Case of the Livermore-Amador Valley."

125. Le Gates and Nikas, "Growth Control through Residential Tempo Controls in the San Francisco Bay Area."

126. Madelyn Glickfeld and Ned Levine, *Regional Growth—Local Reaction: The Enactment and Effects of Local Growth Control and Management Measures in California* (Cambridge, Mass.: Lincoln Institute of Land Policy, 1992).

127. Gerrit J. Knapp, ed., *Land Market Monitoring for Smart Urban Growth* (Cambridge, Mass.: Lincoln Institute of Land Policy, 2001).

128. Knaap and Traci Severe, "Toward a Residental Land Market Monitoring System," Ch. 9; pp. 241–264, and Amy S. Bogdon, "Monitoring Housing Affordability," Ch. 12, pp. 307–332; both in Knaap, ibid.

129. John D. Landis, "Do Growth Controls Work? A New Assessment," in *Institute of Urban and Regional Development Working Paper* (Berkeley, Calif.: Institute of Urban and Regional Development, 1991).

130. Ibid.

131. William A. Fischel, *Do Growth Controls Matter? A Review of Empirical Evidence on the Effectiveness and Efficiency of Local Government Land Use Regulation* (Cambridge, Mass.: Lincoln Institute of Land Policy, 1990).

132. Benjamin Chinitz, "Growth Management: Good for the Town, Bad for the Nation?" *Journal of the American Planning Association* 56 (1990).

CHAPTER 5

Non-Regulatory Techniques to Manage Growth

Some of the most important governmental activities that control the rate, timing and location of growth involve activities of a local government other than the exercise of its regulatory powers. The most typical "non-regulatory" activity of local government is spending money. The annexation of territory or the purchase of land are also activities that, from the perspective of a local government, do not involve its regulatory powers. This chapter includes several such activities under the general heading, "non-regulatory activities." These activities may, of course, be regulated by other levels of government; few activities in the contemporary United States are totally free of regulation. However, from the perspective of the actor, these activities are not regulatory.

Activities described in this chapter include building new highways and sewer lines, agreeing to make land part of a city through annexation and purchasing strategically located land to prevent or control its development.

ANNEXATION

Annexation is the process through which a city or other municipal government expands its territorial boundaries. As two academic analysts concluded, "[T]hroughout the 1970s, as earlier, municipal annexation was the primary means by which local governments, particularly those in metropolitan areas, regulated their physical expansion."[1]

The purpose of annexation finds its roots in the structure of American local government, discussed briefly in Chapter 1. Citing North Carolina law, a 1989 study noted that the express purpose of annexation is to "make municipal that which is urban."[2] Although all territory within a state is subject to the jurisdiction of some form of local government, those local governments vary greatly in their purpose and authority. In the majority of states, the form of local government with jurisdiction over the largest land areas is the county (Louisiana's parishes are similar). The county was created as a branch of state government, with the county courthouse serving as the local office for a variety of state functions when, lacking twentieth-century transportation and communications systems, residents found the state capital relatively inaccessible.[3] Counties continue to handle such state operations as maintaining land records, assessing property for taxation, registering voters, serving legal process (through the sheriff), building and maintaining roads, managing social service (welfare) programs and registering vehicles. All of these require, or at least function better with, some degree of geographical convenience to citizens, something that is not available if the services are only offered from the state capitol.

Some county officials who are elected by county residents have express duties to the state; the sheriff and, in many states, the local prosecuting attorney, are primary examples. Judges, who are often housed in the county courthouse, are typically officers of the state, not the county.[4]

Counties in most states have been given at least limited authority over their own territory. For example, the authority for county zoning and subdivision control in the "unincorporated" territory is common. However, counties in many states lack general ordinance, or local lawmaking, power and the authority to operate a police force. Although counties in some states have the authority to offer such urban services as street lighting, sanitary sewer and potable water service, counties in others do not. Further, even where counties have such authority, there are difficulties in implementation. If a county has within its general jurisdiction an urbanized area next to a city, it faces conflicting pressures regarding service and equity. Should it: provide sewer, water, streetlighting and police services throughout the county in order to accommodate the needs of residents of the urbanized area; provide different levels of service in the two areas and attempt to adjust for the differences through user fees or other fiscal policies; or continue to function largely as a rural form of government, offering few if any municipal services? Although some counties have elected to provide significant urban services, the reasons for not doing so are many.

Thus, new development typically occurs within the boundaries of municipalities. Many municipalities have significant undeveloped areas within their existing borders. New development may take place on such land. In some cases it may be possible for a developer or group of developers to incorporate a new municipality.[5] It is more difficult for a developer to incorporate a new municipality in states, such as California, that provide rigorous administrative or quasi-legislative review of proposed incorporations.[6]

However, an easy way for a developer to ensure the availability of urban services is through annexation to an existing municipality. Not surprisingly, a detailed study of the motives behind annexations in two cities found that a substantial number were initiated by "builders and Realtors."[7] That study found that one-quarter of the requests for annexation to Milwaukee over a 30-year period were initiated by builders and Realtors and that 42 percent of such requests to the City of San Antonio, Texas, were initiated by builders and Realtors. Why do developers want territory annexed? To obtain urban services. A study of annexations to Milwaukee and San Antonio, cited the desire for services as a recurrent theme and found that in virtually all cases, there was in fact an increase in services after annexation.[8] The desire for services is a perfectly logical motivation for developers.[9]

Municipalities initiate or consent to annexation for a variety of reasons. A municipality may annex territory to ensure the availability of land for future development. It may seek an improved tax base. A study of annexations to Charlotte, North Carolina, found that annexation in fact improved the public fiscal circumstances, resulting in reduced taxes with a steady level of services.[10] A broader study, by the author of the Charlotte study and another person, reached a similar conclusion,[11] although a separate study from the same period noted that not every annexation has a positive fiscal impact.[12] The existence of property tax rate limits may accelerate municipal desires to annex.[13] Sales tax revenues from new commercial development also provide significant motivation to annex territory in those states where local governments receive a portion of sales tax revenues directly.

Some annexations are defensive, in the sense that the best defense is a good offense. Thus, annexation wars in growing metropolitan areas may lead to annexation of increased amounts of territory, perhaps far beyond current needs to absorb development.[14] A city may also annex territory simply to assert zoning and regulatory control over the land, to ensure that such high-impact uses as feedlots, adult entertainment establishments and salvage yards are not established on the urban fringe without municipal control. To assert regulatory control, an annexation may be necessary because the county lacks land use control authority or has not exercised it, or because different political values in the county may lead to different decisions than the city might like. Such a protective annexation is less necessary in those states which permit some form of "extraterritorial" zoning or land use control, allowing the city to assert regulatory control along its borders without annexing the territory.

What does all of this have to do with growth management? A great deal. If a developer needs or wants annexation in order to obtain municipal services, a denial of annexation may leave a proposed development without urban services and consequently unbuilt. The corollary is that annexation in many cases makes the development of the annexed territory a good deal more likely than it would be if the property were not annexed. Once territory has been annexed to a city, the city may, as a matter of course, provide urban services. In some states, property owners and potential developers have a right to demand services similar to those provided in other areas. Politically it is difficult for a city not to provide services to an area that has been paying city taxes. For these and other reasons, two social scientists concluded that "[I]t is likely that suburbs which annex territory acquire the space for residential development which attracts in-migrants."[15]

Thus, simply by constraining its borders, a municipality may be able to influence significantly the location of growth around it. That concept forms the basis of state growth management programs in Hawaii and Oregon (see next chapter), but it also provides a lesson for other communities. Refusing to expand territorial boundaries may have little effect on urban form if there are other communities nearby and if one or more of them is willing to annex territory rejected by another.

Annexation policy can be an effective growth management tool, but it is not one that falls entirely under local control. According to a comprehensive analysis in the mid-1980s, only Idaho, Nebraska and North Carolina allowed unilateral municipal annexation. Six other states give the municipality control subject to consent of the annexed area and three more give the municipality control subject to consent of both the annexed area and the municipality. Five states required judicial review of annexation proposals, while ten others had quasi-legislative bodies that review annexations against stated criteria. Sixteen states required a vote of the people for annexation and five required an act of the legislature.[16] Florida growth management expert John De Grove found the cumbersome annexation procedure in Washington to be a significant impediment to the state's growth management strategy. Although the state's policy of urbanization and use of "urban growth boundaries" suggest that most development should take place within city limits, the "triple majority" requirement of state law makes annexation very difficult by requiring approval by a majority of the residents of an area, a majority of the land parcels involved and a majority of the assessed valuation involved.[17]

Despite the fact that a municipality does not exercise complete control over annexation matters, in virtually all states the municipality can prevent an annexation by refusing to approve it; only in the five states where the legislature makes the determination does the system create a mechanism through which to force territory on a community, and such an action seems unlikely even in those states. In other states, the annexation process includes an act of the municipal governing body. If the governing body does not approve the annexation, the proposal goes no further. The additional procedures in those states simply provide an outside review or veto on annexations by a municipality. Thus, in most states a municipal government retains the key element of control of annexation, and that is the power to say, No.

Limiting the amount of annexation will not automatically limit the growth of a community. However, careful management of annexation practices is an important element in an effective growth management program, because extensive annexation of undeveloped territory can reduce rather than increase the degree of control that a community has over the location of growth.

THE GROWTH SHAPERS

The title of this section comes from a 1976 study, subtitled "The Land Use Impacts of Infrastructure Investments."[18] The author was first exposed to the concept several years before that, when a Realtor in southern New Jersey advised him to buy land near proposed interceptor sewer routes, because "growth follows sewers." As Marion Clawson noted, "The nominal planners are often not the real planners; sewer builders, transportation agencies, and other units of government often usurp the role assigned to the planning agency."[19]

An econometric model of development patterns in the Denver, Boston, Washington, D.C. and Minneapolis–St. Paul metropolitan regions during the period from 1960 to 1970 concluded that "public investments in transportation and wastewater facilities have identifiable and measurable effects on urban growth."[20] The study suggested that 10 to 15 percent of single-family construction was correlated with highway construction and a similar amount with sewer construction. However, it found that in some locations, depending on other conditions, up to 40 percent of development decisions might be attributable to such investments. Other variables in the study included land availability and price, zoning and land use controls, income levels of existing residents, existing levels of access and sewer service and vacancy rates. The impact of sewer investments in the study is particularly notable because the data all arose before the adoption of the Federal Water Pollution Control Act Amendments of 1972 (see discussion later in this section).

Growth does follow sewers and highways. Although it may be difficult to see the effects of sewers without a map of the lines, observing the effects of highways is considerably easier. The concentrations of intense commercial activity in a ring around Washington, D.C., the concentration of development in the Denver Technological Center area south of Denver, the elliptical shape of the Des Moines metropolitan region and the enormous growth between Dallas and Fort Worth all follow the paths of freeways that were built before most of the development occurred. In his detailed study of suburban growth in the San Francisco region, Dowall found that "Land development in the 1950s set the pattern for the years to come. Growth spread outward along all major transportation corridors; small towns within commuting range of employment centers became major cities in a few short years."[21]

It was the construction of the Tappan Zee Bridge that opened Rockland County to suburban commuting from New York, resulting in the growth pressure that led Clarkstown to adopt its early growth management program (see Figure 5.1 and Chapter 3). A decade later, in 1965, the opening of the New York State Thruway through Ramapo extended the Rockland County development pressure to that community, leading to the adoption of its own growth management program within four years.[22]

The pattern identified in *The Growth Shapers* is not a new one, nor is it a pattern that is limited to contemporary experience. An earlier book described the relationship between infrastructure investment and suburban Boston development patterns in the latter third of the nineteenth century.[23] It described how the development of streetcar systems by private companies and water and sewer service by public entities made possible the private development of land in the suburbs. Transportation (streetcars) opened the area to suburban development. Water service then made that development possible, and sanitary sewer service followed development pressures.

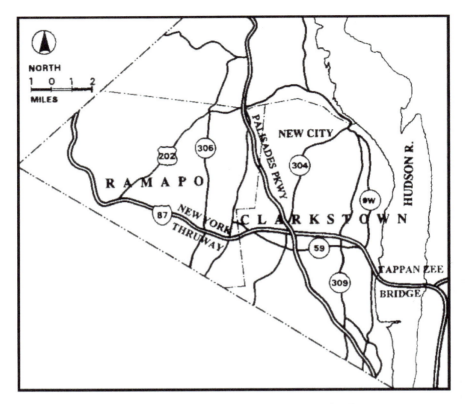

Figure 5.1   Map of southern Rockland County, New York, showing Ramapo,
Clarkstown, the Tappan Zee Bridge and New York Thruway. (*Source:*Adapted for first
edition by Jerzy Lewicki from original Rockland County Planning Department, 1991,
"County of Rockland." Prepared for second edition by Bram Barth.)

The book set out the "consequences" of the expansion of infrastructure to a suburban area covering a 10-mile radius from city hall. "Once a dense merchant
city clustered about an ocean port, Boston became a sprawling industrial metropolis. In 1850 it was a fairly small and unified area, by 1900 it had split into two functional parts: an industrial, commercial, and communications center packed tight
against the port, and an enormous outer suburban ring of residences and industrial
and commercial subcenters."[24]

A much earlier book analyzed the relationship between transit improvements
and land values in New York City in the 1920s.[25] The author found the transit
facilities to be a significant factor in facilitating development, although he did
not find a direct and certain increment in land values resulting from transit improvements. Despite some reservations, that study found essentially the same
thing that other studies did half a century later; the construction of transportation
improvements clearly influenced development pressures and related land values.

In addition to influencing the location of development, infrastructure investment also influences the type of development that will take place. Thus, one finds intense commercial or residential development at critical freeway interchanges and mass transit stations. Not surprisingly, an international study found a high degree of correlation between urban densities in general and use of mass transit, with a corresponding negative correlation between urban densities and highway use.[26] The study made no attempt to analyze cause-effect relationships between urban form and the availability of transit facilities or highways.

The Transportation Link

There are a variety of models of the relationship between transportation and land use patterns. A 1989 study examined a number of models that are based in microeconomics, macroeconomics and spatial theory, and that encompass experience in several of countries.[27] Lowdon Wingo, whose work was cited in the 1989 study, developed a model based on the premise that a consumer would spend a fixed amount on the combination of transportation and housing, including in the cost of transportation the value of commuting time.[28] In a work based in large part on field research, three academics writing in the 1960s noted that, "In urban areas, transportation expenditures and housing costs are substitutable in varying degrees."[29] One of the clear corollaries of such a substitution model is that commuting cost must vary inversely with housing cost.

Wingo's model and the other work cited here owe a debt to William Alonso's landmark work, *Location and Land Use*.[30] That frequently cited book presented an economic model of urban land values, with location and the related transportation costs as key variables. Wingo's work developed Alonso's model in a somewhat different direction.[31] Alonso used transportation costs to project the relative value of different pieces of land. Under Alonso's model, the parcel nearer the urban center would have a higher price than a piece further from the urban center; the price difference would, all other things being equal, be equal to the difference in respective transportation costs between each parcel and the urban center. Wingo's model started from the same conceptual base, but it modeled the choice of housing location for the individual consumer, rather than modeling the entire local land market. That is quite a different model. However, for purposes of this book, the important factor in both is that they recognize the critical link between transportation and the use and value of land.

A simpler "model" than Wingo's, if indeed it can be called a model, is the transportation planner's "circle" around a city, which is not a circle at all but an "iso-time" line. A 1951 Planning Advisory Service report described the analysis of the journey to work through the use of "iso-times," each of which is a "line connecting all geographic locations which are removed from an employment center by the same distance in time by the same means of transportation."[32] Although a geographer may be interested in the distance from the center of the city, a transportation planner uses these strange lines to reflect commuting time. The iso-time lines, of course, extend outward from the center along expressways and come

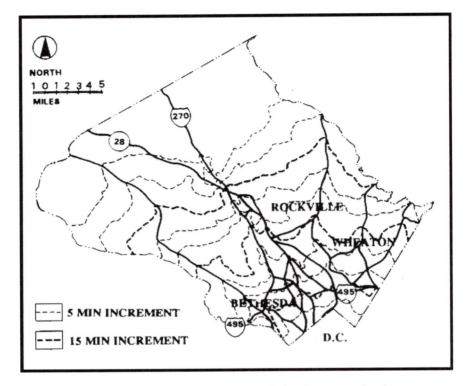

Figure 5.2   Map of Montgomery County, Maryland, showing commuting times to
Washington, D.C. (*Source:* Map from Montgomery County Planning Department, 1987,
*Alternative Transportation Scenarios and Staging Ceilings, a Background Report for the
FY89 AGP*, unnumbered map at p. 212 [original credits Douglas & Douglas, Inc.,
Gorove/Salde Associates, Inc., and Dynamic Concepts, Inc]; adapted for second edition
by Bram Barth.)

back toward the center where access is not as convenient. They reflect the simple
concept that commuting time is more critical than geographical distance to the
commuter. Figure 5.2 shows iso-time lines on routes leading to Washington, D.C.,
from Montgomery County, Maryland. The figure illustrates how a highway makes
land near it more accessible in minutes, even if the land is no closer to the city.

Consider the effect of opening a new freeway under either Wingo's model or a
simple model that simply reflects commuting time. Under Wingo's model, the
new freeway will, in most cases, reduce transportation time and resulting cost,
thus making areas along that route more desirable for development than they previously were. Existing housing along the route would, presumably, rise in value
as market forces restore equilibrium; this notion derives easily from Alonso's
model, if one substitutes the more critical time for the distance that he used for
simplicity. More important, the undeveloped land along that route would become

economically attractive for development. It is obvious that the new road changes the travel-time curves, reducing travel times to some areas and thus making them more attractive for development. Regions have become more complex, however, and now may have multiple centers.[33] Convenience in that context involves a weighing of the relative opportunity at various locations and the accessibility of each of those locations.[34] As a practical matter, most centers of opportunity develop at locations with good accessibility. The critical variable thus is the accessibility from the other end of the trip—where people live. Any increase in the transportation access from an undeveloped, or partly developed, portion of the metropolitan region will make that location more attractive for residential development. That principle holds even with a multi-centered model of the region.

All of this explanation may belabor the obvious. In a busy society, convenience is critical. Chains of "convenience" stores and fast-food restaurants profit greatly by catering to the desire of consumers to save time. Clearly, a new road link that increases the accessibility of an area, particularly when measured in commuting time, will significantly influence the behavior of developers and of the consumers whom they ultimately serve.

The Role of Sewer and Water Service

The explanation of the relationship between sewer lines and land development patterns is perhaps simpler, if somewhat less obvious, than the explanation of the relationship between highways and development.

Few consumers are likely to inquire about the availability of sewer lines when selecting a new residence. However, most consumers buy residences from entities that do concern themselves with such things. A 1976 study summed up the relationship succinctly:

Residential development is dependent on the availability of essential public services. Sewerage, along with highways and water supply, is among the most capital intensive of these services and, therefore, is frequently the most in demand. In the past, the provision of interceptor sewers often trailed behind other services because of low political priorities for environmental quality. Developers of residential housing dealt with the problem of waste disposal through the provision of septic tanks, local package treatment systems, or discharges of raw sewage into local receiving waters.

In recent years, rising public concern for environmental quality has led to strict new water quality regulations. Ad hoc solutions to the pollution problems of new residential development have been severely restricted through the enforcement of zoning restrictions on septic tank use, bans on new connections to existing collection sewer systems, and requirements for advanced wastewater treatment. As a result of these environmental standards, the lack of sewerage has become a real bottleneck to development and, in some localities, has halted residential construction.[35]

Although the quoted study was several years old when the first edition of this book was published, the data and analysis included in the study post-dated the landmark Federal Water Pollution Control Act Amendments of 1972 and thus remains relevant. That act marked the major national policy shift toward cleaning up the nation's waters, a policy shift destined to affect development patterns. The practical and political issues affecting the relationship between sewers and development have changed little.

The study just quoted, *Interceptor Sewers and Urban Sprawl,* found a positive correlation between excess capacity in interceptor sewers and urban sprawl.[36] The authors criticized sewer planning programs for deficiencies that included the tendency of local governments to be overly optimistic in population projections. They also criticized several EPA technical requirements that tended to increase projected demand and the resulting facility size. Among the recommendations of Binkley and his colleagues was that new development should pay all capital costs incident to serving it, a policy that has now been widely implemented.[37]

A study of land values in Clay, New York, found that, all other things being equal, a parcel of land with sewer service would sell for 1.8 to 3.0 times the price of a piece of land without sewer.[38] The authors commented that, "We did not determine the significance of either local roads or water or other utilities because within Clay, these facilities already existed. Sewers were, therefore, the final step in the process of providing required infrastructure for development."[39]

The authors of the New York study also traced the history of sewer lines as a control mechanism in Fairfax County, Virginia, an area that has long felt the suburban effects of growth around the nation's capital. A sewer moratorium there began under a state mandate resulting from water contamination in the area. Early in the process, the task of allocating the limited capacity available fell entirely to the engineers, with some participation from the Board of Supervisors (governing body). However, facing a growing concern among residents about the impacts of growth, the county subsequently used its sewer moratorium as a method to delay growth pressures while it designed and implemented a new "Planning and Land Use System."[40]

A 1989 study suggested that technology may limit the effectiveness of sewers as a growth management tool. A study in Wisconsin found that the improving technology of private sewage treatment systems offers developers a practicable alternative to public sewer, even with contemporary pollution control requirements.[41] Still, such systems are not feasible everywhere and some state health departments are less receptive to them than others.

The relationship between water supply and growth has received much less study than the relationship between sewer supply and growth. Two studies in the 1970s did examine how water affects growth patterns. Both concluded that there was no correlation between the availability of public water service and regional growth. One examined the growth of the Denver metropolitan region[42] and the other examined growth of selected counties in four states; Georgia, Minnesota, Pennsylvania and Oregon.[43]

The similar conclusions in the two studies are hardly surprising, because the influence of all these facilities is on the location of growth *within* a region, not on whether the region grows at all (see discussion later in this chapter). Because both studies simply examined the effect of water supply on total county or regional growth, they found none. In short, those studies asked a different question than the one considered here. There are two other problems with the cited studies. First, the Denver study was prepared for the Army Corps of Engineers as a defense of Corps plans to build the proposed Foothills Dam and Reservoir. The report responded to allegations of critics that the project would contribute to regional sprawl and resulting air pollution. The other study is puzzling because it examined only counties in wet states. Clearly, the influence of water supply is greater in arid states like Nevada and Colorado than in states like Georgia and Pennsylvania, that have extensive surface water supplies and accessible groundwater systems.

One would suspect, although the author found no studies to prove it, that the locational effects of the availability of water in arid states would be similar to the locational effects of sewer service in wet states. In wet states, water is often relatively accessible from shallow and inexpensive wells or from low-technology private systems. That would result in circumstances similar to those reflected in the Wisconsin study that found that the availability of private sewage treatment technology reduced the growth effects of sewer lines.[44] In general, it is in those same wet states in which sewage disposal is the most difficult, because high water tables and extensive surface water systems create greater risks of contamination from septic tanks. Thus, in the wet states, sewer service is the more scarce and thus more valuable commodity. Viewed from another perspective, in those states, a consumer or developer who has difficulty obtaining water can realistically consider drilling and using a well, but that same consumer or developer may find few alternatives for sewer service.

In contrast, in the arid states the priority system of water rights limits the legal ability of many people to drill wells, and the depth to good water limits the practicability of using wells. The same system limits the use of surface water to those who own the rights. However, in those states, there are comparatively large land areas on which septic tanks are unlikely to threaten water supplies, even in cases of marginal soils. In the arid states, water is the rarer commodity. A developer in an arid state who has a water supply can probably find a way to handle sewage, but a developer (or consumer) without water may not be able to build.

Note that there is an operational difference between the effects of sewer and water service on development patterns and the effects of highways. In most cases, highways simply increase the convenience of a particular location and thus make development there more convenient and more attractive. In contrast, the availability of water and sewer service is, in many locations and for many types of development, a prerequisite to development. Even in circumstances where a developer may be able to provide on-site sewer systems or use wells to provide water, it is a rare circumstance in which a developer can do both. Thus, the combination of utility services do not simply make development more convenient; they make it possible.

The Roles of Consumers and Developers

No single authority decides that the location of a new sewer line or new highway will change the patterns of growth in the region. In fact, transportation and utility planners often deny that their decisions affect growth. They are correct in a very technical and narrow sense. For example, one author argued that it is difficult to establish the link between transportation and land use, because the equation includes a third factor, the behavior of individuals.[45] Certainly that is implied in either Wingo's model or in the simple transportation planning iso-time lines.

A study that is now somewhat dated still seems entirely plausible in explaining why new transportation links can influence development patterns so significantly. Given the choice of living in a city of more than 500,000, a city with a population between 50,000 and 500,000, a smaller city within commuting distance of a large city or a small city further away, a majority of respondents (55 percent) preferred the small city within commuting distance of the larger city. Although 51 percent of those then living in a large city preferred to remain in a city, either large (36 percent) or smaller (15 percent), another 37 percent chose the alternative of living in a suburb near a city. A majority of those living in smaller cities preferred the suburban alternative.[46]

In 1956, Tiebout proposed a widely cited model that, among other things, attempted to explain the consumer choice involved in determining what community within a metropolitan area would become home for that consumer.[47] Tiebout created an idealized model in which different communities would offer different mixes of public goods, ranging from recreational facilities to basic public utility services. Each consumer would then select the community that provided the mix of public goods that best fit that consumer's needs and pocketbook. There are three problems with trying to apply Tiebout's model nearly five decades after it was published. First, some public goods are essential to providing the opportunity for anyone to reside in a community. As suggested in this chapter, those include, at a minimum, sewer and water service and reasonable access. Those goods are not readily available in all communities in a metropolitan area and the market thus skews toward the communities that include those basic public goods. Second, there are, at particular times and in particular communities, shortages in some public goods. Those lead to moratoria and other market limitations that further constrain consumer choice. Third, as the following material explains, individual consumers do not simply pick a community in which to live.

Any attempt to analyze urban form or the urban land market based on consumer behavior assumes that consumers may choose freely among all locations within the metropolitan region. That is simply not the case. Few consumers buy raw land and develop their own homesites. In fact, most new housing consumers buy homes from homebuilders.

The location in which a consumer buys a home depends heavily on where homebuilders build. Thus, the behavior of builders is important. A survey of Phoenix-area builders found that the availability of services was a key element in the selection of locations for development.[48] It ranked behind zoning and attractiveness and prestige of the area. However, the survey was somewhat confusing, because it listed "availability of services" as one item and "utility extension not required" as another. The two are closely related, of course. If some respondents listed only one of those items in preference to the other, then the responses should be partially or wholly combined; such a revision to the tabulation would increase the rank of "service," perhaps to first or second on the list. The only surprising thing in the Phoenix study was that "near freeway" ranked relatively low among criteria for selection. The Phoenix findings were entirely consistent with an earlier survey of developers in the Vancouver, B.C., area which concluded that, "Developers require adequate supplies of zoned and sewered land *before* development can be considered."[49]

A separate study suggested one reason why highways may not have ranked higher in either survey:

Although analyses of pooled data [from four case studies] indicated that new highways have an impact on single-family housing construction, analyses of individual regions did not show any strong or consistent effect. In part this was probably because most of the regions analyzed had relatively good highway accessibility even before 1960. Each new highway in a region brings a successively smaller improvement in accessibility. These diminishing marginal changes imply diminishing marginal effects on location decisions and land use.[50]

However, a Minneapolis study concluded that highway access was still important, even by the late 1970s. It found that "general accessibility" was a "limiting factor" at the last two of a developer's three-stage site selection process and that roads and public and private utilities were limiting factors in the third stage, in which the developer typically selects a specific parcel of land (as opposed to a general area in which to develop).[51]

The explanation for the need for zoning relates to the uncertainties of the political process. The explanation for the need for sewer and other services is simpler still, money. As Richard Peiser has noted, "As a practical matter, extending utility services more than a mile or so from the end of existing lines is not economically feasible except for the largest developments."[52] *The Growth Shapers* explained the process simply:

Infrastructure influences local land use by changing the supply of developable land, the demand for development, or both. . . .

It is easiest to look at land use changes from the point of view of developers. They are the chief actors in the urbanization process, and deal with the market forces of supply and demand in the most direct and practical way. Developers acquire land, remove or modify any existing structures, build their projects and then seek tenants or buyers. They are, of course, interested primarily in profits. . . .

Infrastructure investments can lead to local increases in demand for development or reductions in development costs, and thus create a strong incentive for developers to locate their projects nearby. The presence of infrastructure can both reduce risk and increase profits for developers. While this is obvious, it is seldom adequately considered by infrastructure planners.[53]

A California researcher noted, perhaps unnecessarily, that highways do not *produce* (population) growth; they simply shift it from other locations within the region.[54] A University of Iowa study team found that highway construction alone would not produce economic development, although good transportation is clearly important to economic development.[55] Those positions are, of course, entirely consistent with the discussions here of developer behavior and consumer behavior. None of the discussions above analyzed the decision of a consumer choosing a new job and a new community in which to live; all of the studies tacitly but clearly presumed that the consumer had a job or other reason for being in the region and was selecting a location for a home within that region. Similarly, the decision of a developer about whether to develop in a particular region must be based on complex market analyses of the region. *The Growth Shapers* acknowledged that, "[G]rowth seems to be created by the installation of new infrastructure; actually, the infrastructure merely concentrates growth which might otherwise have been located elsewhere in the region."[56]

Having considered all of that, it is important to recognize two things. First, for a particular community within a larger region, a highway may indeed "produce" growth. In economic or regional planning terms, it will simply attract growth that would occur somewhere in the region, anyway. Further, the highway may very well induce growth in travel and resulting traffic totally separate from growth in population. By making travel more convenient, the highway encourages people to travel longer distances or to make new trips. Thus, the highway does indeed "create" certain types of growth, though neither a highway nor a utility line will actually create regional population growth. They simply influence its location.

Although the capacities of the transportation and utility systems are powerful determinants of growth patterns within a region, they have relatively little impact on the total amount of growth in the region as a whole. It was the developer's selection of a location within the region, not the selection of a region within which to be active, that was the subject of the studies in Phoenix and Vancouver.

In short, the direct impact of the location of sewer and water lines and highways is not on growth itself or even on consumer behavior. The direct impact affects the behavior of developers, who play the most active role in determining urban form. Individual consumers simply buy from those developers or from homebuilders who buy lots from the developers and then build homes on them. Consumer desires influence developer behavior, but it is the developer—not the consumer—who decides to build next to the new sewer line or highway and not on the other side of town. The developer selects a site near a highway, because the convenience is important to sales. The developer selects a site with water and sewer service, because local government will generally not approve building homes without those services and it is cheaper to tie into existing systems than to build new ones.

Sewer lines and highways are obvious "growth shapers." They can be powerful elements of a growth management program. Perhaps, more typically, the construction of such facilities without regard to growth management and other plans of the community can thwart, or at least substantially impede, those plans.

One important variable not considered in any depth up to this point is the issue of who makes important decisions about these facilities. Local growth management programs are generally implemented by local governments interested in local issues. Although the city councils and other governing bodies of those local governments generally control their own comprehensive plans, zoning ordinances and subdivision regulations, in many cases, they do not have direct control over other crucial decisions. Local officials typically have little, if any, influence over highway decisions. The most important highways are built by state agencies, using federal funds and following state and federal guidelines. Political decisions regarding the relative priority of roads and even their location are generally made at the state level.

That is gradually changing. In 1991, Congress finally acknowledged the significance of decisions about highways to local land use and planning concerns. The Intermodal Surface Transportation Efficiency Act of 1991[57] (its acronym, "ISTEA," was widely pronounced as a homonym for "iced tea") included strong planning provisions, with specific reference to land use issues. The title of the act itself was important, because it suggests a significant departure from the "highway bills" of past years. "Intermodal" indicates the emphasis of the new Act on multiple modes of transportation, including bicycle and pedestrian ways; bus, light rail and other forms of (mass) transit; and automobiles. It is "intermodal" rather than "multimodal," because the modes should connect to one another as part of a total system. "Surface transportation" simply distinguishes it from separate bills addressing air and transportation.

The new act continued the provision for regional planning by designated "Metropolitan Planning Organizations" and required the designation of an MPO for each urbanized area of more than 50,000.[58] The Act also broadened the planning requirements to be considered by the MPO. Among the fifteen "factors to be considered" in developing a metropolitan transportation plan are:

3. The need to relieve congestion and prevent congestion from occurring where it does not yet occur. . . .

4. The likely effect of transportation policy decisions on land use and development and the consistency of transportation plans and programs with the provisions of all applicable short- and long-term land use and development plans.[59]

The Act added a new requirement for state-level planning function. The states are responsible for coordinating metropolitan-level planning activities and developing a state implementation plan.[60] Among the factors to be considered by the states are:

3. Strategies for incorporating bicycle transportation facilities and pedestrian walkways in projects where appropriate throughout the state. . . .

6. Any metropolitan area plan. . . .

12. Methods to reduce traffic congestion and to prevent traffic congestion from developing in areas where it does not yet occur, including methods which reduce motor vehicle travel, particularly single-occupant motor vehicle travel.

13. Methods to expand and enhance transit services and to increase the use of such services.

14. The effect of transportation decisions on land use and land development, including
the need for consistency between transportation decisionmaking and the provisions of
all applicable short-range and long-range land use and development plans.[61]

   As the title suggested, the Act was not just another highway bill. Of the $151
billion authorized in it, $31.5 billion was specifically designated for mass transit.
Of the $119.5 billion remainder, $23.9 million was allocated to the "surface
transportation program," from which funds can be used for highways, transit or
bicycle and pedestrian ways. States with Clean Air Act "non-attainment" status
related to ozone can use all of those funds for mass transit and others can use
up to 75 percent of the funds for that purpose.[62] Of the total appropriation,
$3 billion, or about 2 percent, was designated for a "transportation enhancement
program." Those funds may be used for acquisition of scenic easements and historic sites, pedestrian and bike trails along abandoned rights-of-way or as part of
new projects, and control and removal of billboards, among other purposes.[63]

   Since the beginning of the federal highway program, highway planning, one of
the most powerful determinants of growth patterns, has been largely beyond the
control of local officials concerned with land use, growth management and related
issues, although they have had limited input through the old MPO planning
process. The land use and planning provisions of ISTEA were continued in its
successor, TEA-21 (Transportation Efficiency Act for the twenty-first century).[64]
As this book went to the publisher, there appeared to be bi-partisan support for an
extension of the intermodal philosophy in a new transportation act, being called
"Transportation Equity Act: A Legacy for Users," or, by some, "Tea-3."[65]

   With its emphasis on intermodal transportation and on coordination with local
planning, ISTEA and its successor(s) have provided a very different scenario for
transportation funding. Although California has experimented with turning over
much of its state transportation decision-making process to the regional MPOs,[66]
there has yet to be a significant shift to local or regional control in most of the
nation.[67] At this point, the effect of the land use and local planning provisions of
these acts appears to be similar to the effect of the National Environmental Policy
Act's requirement for environmental impact statements; the same agencies (state
transportation departments) remain in charge of the decision-making and appear
only to have adjusted their decision-making processes to accommodate the technical requirements of the law. The basic outcomes, however, appear to be similar to
those before the laws were passed. Federal money continues to be spent to expand
urban freeways, thus encouraging commuting by automobiles, even in cities with
substantial investments in mass transit systems. In Indiana, the state DOT in 2003
proposed a largely "greenfields" route for an I-69 extension from Indianapolis to
Evansville; the alternate, lower-cost route would have followed existing interstate
and U.S. highways, providing improved service to existing communities, rather
than opening several largely rural counties to highway-oriented strip development.[68]
Although there were certainly arguments in favor of each of the routes, it was clear
that land-use considerations carried virtually no weight in the decision process.

The control of sewer and water systems is more complex. Some sewer and water systems belong to regional entities that make decisions, much as highway departments do. One factor that led to the ultimate failure of the Ramapo growth management program was the fact that it did not control its own sewers. Sewer construction by the regional authority fell behind the schedule outlined in the original plan, posing major problems for the growth management program. Ramapo officials then elected to solve that problem by ignoring sewers as a factor in the program, an ironic twist indeed.[69]

Engineering and cost considerations are major factors used by regional authorities to make decisions about sewer system expansion. A dominant consideration in such decisions is the desire of engineers to ensure that sewage all flows downhill by gravity to the central treatment plant.[70] Many local governments control their own sewer and water systems. However, unlike the zoning and subdivision regulations and other growth-influencing tools, such systems typically do not remain under direct control of the policy makers. They are usually operated by "enterprise departments," run by technical experts who are charged with the duty to operate the systems safely, effectively and at a profitable or break-even level.[71] Thus, money drives everything. Engineers can easily make sewage flow uphill, if there is a reason to do so; however, it costs more. Thus, money, in the form of a profit from the enterprise department, is more important than many of the engineering considerations. A candid utilities director in a southwestern community once told the author, when asked why he was willing to provide utility service in an area shown on the comprehensive plan as inappropriate for growth, "I am running an enterprise department. I will provide service anywhere that I can make a profit. I will continue to do that until the city council tells me otherwise."

In theory, effective planning should eliminate conflicts between infrastructure construction plans and growth management plans. In practice, the planning processes are separate, even when a single local government makes most of the decisions. Plans for local roads and for sewer and water lines are typically included in a Capital Improvements Program (CIP). A good CIP is a rolling five-year or six-year plan for construction of new capital facilities, ranging from swimming pools to a new city hall to roads and sewer lines. The CIP is largely budget-driven.[72] The governing body, together with the chief administrative or executive officer and the chief budget official, typically control the process. They establish costs and priorities on the advice of the technicians responsible for the projects. Those technicians then control the implementation—the utilities director and traffic engineer in the case of sewer, water and road facilities.

In contrast, growth management programs typically evolve from the comprehensive planning process. Responsibility for the comprehensive plan lies with the planning commission. The planning director typically assists the commission in the process. Early model legislation, still in effect in most states, called for the planning commission simply to deliver the finished plan to the governing body. That process is not likely to generate any real interest of the governing body in the document. Although many jurisdictions now wisely involve the governing body in developing the comprehensive plan, the process is too seldom linked to the CIP and budgeting process.

Thus, dollars and engineering studies drive critical local decisions about the location and capacity of new sewer and water lines, just as dollars and engineering studies drive critical state decisions about the location and capacity of new freeways. There is nothing inherently wrong with that fact, except that it will often lead to results inconsistent with local growth management plans and may at times serve to thwart those plans.

If the only consideration of the local government is ensuring adequate highway and sewer capacity, then the loop will close nicely. Growth will follow the sewers and highways, which will then be available to serve the growth. However, if the new highway goes north of town and the new interceptor sewer line flows southwest from town, problems arise. If the growth management plan calls for directing development to the east of town, where capacity in schools and parks is greatest, the problem is substantial indeed.

Even where the governing body decides to use infrastructure construction policy as a growth management tool, it may encounter problems in doing so. First, within the city limits, it may be legally difficult to refuse to extend service. Outside the municipal boundaries, the community typically has more flexibility to set policy, although that flexibility is not unlimited.[73] Boulder lost a court challenge to its refusal to grant service to a developer with property adjoining a city-controlled system outside the city limits.[74]

Although a community may not be as free as it might like to be to deny service when there is adequate capacity or to refuse to connect users to existing lines, water and sewer lines can still be important tools in growth management. Courts in Colorado, including the Colorado Supreme Court, sustained Westminster's growth management program when it refused service because it lacked adequate capacity.[75] Professor David Callies cited the lack of infrastructure in large areas of Hawaii as one of three major factors that contributed to maintaining 95 percent of the land in that state in non-development categories, despite substantial pressures for tourist development.[76]

What can the growth managing community learn from all of this? In deciding to extend sewer and water lines into undeveloped areas, community officials should consider seriously whether the community wants those areas to develop. Although it has been relatively rare in the 1980s and early 1990s for local governments simply to extend such services *to* undeveloped territory, it is not at all unusual for them to extend services *through* undeveloped areas. The line may pass through undeveloped areas on the way to a new airport or a new industrial park or as a shortcut from one part of town to another. In some cases, the intervening lands are entirely suitable for development; in others they are not. Those suitability factors can and should be considered in the decision to extend the services through the area. As the authors of *Interceptor Sewers and Urban Sprawl* found, one of the major problems is the existence of excess capacity in lines.[77] A community could choose to extend to the new airport a line with exactly enough capacity to serve the airport. As the cited study indicates, engineers typically prefer a larger line with the capacity to serve future needs. However, those theoretical future needs are likely to become self-fulfilling predictions. Thus, the question of whether development is desirable along the route of the line is a critical question that should influence both the location and the size of the line.

The scope of the problem can be great indeed. Airports and residences are fundamentally incompatible, and communities take many steps to buffer airports from residences. However, if by extending major water and sewer lines to the airport or to an adjacent industrial park, the community opens the area to all kinds of development, it will create just the problems that it hoped to avoid. Building a good access road to the airport simply compounds the problems. Officials in the Washington, D.C., metropolitan area tried to avoid that problem by building an expressway to Dulles Airport that had no exits to Reston, Virginia, and other residential areas on the outbound lanes and no entrances from them on the inbound lanes. After years of watching commuters get on the roadway going toward the airport and then turn around at the airport to drive to Washington, officials gave up in the early 1990s and created a parallel commuter toll road in the original airport expressway right-of-way. Infrastructure-induced development will continue around the airport, increasing the probability of future conflicts between the airport and its neighbors.

Sometimes project planners themselves create the problems. In their zeal to minimize operating costs and problems by ensuring that everything flows by gravity, engineers seek the lowest possible location for each link in a sewer system. Interceptor sewers, the major lines in the system, thus wind up in the river bottoms. Those lands, of course, constitute the centers of floodplains. At the same time that they try to discourage development in floodplains, public officials allow people who work for them to build major growth magnets in the middle of those problem lands.

There is obviously no perfect solution to these complex problems. Clearly, interceptor sewer lines should not run along high ridgelines just to avoid floodplains. Equally clearly, a good airport must have good road access. However, by understanding the growth-shaping role of infrastructure investments and considering the secondary impacts of those investments, a community can make far better decisions. By understanding the process and attempting to implement a rational planning program, a local government certainly has the opportunity to do better than did those in California's Amador Valley who, according to one study, facilitated virtually uncontrolled growth through the provision of transportation, sewage collection and treatment and other public facilities "within a fragmented political structure in which there was virtually no overall coordination and planning."[78]

LAND ACQUISITION

Both Boulder, Colorado, and Montgomery County, Maryland, have recognized that owning land or rights in land can be an important element of an effective growth management program.[79]

Boulder has used land acquisition to establish a city-owned greenbelt around the city. Using revenues from a special sales tax passed by the voters in 1967 and from several subsequent bond issues, by 2003, the city acquired more than 43,000 acres of open space.[80] The city leases some of the open space to farmers for continued agricultural use and maintains other areas of open space as part of its active park and recreation system. Some open space is simply passive.[81] Open space owned by Boulder County, as well as mountain parks owned by both the city and the county, link with the open space to provide green space on most of the mountain backdrop to Boulder and for several miles to the south, blocking suburbanization from sprawling Denver suburbs. By 2003, the open-space system formed a complete and substantial greenbelt around the city (see Figure 5.3).

A publicly owned greenbelt stops continuous sprawl more effectively than any other technique, because it absolutely precludes development. In order to ensure that its greenbelt will continue to function as intended, Boulderites approved an amendment to the city charter in 1986, severely restricting the ability of the city to sell open-space land. Under the charter provision, any proposed sale of open-space land requires the affirmative vote of three of the five members of the open-space board as well as by the city council. Even after city council approval, citizens have a period of 60 days within which they can force a referendum on the sale by obtaining signatures of 5 percent of the eligible voters on a petition seeking such a referendum.[82]

Although a greenbelt is the strongest tool in the local arsenal for attempting to control urban form, it is not perfect. If the greenbelt is too narrow or the area within it too constrained, it may cause leapfrog development (see discussion in Chapter 7). There is evidence in Boulder County that the combination of growth management programs in Boulder and the effective programs precluding growth on the fringe of the city have redirected some growth to nearby Louisville, Longmont and Lafayette;[83] this topic is considered in some depth in Chapter 10. However, Boulder itself has a well-defined urban edge without the contiguous sprawl characteristic of many communities.

Montgomery County has used a combination of land acquisition and development rights acquisition to attempt to shape its urban areas. It has tried to preserve greenways along creeks as well as major agricultural areas.[84] Other communities have used the acquisition of development rights to preserve farmland.[85] Professor Ann Louise Strong described the efforts of a private group to preserve parts of the Brandywine Valley through development rights acquisition.[86] Although the project was not a complete success, her documentation of it provides valuable lessons for others interested in using similar techniques. Private groups have also been active in land acquisition in other communities, including Palm Beach County.[87]

The purchase of property is relatively simple, although it can also be expensive. Boulder has dedicated revenues from a special sales tax for that purpose. The acquisition of "development rights" may offer a less expensive alternative. The theory of purchasing development rights is that the acquiring entity does not purchase the entire bundle of the owner's land interests; rather, it acquires simply that part of the owner's interests representing the ability to develop the land. That

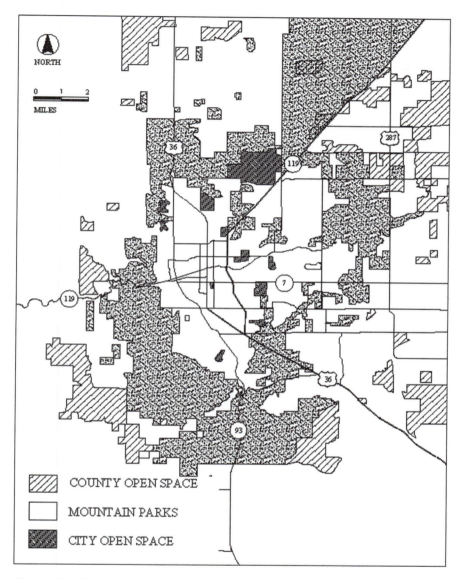

Figure 5.3 Map showing the city-owned greenbelt around Boulder, Colorado. (*Source:* City of Boulder, Colo., "City of Boulder Open Space and Mountain Parks 2001" [map]; adapted for second edition by Kyle Lueken.)

transaction leaves the seller with the residual land interest, which typically permits an agricultural use. The acquisition cost of development rights should consequently be less than the acquisition costs of the land by the amount of the residual value.[88] The acquisition of development rights makes the most sense where agricultural (or other residual) values are relatively high and where public services and growth pressures have not placed a high value on the land for development.[89]

Although the term "development rights" is used rather freely by planners, it does not refer to anything in particular. Water rights and mineral rights have been well defined through the common law in this country and in England, from which U.S. property law originates. In contrast, "development rights" are a modern invention. The legal mechanism through which they are acquired, however, is based on another common law concept, the easement. Under an easement, the holder of the easement (the "dominant estate" in legal terms) has the right to make limited use of another's property; the holder of the property (the "burdened estate") has free use of the property, except to the extent that it would interfere with the rights of the dominant estate holder. Classic uses of easements are for roadways, waterways and utility lines. William H. Whyte suggested the application of easement law to the acquisition of partial interests in open space in a short but very influential publication in the late 1950s.[90] Since that time most states have adopted legislation permitting the use of "conservation easements" or something similar, and the Internal Revenue Service has adopted regulations under which the value of the gift of a conservation easement is recognized.

One problem with property (or development rights) acquisition as a control technique is that the budget in any given year is limited and the short-term impact is thus limited, even in cases, such as Boulder, where the long-term impact is significant. One device that communities in many states might consider to make land acquisition programs more effective is the *Official Map Act*, originally included as part of the *Standard City Planning Enabling Act.*[91] Under that act, a local government can reserve property for future acquisition without acquiring it immediately. Although the primary use of the device over the years has been for reserving enlarged rights-of-way along existing roads, the act as adopted in many states includes "open space" or is otherwise broad enough to permit its use to reserve open space. A carefully drafted local ordinance can create an acquisition "trigger" that is pulled by a development application, thus forcing the community to acquire the property within a specified period. Such a device could, in effect, give a local government a broad option on targeted lands, with the priority always given to those lands threatened by development.

There are two disadvantages to the proposed scheme. First, as Strong pointed out, it is desirable and logical to try to acquire agricultural and other rural property before development pressures occur, to avoid paying the inflated price that development pressure brings to land.[92] Second, under a series of U.S. Supreme Court decisions, a local government that establishes such a system and then fails to acquire reserved property after the event triggering the reservation is likely to be held liable for "interim damages," representing the value of the loss of use of the property for whatever period use or development was delayed by the failure of the government to act.[93] A local government can mitigate the impact of those decisions, however, by providing a prompt determination of whether it intends to buy the property or forego its "option" in response to a development application.

One method of financing the preservation of open space is to require that development in particular areas—or affecting certain types of sensitive lands—be clustered, so that specified types or percentages of land area can be preserved as open space. A 2002 analysis by a land economist found that preservation of land as private open space added value to surrounding residential property, whereas preservation of the same land as public open space added less value and development of the land for residential uses actually detracted from the value of neighboring property.[94]

The acquisition of land or development rights can play an important part in an effective growth management program. Boulder and Montgomery County provide good examples. Land acquisition is the most effective technique for drawing a firm urban edge around a community. Because of its cost, it is not likely to become a dominant growth management tool, but it will remain an important one for those communities that have the fiscal will and/or the ability to use it.

CONCLUSION

The question that communities must face is not whether these non-regulatory techniques will affect the timing and location of growth, but whether the community has the power and the political will to use these tools to influence the timing and location of growth. Some authors routinely include such tools in their definitions of growth management.[95] Two years before *The Growth Shapers* called attention to the important role that infrastructure improvements play in shaping communities, Clawson recognized that they not only could be inadvertent growth shapers but that, "Extension of various public improvements, such as roads, sewer lines, water lines, schools and others, and even such privately provided services as electricity, gas and telephones, in coordinated fashion into suburban areas ripe for development could be a powerful tool affecting the location and rate of such suburban development."[96]

A community that has the authority to control all of these techniques clearly should use them to implement planned growth strategies. The growth-shaping power of infrastructure investment is so great that infrastructure investments may overwhelm regulatory efforts to direct growth. Similarly, the legal and political pressure to provide services to annexed lands is so great that the decision to annex should be viewed as a decision to develop. Conversely, the decision to purchase land is the most certain way to ensure that the land will not develop without public sector support.

Some communities control virtually none of these non-regulatory tools that affect their growth patterns. Those communities clearly have less opportunity to manage growth than do communities with more techniques under their control. However, every community should coordinate the non-regulatory decisions that it does or can make with its total strategy of community planning and growth management.

NOTES

1. Thomas Galloway and John D. Landis, "How Cities Expand: Does State Law Make a Difference?" *Growth and Change* 17 (1986): 27.

2. Anthony J. Mumphrey, Jr., John Wildgen, and Louise Williams, "Annexation and Incorporation: Alternative Strategies for Municipal Development" (New Orleans, La.: University of New Orleans College of Urban & Public Affairs, 1990).

3. C. Dallas Sands and Michael E. Libonati, *Local Government Law* (Wilmette, Ill.: Callaghan, 1981), sects. 2.13, 8.01; Frank S. Sengstock, *Annexation: A Solution to the Metropolitan Area Problem*, reprint of 1960 edition published by University of Michigan Law School ed. (Buffalo: William S. Hein & Co., 1960), 1–9.

4. Sands and Libonati, *Local Government Law*, sect. 8.01.

5. See discussion in Mumphrey, Wildgen, and Williams, "Annexation and Incorporation: Alternative Strategies for Municipal Development," 15. Also in John Rahenkamp, "Boroughing Isn't Boring," *Pennsylvania Planner* 46 (1991).

6. Stephen L. Mehay, "The Expenditure Effects of Municipal Annexation," *Public Choice* 36 (1981).

7. Arnold Fleischmann, "The Politics of Annexation: A Preliminary Assessment of Competing Paradigms," *Social Science Quarterly* 67 (1986).

8. Ibid.

9. Michael A. Goldberg and Daniel D. Ulinder, "Residents Developer Behavior 1975: Additional Empirical Findings," *Land Economics* 52 (1976).

10. Mumphrey, Wildgen, and Williams, "Annexation and Incorporation: Alternative Strategies for Municipal Development."

11. Rodolfo A. Gonzalez and Stephen L. Mehay, "Municipal Annexation and Local Monopoly Power," *Public Choice* 57 (1987).

12. Charles K. Coe, "Costs and Benefits of Municipal Annexation," *State and Local Government Review* 15 (1983).

13. Arthur T. Johnson, "Intergovernmental Influences on Local Land Use Decisions" (Washington, D.C.: National League of Cities, 1989).

14. Ibid., 39–42. Westminster, "Growth Management Plan: Phase II Report."

15. John M. Stahura and Harvey H. Marshall, "The Role of Annexation in the Growth of American Suburbs," *Sociological Focus* 15, no. 1 (1982): 21.

16. Galloway and Landis, "How Cities Expand: Does State Law Make a Difference?" 32; Sengstock, *Annexation: A Solution to the Metropolitan Area Problem*.

17. John Melvin De Grove, *Land, Growth & Politics* (Washington, D.C.: Planners Press American Planning Association, 1984), 271.

18. Urban Systems Research & Engineering, "The Growth Shapers: The Land Use Impacts of Infrastructure Investments."

19. Clawson, *Suburban Land Conversion in the United States: An Economic and Governmental Process*, 6.

20. Environmental Impact Center Incorporated, "Secondary Impacts of Transportation and Wastewater Investments: Research Results" (Washington, D.C.: Council on Environmental Quality, 1975), 76.

21. David E. Dowall, *The Suburban Squeeze: Land Conversion and Regulation in the San Francisco Bay Area, California Series in Urban Development; [3]* (Berkeley, Calif.: University of California Press, 1984), 17.

22. Hammer Siler George Associates, "Unpublished; Prepared for National Association of Homebuilders; Cited Copy Hand-Labeled 'Draft,'" 1.

23. Sam B. Warner, Jr., *Street Car Suburbs: The Process of Growth in Boston, 1870–1900,* Publications of the Joint Center for Urban Studies (Cambridge, Mass.: Harvard University Press/M.I.T. Press, 1962).
24. Ibid., 153.
25. Edwin H. Spengler, *Land Values in New York in Relation to Transit Facilities* (New York, London: Columbia University Press; P. S. King & Sons, Ltd., 1930).
26. Newman and Kenworthy, *Cities and Automobile Dependence: A Sourcebook.*
27. Tomas de la Barra, *Integrated Land Use and Transport Modeling: Decision Chains and Hierarchies,* ed. Leslie Martin and Lionel March, *Cambridge Urban and Architectural Series* (Cambridge, UK: Cambridge University Press, 1989).
28. Lowdon Wingo, *Transportation and Urban Land* (New York: AMS Press, 1983).
29. J. R. Meyer, J. F. Kain, and M. Wohl, *The Urban Transportation Problem,* 1972 trade paperback ed. (Cambridge: Harvard University Press, 1965), 119–30.
30. William Alonso, *Location and Land Use: Toward a General Theory of Land Rent* (Cambridge, Mass.: Harvard University Press, 1964).
31. Wingo, *Transportation and Urban Land.*
32. "The Journey to Work: Relation Between Employment and Residence," in *Planning Advisory Service* (Chicago: American Society of Planning Officials, 1951).
33. Robert Cervero, "Jobs-Housing Balance and Regional Mobility," *Journal of the American Planning Association* 55 (1989).
34. Shunfeng Song, "Some Tests of Alternative Accessibility Measures: A Population Density Approach," *Land Economics* 72, no. 4 (1996).
35. Binkley, *Interceptor Sewers and Urban Sprawl,* 1.
36. Ibid.
37. Advisory Commission on Regulatory Barriers to Affordable 'Housing, "'Not in My Backyard': Removing Barriers to Affordable Housing," Frank and Rhodes, eds.; *Development Exactions,* Robinson, ed.; *Financing Growth: Who Benefits? Who Pays? And How Much?* A brief discussion of this subject occurs near the end of Chapter 4 of this book.
38. Tabors, Shapiro, and Rogers, *Land Use and the Pipe: Planning for Sewerage.*
39. Ibid., 161.
40. Ibid., 133–45.
41. Hanson and Jacobs, "Private Sewage System Impacts in Wisconsin: Implications for Planning and Policy."
42. Llewelyn-Davies Carson Ltd., "Relationship of Water Supply and Urban Growth in the Denver Region" (Denver: U.S. Army Corps of Engineers, 1978).
43. John Michael Carson, Goldie W. Rivkin, and Malcolm D. Rivkin, *Community Growth and Water Resources Policy* (New York: Praeger, 1973).
44. Hanson and Jacobs, "Private Sewage System Impacts in Wisconsin: Implications for Planning and Policy."
45. Daniel Brand, "Research Needs for Analyzing the Impacts of Transportation Options on Urban Form and the Environment," in *Transportation, Urban Form and the Environment, Special Report* (Washington, D.C.: Transportation Research Board, 1991).
46. Glenn V. Fuguitt and James J. Zuiches, "Residential Preferences and Population Distribution," *Demography* 12 (1975).
47. Charles M. Tiebout, "A Pure Theory of Local Expenditures," *The Journal of Political Economy* 64 (1956).
48. George F Hepner, "An Analysis of Residential Developer Location Factors in a Fast Growth Urban Region," *Urban Geography* 4 (1983).

49. Goldberg and Ulinder, "Residents Developer Behavior 1975: Additional Empirical Findings," 364.

50. Environmental Impact Center Incorporated, "Secondary Impacts of Transportation and Wastewater Investments: Research Results," 6.

51. Thomas J. Baerwald, "The Site Selection Process of Suburban Residential Builders," *Urban Geography* 2 (1981). See table on p. 350 and accompanying text.

52. Richard B. Peiser, "Density and Urban Sprawl," *Land Economics* 65 (1989): 202.

53. Urban Systems Research & Engineering, "The Growth Shapers: The Land Use Impacts of Infrastructure Investments," 18.

54. Elizabeth Deakin, "Jobs, Housing and Transportation: Theory and Evidence," in *Transportation, Urban Form and the Environment, Special Report: Proceedings of a Conference* (Washington, D.C.: Transportation Research Board, 1991).

55. David J. Forkenbrock, et al., "Road Investment to Foster Local Economic Development" (Ames, Iowa: Midwest Transportation Center, 1990).

56. Urban Systems Research & Engineering, "The Growth Shapers: The Land Use Impacts of Infrastructure Investments," 5.

57. H.R. 2950.

58. H.R. 2950, Sect. 1024(a); 23 U.S.C. 134.

59. H.R. 2950, Sect. 1024(a); 23 U.S.C. 134(f).

60. H.R. 2950, Sect. 1025; 23 U.S.C. 135.

61. H.R. 2950, Sect. 1025; 23 U.S.C. 135(c).

62. Marya Morris, "New Transportation Law Benefits Planning," *PAS Memo*, February 1991, 1.

63. Ibid., 4.

64. Like its predecessor, this law has been codified at 49 U.S.C. §101, et seq.

65. 108th Congress, H.R. 3550.

66. Steve Kinsey, "California's Successful Experiment with Sub-Allocation," *Surface Transportation Policy Project Progress*, March 2003.

67. Sarah Campbell, "Tea-3 and Local Control: The Final Frontier," *Surface Transportation Policy Project* 2003.

68. *Selected I-69 Route Would Pass near Bloomington* (theindychannel.com, January 9, 2003 [cited November 2003]); available from www.theindychannel.com/news/1878809/detail.html.

69. Hammer Siler George Associates, "Unpublished; Prepared for National Association of Homebuilders; Cited Copy Hand-Labeled "Draft," 11.

70. Tabors, Shapiro, and Rogers, *Land Use and the Pipe: Planning for Sewerage*. It offers a description of the design process, beginning at p. 1.

71. Lawrence W. Chip Pierce and Kenneth L. Rust, "Government Enterprises," in *Local Government Finance: Concepts and Practices*, ed. John E. Petersen and Dennis R. Strachota (Washington, D.C.: Government Finance Officers Association, 1991).

72. Robert A. Bowyer, "Capital Improvement Programs: Linking Budgeting and Planning," in *Planning Advisory Service* (Chicago, Ill.: American Planning Association, 1993).

73. "Note: Public Utility Land Use Control on the Urban Fringe," *Iowa Law Review* 63 (1978); Catherine R. Stone, "Prevention of Urban Sprawl through Utility Extension Control," *The Urban Lawyer* 14 (1982).

74. *Robinson v. City of Boulder*, 547 P.2d 228 (Colo. 1976). The case was discussed in Kelly, "*Robinson v. Boulder*, a Balance to *Ramapo* and *Petaluma*"; interesting opinion

of the trial court was published in Scott et al., *Management & Control of Growth: Issues, Techniques, Problems, Trends*, vol. II, 237 et seq.

75. *P.W. Investments v. City of Westminster*, 655 P.2d 1365 (Colo. 1982). For discussion, see Kelly, "Comment on Westminster Growth Control Cases"; Kelly, "Piping Growth, the Law, Equity and Economics of Sewer & Water Connection Policies."

76. Callies, "Dealing with Scarcity: Land Use and Planning."

77. Binkley, *Interceptor Sewers and Urban Sprawl*.

78. Greenberg, "Growth and Conflict at the Suburban Fringe: The Case of the Livermore-Amador Valley," 152.

79. Hamblen, "Montgomery County at the Crossroads"; Donald V. H. Walker, "Boulder Preserves Open Space," in *Growth Management: Techniques in Application*, ed. Frank Schnidman, Jane Silverman, and Rufus D. Young, Jr. (Washington, D.C.: Urban Land Institute, 1978).

80. City of Boulder, "Some Facts About Boulder's Open Space," (1992).

81. Ibid.

82. Charter, City of Boulder, Sec. 177.

83. "Growth Masks Out-Migration of Young Families; in-Migration of Established Families," *Research Perspectives (City of Boulder)*, Winter 1992.

84. Hamblen, "Montgomery County at the Crossroads."

85. Ibid.; Craig A. Peterson and Clare McCarthy, "Farmland Preservation by Purchase of Development Rights: The Long Island Experiment," *De Paul Law Review* 26 (1977); Ann L. Strong, "Vermont's Act 250 and Prime Farmland" (Philadelphia, Pa.: Regional Science Institute, 1991).

86. Ann L. Strong, *Private Property and the Public Interest: The Brandywine Experience, Johns Hopkins Studies in Urban Affairs* (Baltimore, Md.: Johns Hopkins University Press, 1975).

87. Will Abberger, "Growth Management through Land Acquisition" (International City Management Association, 1991).

88. Peterson and McCarthy, "Farmland Preservation by Purchase of Development Rights: The Long Island Experiment"; Strong, "Vermont's Act 250 and Prime Farmland."

89. Ann L. Strong, *Land Banking: European Reality, American Prospect, Johns Hopkins Studies in Urban Affairs* (Baltimore, Md.: Johns Hopkins University Press, 1979).

90. William Hollingsworth Whyte, *Securing Open Spaces for Urban America: Conservation Easements* (Washington, D.C.: Urban Land Institute, 1959).

91. United States Department of Commerce Advisory Committee on City Planning and Zoning, *A Standard City Planning Enabling Act by the Advisory Committee on City Planning and Zoning Appointed by Secretary Hoover*.

92. Strong, *Land Banking: European Reality, American Prospect*.

93. *Lucas v. South Carolina Coastal Council*, 112 S. Ct. 2886 (1992); *First English Evangelical Lutheran Church of Glendale v. County of Los Angeles*, 107 S. Ct. 2378 (1987). See also *San Diego Gas & Electric Co. v. City of San Diego*, 101 S. Ct. 1287 (1981).

94. Elena G Irwin, "The Effects of Open Space on Residential Property Values," *Land Economics* 78, no. 4 (2002).

95. Glickfeld and Levine, *Regional Growth–Local Reaction: The Enactment and Effects of Local Growth Control and Management Measures in California*; Landis, "Do Growth Controls Work? A New Assessment."

96. Clawson, *Suburban Land Conversion in the United States: An Economic and Governmental Process*, 347.

CHAPTER 6

Statewide Efforts
to Manage Growth

The complexity of most metropolitan regions makes it difficult for local governments to manage some aspects of growth effectively. With the broad extent of their territorial controls, states have a greater opportunity to address such growth-related issues as the actual shape of the metropolitan area. This chapter examines briefly the implementation of several state-level programs to manage growth.

THE LITERATURE ON THE STATE ROLE

In 1972, Fred Bosselman and David Callies wrote about *The Quiet Revolution in Land Use Control*:

The *ancien regime* being overthrown is the feudal system under which the entire pattern of land development has been controlled by thousands of individual local governments, each seeking to maximize its tax base and minimize its social problems, and caring less what happens to all the others.

The tools of the revolution are new laws taking a wide variety of forms but each sharing a common theme, the need to provide some degree of state or regional participation in the major decisions that affect the use of our increasingly limited supply of land.[1]

There was a flurry of interest in state land use activity in the mid-1970s. Under contract with the U.S. Department of Housing and Urban Development, the American Institute of Planners prepared a comprehensive review of state planning activities in all fifty states.[2] That study included in its compilation state planning and budgeting activities, as well as land use enabling powers and broader state land use programs.

Also under contract to the U.S. Department of Housing and Urban Development, the Council of State Governments prepared a report entitled "State Growth Management."[3] That report was (and is) interesting because it included both economic development programs and regulatory programs, the latter ranging from energy facility citing legislation to zoning. It thus provided an extremely broad, if brief, examination of the growth management issue at the state level.

In the same year, an individual author prepared a report entitled *Land Use and the Legislatures*.[4] It examined three major areas of activity: "growth management"; citing legislation for power plants, surface mines and other large-scale activities; and natural areas legislation, protecting areas such as wetlands and shorelines. Rosenbaum's use of the term "growth management" was broad and focused on state laws requiring that local governments engage in planning, zoning or subdivision regulation.

Also in 1976, Resources for the Future published the first edition of *Land Use and the States*,[5] updated three years later.[6] The first edition provided the first in-depth view of several state land use programs and an examination of their common themes. It focused on Vermont, California and Florida. In the same period, the Conservation Foundation sponsored a series of short publications on state programs, including Vermont[7] and Hawaii.[8]

Callies and Bosselman's original report featured statewide programs in Hawaii and Vermont, along with specialized and regional programs in other states. The Hawaii system remains little changed since the report was published. Vermont has added a new piece to its state control program. Florida and Oregon joined them in adopting strong statewide programs during the 1970s. Georgia adopted a state planning law in 1990, and Washington began implementation of a new state planning program in 1991. Other states have tinkered with their enabling acts, some of them strengthening the role of planning. The states with a strong state presence in land use control and growth management, however, remain a distinct minority.

The revolution is not one that has swept the nation, as some thought it would. Even by 1979, one author noted of the so-called "quiet revolution": "[T]his early momentum has been lost. . . . State legislatures are reluctant to pass more laws that seem 'comprehensive' in affecting all lands in the state or a wide range of types of development."[9]

The development of the literature on state planning paralleled both the development of the initial state programs and the development of the influential growth management literature (see material in Chapter 3). As the examples above suggest, most of the original literature on the state role was published in the 1970s. At first impression, John De Grove's 1984 book, *Land, Growth & Politics*, appeared to be an exception.[10] However, most of the interviews and source materials in the book dated from the late 1970s; a small proportion of the dates was from 1981 and 1982. Thus, the book substantially overlapped the time covered by the Resources for the Future books.[11] It was a far different book from theirs, with more emphasis on the politics. It contained thorough analyses of the politics of state land use control in Vermont, Florida, California and Oregon, as well as in

Colorado and North Carolina, which have more limited programs.[12] Callies updated the literature on Hawaii with a book and a short chapter on land use controls in a larger book about Hawaiian politics.[13]

Three 1991 working papers from the University of California–Berkeley provided interesting, if limited, perspectives on issues in state-level growth management. Two scholars at Berkeley contributed to the literature on the state role. Michael Teitz analyzed the practical and policy issues confronting California in his plea for development of a state growth policy.[14] Judith Innes examined the role of state growth management programs in increasing planning coordination among different levels of government and for enhancing the role of citizens in planning decisions.[15]

The only broad examination of the state role in growth management during the 1980s and based on information dating later than the period around 1980 was a short twenty-page article by John De Grove.[16] Although the "quiet revolution" did not spread across the nation, as some had anticipated that it might, the implementation of evolutionary controls continued in the "quiet revolution" states and in several others. A considerable body of literature in the 1990s and early 2000s dealt with more general topics of controlling sprawl and implementing concepts of "smart growth." That literature is discussed near the end of this chapter.

THE STATE OPPORTUNITY IN GROWTH MANAGEMENT

Despite the limited number of statewide programs of planning and growth management, it is important to examine these programs. One of the difficulties facing local governments in developing growth management programs is that the typical local government does not control enough territory to manage growth on a meaningful scale. Petaluma and Ramapo, famous for their growth management programs, are both exurbs of major metropolitan areas that faced regional growth pressures beyond the control of any single municipality. Boulder is somewhat more independent, lying outside the "normal" commuting range of Denver. However, it is still less than half an hour from the north Denver suburbs, and people commute back and forth to work between Boulder and the Denver area every day.

Clearly a state, with its broad area of control, can address some issues that a local government simply cannot. It is important to examine, at least briefly, some significant state programs and their apparent effectiveness.

Although the majority of states have not adopted comprehensive planning or land use policies, every state significantly influences local land use patterns and practices through amendments to enabling acts, investments in highways and regulation of air and water pollution. Thus, even in those states in which there is no express policy, the state does play a role. That role can perhaps best be understood by examining, however briefly, the experience of several states with express land policies. Furthermore, local governments can learn from, and even use, some of the techniques applied by those states. There are lessons from some

of the programs even for local governments that prefer not to have the state inter-
vene further in their land use affairs.

HAWAII

Hawaii does not call its program "growth management," but it works like a
growth management program. Its statewide program originates in a "land use
law" that predates the national interest in growth management. The land use program, which is called just that, looks a lot like statewide zoning. However, what
it does is to control the timing and location of growth more effectively than any
form of local zoning. It thus constitutes a statewide growth management program, regardless of the name.

To understand why Hawaii had the earliest statewide control system and why it
remains one of the strongest, it is important to understand Hawaii. It is unique in
more ways than just being the island state. It was under a monarchy until 1890.
Concentrated land ownership and strong central authority were a part of the
Hawaiian tradition before statehood. According to one writer, by the 1950s, "72
major landholders (owners of more than 1,000 acres) held title to 47 percent of
the land. The state owned 38 percent of the land, and the federal government, by
lease or ownership, controlled 10 percent (including 25 percent of the island of
Oahu)."[17] That leaves only 5 percent of the land for the other 99.9 percent of the
population. The land ownership pattern created one unique set of circumstances.

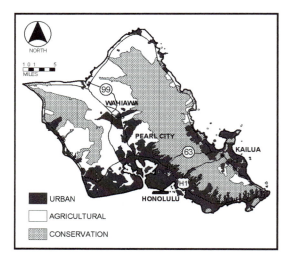

Figure 6.1   City and County of Honolulu (island of Oahu) land use districts as
established by Hawaii Land Use Commission. (*Source:* Hawai'i Land Use Commission,
Land Use Map, Oahu, 2003, http://luc.state.hi.us/maps/oahu2003.pdf; adapted for second
edition by Bram Barth.)

Technology created the other. Agriculture, particularly sugarcane and pineapple, was the mainstay of the Hawaiian economy through the 1950s. Although there was some tourism, it was not a large factor in the economy. However, at about the time that Hawaii achieved statehood, the jet aircraft made Hawaii considerably more accessible to tourists than it had been. Speculators began to acquire inexpensive agricultural land, with the apparent intent to develop it. Many in Hawaii saw excessive tourist-driven development as a threat to the economic base. It was from that political source that the support for the strong state land use law arose.[18]

The Land Use Law, adopted just two years after Hawaii became a state in 1959, created a state Land Use Commission.[19] The governor appoints the nine-member commission. The commission determines the boundaries of four types of districts in the state:[20]

Urban. Lands in this district fall entirely under local control. Local governments may permit all sorts of urban uses. Operation of local planning and zoning within these districts is similar to those activities in other communities in the mainland states.

Rural. Rural lands permit residential uses on relatively large lots of one-half acre or more. The Land Use Commission establishes permitted uses within this district. The original law did not include this district, which was added in a 1963 amendment.

Agricultural. The agricultural district contains lands most suitable for the principal agricultural activities of the islands, sugarcane and pineapple plantations, as well as for less intensive agricultural uses and agricultural industries such as sugar mills. The commission also establishes the permitted uses within this district.

Conservation. The Department of Land and Natural Resources regulates uses within this district. The initial district boundaries contained only public land, but the Land Use Commission subsequently enlarged them to include significant areas of private land.[21]

See Figure 6.1, which shows the state-designated boundaries around Honolulu.

The Land Use Commission has the sole authority to make boundary changes. That process appears to differ little from rezoning pressures in other communities. Bosselman and Callies may have understated the problem somewhat when they noted that, "Applications for boundary changes and special permits keep the Land Use Commission quite busy."[22] During the 10 years after the Commission established the initial boundaries (1964–74), the Commission granted boundary change requests that increased the urban district by 30,000 acres, or 25 percent.[23] During that period, the Commission considered petitions to change the classification of 133,438 acres and approved a change for 66,670, or 50 percent, of the amount included in the petitions.[24] Two researchers examined the files of the Commission over the first 20 years and found 264 applications for boundary changes involving at least 5 acres and a presumed profit motive (the authors ignored petitions from public and nonprofit agencies); of those 264 petitions, the Commission granted 202.[25] John DeGrove gave the Commission generally good marks for its role in implementing the act ("a creditable job in the face of substantial handicaps") in its first several years, somewhat mixed reviews for the next 5 years and a reservation of judgment for the following 5 years, which was the last period included in his book.[26]

The two researchers who studied the program alleged that the boundary change process is highly political and documented the relationship of public officials with major landowners affected by the process. They found a 91 percent approval rate for those 185 applications (of the 264 cited above) with which public officials had direct ties as officers, trustees, lawyers or otherwise.[27] However, the problem may not be as severe as they allege. An official report for Oahu (Honolulu County) shows that 13 amendments that were approved during the previous year removed as many acres from the urban zone as they added, thus resulting in no net change.[28]

Has the Hawaii program worked? Healy concluded, "The record shows that Hawaii's land use law has been relatively, but not completely, effective in stopping the urbanization of agricultural lands. . . . Nevertheless, the law has had a striking effect on the pattern of Hawaii's growth, making urban expansion far more compact and orderly than it would have been without the law."[29] In 1992, after more than three decades of operation of the new law, 95 percent of the land in the state remained in the rural and conservation classifications.[30]

The effect is dramatic on Oahu, where the high density of Waikiki Beach exists within two or three miles of areas showing no signs of development (see Figure 6.1). However, De Grove suggested that the policies underlying the state law require reconsideration, because of the significant decline of agriculture as a factor in the economic base and because of pressures for increased housing opportunity. By 1991, a City and County of Honolulu report noted that "Oahu's economy is currently dominated by tourism and defense expenditures."[31] The fact remains, however, that the state of Hawaii has exercised far more effective control over the patterns of development in the state than have any of the other 49 states.

VERMONT

The second state to join "the quiet revolution" was Vermont. In 1970, some ten years after Hawaii adopted its landmark Land Use Law, Vermont adopted Act 250. That law, the first in a series of land use reform measures adopted in the state, established a statewide development permitting system, with substantial control at the regional level.

Each state is, in a sense, unique. However, Vermont and Hawaii, the first two states in this movement, are particularly so. Vermont is one of the smallest states in the nation in both land area and population, with a 2000 population of 608,827, up only 4.5 percent from 1990.[32] One author noted that "one symbol of change, according to some observers, came in the early 60s, when for the first time, Vermont had more people than cows."[33] Its largest city, Burlington, had a 1990 metropolitan area population of 169,391, up 23 percent from 1990; but note that the population of the city itself remained a modest 38,889.[34] In short, Vermont is unique in part because of its rural character and relative dearth of major urban areas; the fact that, from 1990 to 2000, there was substantial growth in the Burlington MSA and little growth elsewhere, however, indicates that even in Vermont there is urbanization.[35]

It is also unique in its form of government. The town meeting remains a form of government for a number of its 292 municipal and township governments. It is noteworthy that, disregarding Burlington, the average population served by one of those local governments is roughly 1,500 people, a fact bound to affect the style of government.[36] Not surprisingly, planning and zoning were not widespread in Vermont as the quiet revolution began.[37]

Act 250: The First Shot in the Vermont Revolution

One thing Vermont shared with Hawaii in the "quiet revolution" was the history of the adoption of its revolutionary legislation. The threat of tourism development to agriculture clearly fueled the drive for the new land use law. In particular, a 1968 proposal by International Paper for a second-home development on 20,000 acres, created a political outcry that led the 1970 legislature to adopt Act 250.[38] Healy also cited a proposal to add 2,000 condominium units to Wilmington, a town of 2,000, and a survey of Wilmington and adjacent Dover that found "a total of seventy-three developers in business, one for every twenty-five residents."[39] Despite some early opposition, the act, which was proposed by a study commission appointed by the governor, finally passed the state senate by unanimous voice vote.[40]

The new law required a development permit for: industrial or commercial development on tracts of greater than 10 acres (or 1 acre where the town has not adopted zoning or subdivision controls); housing projects of ten or more units within a 5-mile radius; and any development above 2,500 feet. It also required a permit for any subdivision into ten or more lots of less than 10 acres each.[41]

Primary control of the issuance of development permits falls to nine district commissions created under the law, with a coordinated review process at the state level. The law is clearly supplemental to local regulation. Thus, approval through the state process does not ensure approval by the town under its zoning ordinance or other regulations.

The act included ten standards for approval of development permits. Five of them amounted to the first statewide adequate public facilities requirements in the nation:

2. Does have sufficient water available for the reasonably foreseeable needs of the subdivision or development.

3. Will not cause an unreasonable burden on an existing water supply, if one is to be utilized. . . .

5. Will not cause unreasonable highway congestion or unsafe conditions with respect to use of the highways, existing or proposed.

6. Will not cause an unreasonable burden on the ability of a municipality to provide educational services.

7. Will not place an unreasonable burden on the ability of the local government to provide municipality or governmental services.

The other standards addressed environmental issues and conformance with plans:

1. Will not result in undue water or air pollution. . . .

4. Will not cause unreasonable soil erosion or reduction in the capacity of the land to hold water so that a dangerous or unhealthy condition may result. . . .[42]

8. Will not have an adverse effect on the scenic or natural beauty of the area, aesthetics, historic sites or rare and irreplaceable natural areas.

9. Is in conformance with a duly adopted development plan, land use plan or land capability plan.

10. Is in conformance with any duly adopted local or regional plan or capital program. . . .[43]

Act 250 required the adoption of three plans, all of which required ultimate legislative approval: an interim plan; a land capability and development plan; and a state land use plan. The legislature and the governor approved the interim plan in 1972 without apparent difficulty. Two years later, it approved the land capability and development plan, which established stronger environmental standards but also increased local control over issues within the borders of a particular community. The state land use plan failed in two major legislative efforts. There are several good histories of the political activity surrounding all three plans.[44]

Although Act 250 created a strong system of statewide development control, note that two major types of development are exempt: small commercial development (under 10 acres in most circumstances) of the type that generally creates commercial "strips" along highways; and subdivision of land into parcels larger than 10 acres. Healy referred to these as "gaps" in the law[45] and De Grove cited examples of developments with lots of "10+ acres."[46] From a policy perspective, the above-10-acre exemption is particularly troublesome, because it encourages the worst developers (those who want to avoid regulation) to consume the most land per unit sold.

Has Act 250 worked? It certainly increased the control of development in a state in which many communities lacked basic zoning and subdivision controls before its adoption. De Grove offered this assessment:

Certainly as a growth-management measure capable of directing growth into desired areas and preventing it in areas marginal or unsuitable, Act 250 has yet to be fully utilized and probably cannot be so utilized without changes in the law. . . .

Within the framework of its objectives, there is broad consensus that Act 250 has been successful. Observers and participants agree that while the law has not had a significant impact on the rate of growth in the state. . . , it has significantly improved the quality of the growth that has taken place.[47]

Healy offered a slightly different perspective. He agreed with De Grove's assessment that it had affected the quality of growth more than the quantity. He also found it to be "more effective in regulating second homes and suburban tracts than in stopping commercial sprawl,"[48] a result that is not surprising in light of the fact that the pressure of second-home developments led to its adoption. However, he also noted, "Perhaps the most interesting feature of Vermont's experience is that the policy has evolved over time. . . . For the future then, the question is not how to revamp Vermont's land regulatory process, but whether it can continue to evolve as the process itself uncovers new kinds of issues."[49]

Myers found that the early days of implementing Act 250 were characterized by a process of negotiation that generally led to project approvals. However, she cited anecdotal evidence that the law provided more protection than it might appear through the imposition of large numbers of conditions on most permit approvals.[50]

Writing six years after its adoption, Strong assessed Act 250 as follows, correctly anticipating the need for further action. "Act 250 has resulted in creation of a permit system applicable to some development. It has not resulted directly in preservation of any prime farmland, one of the Act's stated objectives."[51]

Strong saw it as "part of an effective farmland retention program." The type of broader program that she suggested emerged some 11 years later with the adoption of Act 200.[52] As Healy correctly predicted, the system has continued to evolve in Vermont. The land gains tax, discussed immediately below, was included in Healy's assessment of the Vermont program, but the adoption of Act 200, discussed below, proved the accuracy of his prediction that the system would continue to evolve.

The Land Gains Tax

In 1973, Vermont adopted a unique, progressive land gains tax under which the tax rate varied depending on the length of time that the owner held the land and on the amount of the gain. The maximum rate is 60 percent of the gain, for land held less than one year with a 200 percent or greater gain in value. The tax declines to 5 percent for property held more than five years on which the gain is less than 100 percent, and it disappears after six years.[53] The legislature adopted the tax as part of a tax reform package that included property tax credits and a change in the method of assessing agricultural property. Buildings and other improvements, as well as the site of a principal residence, are exempt from the tax. The land gains tax is clearly an anti-speculation tax. Because it applies to subdividers and developers, as well as to those who simply hold land for its unearned gain, it may affect the amount of subdivision and development activity. However, the evidence on that issue is not clear.[54]

Act 200

Renewed development pressures in the 1980s led to the adoption of Act 200, a statewide planning Act.[55] Adoption of the Act followed the 1988 publication of a *Report of the Governor's Commission on Vermont's Future: Guidelines for Growth*, prepared by a commission appointed by Governor Madeleine M. Kunen and chaired by Douglas Costle, former administrator of the U.S. Environmental Protection Agency and then Dean of the Vermont Law School.[56] Citing concern over the failure of the planning aspects of Act 250 and the continued growth of the state, the commission made a number of legislative recommendations. The recommendations included streamlining the development review process; improving planning at local, regional and state levels; and adopting statewide planning guidelines.

The legislature acted on the recommendations, although like most legislation, the action represented a compromise. The legislature did adopt twelve statewide goals.[57] Compliance with those goals is mandatory for state and regional agencies, although an agency can disregard a specific goal if it expressly determines that it should not follow that goal in particular circumstances.[58] However, the law failed either to make planning mandatory[59] or to require that local plans be consistent with state goals.[60] The act does provide a financial incentive for communities to follow state goals. It authorizes impact fees as a form of exaction only for those local governments whose plans have been confirmed by the regional planning commission.[61]

De Grove said of Act 200, "The new Vermont law goes a long way toward establishing an integrated policy framework to guide growth in Vermont, but it fails to take the final, and crucial, step of mandating municipalities to prepare plans and implementing regulations."[62]

A state report published the year before the second edition of this book suggested that implementation of Vermont's laws is incomplete, particularly among state agencies.[63] No comprehensive evaluation of the implementation of the state's laws at the local level was found during the literature review in support of the second edition. Thus, it is not clear at this time to what extent these laws have improved planning practice in Vermont. The state remains, however, a good example of one that has taken an active role in attempting to manage growth.

FLORIDA

Florida joined the revolution later than the others, but when it did join, it moved quickly on many fronts. This state that was not included among those featured in *The Quiet Revolution in Land Use Control* now arguably has the most comprehensive statewide land use program.

The revolution in Florida began differently than it did in Vermont and Hawaii. The state had a century-long history of promoting growth. Florida had used massive land grants to attract railroads into South Florida and to encourage draining of the swamplands. However, rapid growth began to overwhelm the state. It grew from twentieth among the states in population in 1950 to eighth in 1976.[64] Healy offered other figures that put the growth in perspective. "At times during the 1970s as many as 25,000 persons a month moved to Florida. . . . In 1973, for example, one out of every seven new homes built in the United States was built in Florida."[65]

As an indication of the scale of the growth, Healy noted the proposed Palm Coast development in Flagler County, which then had a population of about 4,500. ITT's Palm Coast originally proposed plans for enough housing for 750,000 people.[66]

According to De Grove, who was deeply involved in the development of the Florida system, the change of heart began in Florida in 1969 when environmental groups successfully mobilized to stop a proposed new jetport west of Miami in the Everglades.[67] Growing concern with growth and the actual and potential environmental destruction from it, combined with a serious drought in 1971, led to the adoption of the Land Conservation Act in 1972. This act combined new regulatory concepts with a proposal to float state bonds to finance the acquisition of certain areas. The voters subsequently passed the $200 million bond issue.[68]

The new regulatory concepts in the Land Management Act addressed "areas of critical state concern" and "developments of regional impact." Both concepts were based on the *Model Land Development Code* prepared by a committee and distributed by the American Law Institute.[69] "Areas of critical state concern," as the name implies, are designated land areas of particular concern, those environmentally sensitive areas "affected by or having a significant effect on" a major public facility, or a "proposed area of major development potential."[70] The Big Cypress Area, Green Swamp, Apalachicola Bay and Florida Keys were the subject of subsequent designations as critical areas under the revised process.[71]

The targets of the "developments of regional impact" regulations were, on the other hand, large projects such as power plants, large commercial centers or particularly large housing projects likely to have an impact on an area greater than the community that controlled it. The state law defined such a development as "any development which, because of its character, magnitude or location, would have a substantial effect upon the health, safety or welfare of citizens of more than one county."[72]

The law regarding developments of regional impact remains in effect in essentially its original form. The Florida Supreme Court struck down the law regarding areas of critical state concern as an unconstitutional delegation of authority (the designation of the areas) to an administrative agency. It was, however, readopted with provisions for legislative action on future designations and with some other revisions.[73] Both concepts remain in Florida law today.

The basic idea behind the regulation of critical areas and developments of regional impact is similar. Both are based on the concept that, while land use control should remain largely a local affair, certain types of activities and areas affect the region or the state as a whole and thus should have some participation in the regulatory process beyond that of the local government.

However, the regulatory approach to the two is quite different. "Areas of critical state concern" are subject to a "designation" process, created in the ALI *Model Land Development Code* and involving the state.[74] Once such an area is designated, the state supervises local preparation and enforcement of regulations and can step in to take over the process if the local government does not adequately protect the area. In contrast, the developments of regional impact, or DRI, process is simply a procedural one. The DRI regulation is on the same article of the ALI model code as the areas of critical state concern concept.[75] Projects meeting the regulatory definition are subject to review by designated regional agencies, which then submit their comments to the local government that has regulatory authority over the project. The local government retains the final approval or denial authority, but the state law requires that it give serious consideration to regional concerns as reflected in the comments of the regional agency.

Although the critical areas and DRI provisions remain law in Florida, in many ways the most interesting provisions of Florida law are ones adopted in 1985. There were several legislative acts regarding planning and growth management in the 1984–86 period, including the adoption of a state comprehensive plan as Chapter 187 of the Florida statutes.[76] In 1985, Florida amended Chapter 163 of the Florida statutes, governing local planning and development regulation, to:

- Make local comprehensive plans mandatory;[77]
- Specify, in some detail, the required elements of local plans;[78]
- Require completion of such plans on a specified schedule, beginning on July 1, 1988, and concluding July 1, 1991;[79]
- Require that each county and municipality "adopt or amend and enforce land development regulations that are consistent with and implement their updated comprehensive plan" within one year after completing the plan;[80]
- Establish a process for state review of both the plans and the development regulations to determine whether they comply;[81]
- Give the state strong enforcement authority; and
- Require that local governments develop regulatory requirements limiting the approval of new developments unless there is evidence that adequate public facilities to serve such new development will be available "concurrently" with the demand generated by the development.[82]

Other states have established mandatory planning requirements and eliminated the confusion from the old enabling acts by requiring that local zoning and subdivision regulations be consistent with adopted plans.[83] However, with the 1985 Act, Florida became the first state to require affirmative acts by local governments to bring their local regulations into conformance with mandatory new plans. One of the changes that has occurred since then is that an increasing number of states now require some sort of action to achieve consistency between the plan and local actions.[84] Although it may seem entirely logical that a local government updating its plan would also update its regulations, that is frequently not the practice. For example, a major study of the implementation of plans within the Portland, Oregon, urban growth boundary found that some communities had failed to update their zoning and had thus approved developments inconsistent with state-mandated plans.[85] As the discussion below indicates, Oregon is a state with a strong commitment to planning and such a finding there is particularly significant.

Even where a local government has the will and the means to continue working on planning issues after a major planning effort (and many do not have the will and/or the means), there are often political difficulties in implementing the new plan. For example, the new plan may suggest that certain areas should be "down-zoned," or zoned to a less intense or otherwise less valuable category than they hold under current zoning. Adopting such a policy in a typically non-binding plan is easier for most local governments than actually amending the zoning map to tell the landowner that she or he can no longer build apartments or industry on his or her property. Further, many good ideas in comprehensive plans remain unimplemented. Policies favoring increased open space and new bufferyards are provisions that local governments often include in plans but less often include in actual regulations.

In some ways, however, the "concurrency"[86] requirements of the updated Florida law are even more significant than the planning requirements.[87] The requirements for concurrent availability of public facilities with new development, of course, amount to adequate public facilities standards (see Chapter 4) imposed on a statewide basis.[88] There was precedent for that. Vermont's Act 250 required affirmative findings regarding the availability of water and road access in its development permit review (see above). Colorado had earlier required that counties make affirmative findings regarding the availability of water supply and waste treatment in approving subdivisions.[89]

However, Florida went further in two respects. First, the requirement in the Florida law applied to every type of project reviewed by any local government. In contrast, the Vermont provision applied only to those larger projects subject to the regional review process, and Colorado's requirement applied only to new subdivisions under county jurisdiction. Florida also went further in another respect. It tied the standards for facilities and improvements to a mandatory capital improvements element in the local comprehensive plan.[90]

Although that requirement is a little unusual, nothing about it is particularly radical. It simply requires that a local government develop specific standards to define adequate public facilities or adequate levels of service as part of its capital improvements program. Local governments have long engaged in such activity. Establishing street widths, requiring 4 to 8 percent of an area to be open space and requiring that water pressure provide a minimum "fire flow" are all typical standards contained in local regulations and affecting the design of public improvements.

The twist in the Florida law is the complementary provision that required that the capital improvements element that set these standards also include "principles for correcting existing public facility deficiencies, which are necessary to implement the comprehensive plan."[91] That provides a very significant balance to the standard-setting procedure. The general trend of local government practice has been to increase standards over time. Thus, a project approved in 1991 typically faced greater improvement requirements than one approved in 1981; increased street widths, requirements for increased open space and requirements for such amenities as street trees have been typical additions.[92] However, a community in Florida considering an increase in the amount of park land it requires for each resident must also consider how to acquire and pay for enough additional park land to bring existing areas of the community up to that standard. There is a nice symmetry to the Florida approach, which seems likely to bring considerable balance back to the establishment of development standards.

De Grove, who has been heavily involved in the implementation of growth management in Florida, published his book including the assessment of the

Florida situation shortly before the latest legislation was passed in the mid-1980s. He posed the question of whether the growth management program then in place was adequate and answered his own question with a No. He cited as a "critical issue" the "lack of an integrated planning and policy framework that can assure that clear state policies frame regional policies and equally clear regional policies frame local government plans and policies."[93]

Although the 1985 act included exactly that sort of structure and the legislature adopted the first state comprehensive plan at about that time, the jury remains out some seven years later. Writing four years after its adoption, Fulton noted that the fiscal impacts of growth and their solutions remained major issues in the state.[94] DeHaven-Smith, in a somewhat radical critique of growth management in Florida, wrote in 1991 about "why growth management failed."[95] DeHaven-Smith's thesis was that growth management is misdirected at the rate and amount of growth (a thesis for which he provides little documentation) and that it has thus failed to address the critical issues. To deHaven-Smith, those critical issues were the location and patterns of growth. He argued that the only real problem that Florida faces is urban sprawl and its side effects, including the negative fiscal impacts of sprawl.[96] He urged the adoption of statewide zoning based on the Hawaii model in order to create development patterns that are efficient to serve and that are less threatening to the natural environment.[97] He also recommended the adoption of urban service area boundaries.[98] The consulting team led by Duncan reached the same conclusion in their recommendations regarding more efficient development patterns.[99]

Those involved in implementing Florida's program may not agree with deHaven-Smith's proposed solution, but they recognize the problem. The Department of Community Affairs promulgated a document entitled "Techniques for Discouraging Urban Sprawl" in 1989.[100] Also that year, the state commissioned a group of consulting firms, led by long-time Florida planner James Duncan and his firm, to conduct a major study entitled *The Search for Efficient Urban Growth Patterns.*[101]

As figures at the beginning of this section indicate, Florida's growth rate has been daunting. Some may question whether Florida can manage its growth without some type of limitation. The fact that much of the state's growth consists of retirees limits the impact on schools, a fact that makes it easier for the state to absorb growth. On the other hand, the substantial immigrant population places an extra burden on schools and social welfare programs in urban areas like Miami. Perhaps implementation of deHaven-Smith's suggestion of a state income tax might have some growth-limiting effect, by limiting the number of retirees. An income tax would do nothing to stem the number of immigrants, although it would generate revenues to help provide services for them.

On the one hand, the fact that Florida absorbed virtually a tripling of its population from 1960–1990 and continued to operate at all is a remarkable achievement. On the other hand, the issues of the fiscal and environmental impacts of continued growth, at least in present development patterns, remained in 1992 much the same as they were when the first major Florida legislation was adopted 20 years before. Just as De Grove urged that the state take additional initiatives to manage growth when he wrote his major assessment of growth management in Florida in the early 1980s, Florida must continue to seek improved and more effective solutions to manage the environmental and fiscal effects of growth on the state. Whether the state can accomplish that through the existing structure of local control under state supervision or whether it will take a stronger state hand, as deHaven-Smith urged, is not clear.

OREGON

Oregon adopted a statewide land use law in 1973, two years after the publication of the Bosselman and Callies work.[102] The coalition that led to the adoption of the Oregon law included environmentalists concerned about logging in the eastern part of the state and others concerned about typical growth issues around the urban areas along the Pacific Coast and in the Willamette Valley. De Grove said that, of those issues, the concern about the loss of farmland around growing Portland was perhaps the greatest.[103]

Oregon's law, which remained in effect in 2004 substantially in its original form, contained some unique features. It established a state Land Conservation and Development Commission with the duty to adopt state goals and guidelines.[104] Local governments then had one year to bring their local plans into compliance with the state goals and to submit them to the Commission for review and "acknowledgment" or rejection.[105]

The Commission adopted the initial goals in December 1974.[106] The process of reviewing local plans for compliance took far longer than projected. After seven years, the state had acknowledged about half of the local plans and reviewed another 30 percent without accepting them. Roughly 15 percent of local governments had submitted no plans at all by that time.[107]

Probably the most interesting features of the Oregon program are its dual emphases on the preservation of agricultural and forest lands, on the one hand, and the control of urban form, on the other. Goal 14 required that each community establish an "urban growth boundary" in a perimeter around the city. Land within the boundary was to be sufficient for 20 years of urban development. Goal 3 provided an extremely limited set of uses in the agricultural areas. Those restrictions are, in part, tied to the suitability of the land for farming, based on Soil Conservation Service classifications.

The program bears some philosophical resemblance to the Hawaii system, because it provides a method of limiting sprawl and containing urban development within a limited area. However, there are some marked differences. First, the local government establishes the initial boundary and retains control over any changes in it, subject to LCDC review. That is very different from Hawaii, where the state Land Use Commission establishes the boundaries of the urban districts. Interestingly, perhaps because the boundaries were established to include so much

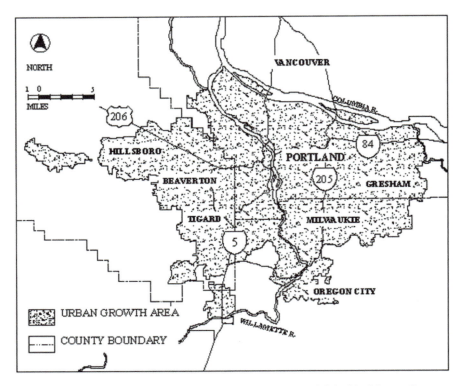

Figure 6.2 Portland, Oregon, urban growth boundary, as established by Metropolitan Service District. (*Source:* Map adapted by Kyle Lueken from Portland Metropolitan Service District, "Urban Growth Boundary," December 12, 2002 http://www. metro-region.org/library_docs/land_use/current_ugb_map.pdf)

land or perhaps because of a lower rate of growth, Oregon has not faced the problem of constant amendments, as Hawaii has. A researcher who studied the Oregon program noted in 1990 that, "So far, only a handful of disputes have arisen in regard to whether or not to expand [urban growth boundaries], but this may be due in large part to the sluggish economy in Oregon."[108]

The next chapter discusses the effects of the Oregon program on urban form. It has been far more effective than most in determining the shape of metropolitan areas. It has also resulted in increasing the intensity of development in some communities.[109]

Has the Oregon program worked? De Grove found it a political and practical success.[110] One researcher gave this anecdotal evidence of his assessment of the program as "one of the most successful statewide programs":

Drive south on I-5 from Portland, a city of 1.3 million, to Salem, the state capital less than 50 miles away, and you won't see the typical commercial strip sprawl, runaway roadside development and far-flung subdivisions that characterize many other highly traveled corridors in the U.S. What you see instead are pastoral landscapes of farms and fields in the fertile Willamette Valley, broken by occasional copses of evergreens. Make no mistake about it: the fact that much of the countryside is still rural can largely be attributed to Oregon's statewide land use planning program, which restricts development to areas within urban growth boundaries. . . .[111]

Three faculty members at Portland State University compiled an excellent collection of essays evaluating the Oregon program some 20 years after it began. Although another ten years has elapsed between the publication of that book and the publication of the new edition of this one, theirs remains an excellent analysis of the comprehensive Oregon program.[112] Professors Gerrit Knaap and Chris Nelson produced a separate work addressing the same general subject.[113]

OTHER STATES AND THE EVOLUTION OF THE 1990S

The most notable achievement in state policy for land use during the 1990s was the publication of the *Growing Smart Legislative Guidebook.*[114] An accompanying *User's Manual* explains the purpose of the project that developed the guidebook:

A number of states are now taking innovative steps to reform their planning and zoning enabling statutes so that they help to revitalize neighborhoods, improve housing affordability, direct the pace and location of development, and ensure wise public expenditures for capital facilities. In other states, public and private groups need answers now about how to improve their communities and deal with issues of growth and change, and objective information on what planning and land use control approaches work. It is time for more states to join the innovators that have already recognized that reforming state planning and land use enabling statutes holds the key to attaining contemporary public and private objectives.[115]

Like the American Law Institute's *A Model Land Development Code,*[116] the Growing Smart project produced model state land use legislation. Whereas the ALI model had given one model that, its authors hoped, would be used by all states, the Growing Smart project included a range of legislative options on most substantive topics, thus allowing state legislatures to pick the approaches that best fit their states.[117] Several of the fifteen articles included in the model legislation address topics directly relevant to this book:

Chapter 4, State Planning

Chapter 5, State Land Use Control

Chapter 6, Regional Planning

Chapter 12, Integrating State Environmental Policy Acts into Local Planning.[118]

A key element of Chapter 5 addresses how a state sites major facilities such as airports and waste disposal sites. Despite the title, the chapter does not suggest a top-down state role in planning.

A 2002 progress report on the Growing Smart project indicated that, in the brief period from 1999 to 2001, there were 2,000 planning-related bills introduced in state legislatures, legislative committees to examine smart growth in eight states and nineteen smart growth executive orders issued by governors of seventeen states (see discussion of "smart growth" near the end of Chapter 6).[119] What may be most broadly significant about the legislative evolution of planning in the 1990s, however, is the increased commitment to planning as the basis for decisions:

Approximately one-quarter of the states are implementing moderate to substantial statewide comprehensive planning reforms: Delaware, Florida, Georgia, Maryland, New Jersey, Oregon, Pennsylvania, Rhode Island, Tennessee, Vermont, Washington and Wisconsin.

One-fifth of the states are pursuing additional statewide amendments strengthening local planning requirements, or they are working to improve regional or local planning reforms already adopted: Arizona, California, Hawaii, Maine, Nevada, New Hampshire, New York, Texas, Utah and Virginia. . . . Half of the 25 states where active reform efforts are underway do not border an ocean: Arizona, Arkansas, Colorado, Idaho, Illinois, Iowa, Kentucky, Michigan, Minnesota, Missouri, Nevada, New Mexico and Utah.[120]

The latter finding distinguishes the more recent evolution from the earlier revolution which, with the obvious exception of Vermont, occurred primarily in coastal states—Hawaii, Florida, Oregon, Washington, Maryland.

Another key finding of the 2002 status report on state planning legislation was that, "In many states where reforms have been previously enacted, recent efforts have focused on implementation. States are continuing to experiment with the right mix of incentives, mandates and initial investment costs associated with implementation."[121]

The Growing Smart project and its supporting documents represent contributions to public policy and the literature that will influence planning and planning legislation for a decade or more. Another significant contribution to the literature from the same period was a book by planner Jerry Weitz; entitled *Sprawl Busting,* its subtitle better represents its content, "State Programs to Guide Growth."[122] The book revisits and provides updates on the state efforts in Florida and Oregon, which have been well-documented elsewhere, but it adds critical examinations of more recent efforts in Georgia and Washington. About half of the book is used for synthesis of concepts from the programs, ranging across such topics as the state role, the regional role, standards for planning and the structure of state (or regional) review of local plans.[123]

There are other states in what planning writer/reporter Bill Fulton has called "the second revolution,"[124] and Jerry Weitz has termed the "third wave," having given the "second" designation to efforts in the 1980s.[125] Several are worthy of brief mention.

Georgia

The development of the state role in Georgia is interesting. In 1989, the governor signed legislation that he had urged the legislature to adopt. It created a three-tiered planning structure:

At the state level, the law created two new state bodies:

- **Governor's Development Council,** a body chaired by the governor and including representatives of key state agencies. It is responsible for long-range planning at the state level and for the location of public facilities by state agencies.[126]
- **Board of Community Affairs,** a reconstituted body appointed by the governor. Its role is to establish state planning guidelines, both procedural and substantive, and to establish the territories of each of the regional bodies.[127]

To carry out regional planning functions, the law created Regional Development Centers and required that every local government become a dues-paying member of one of the centers.[128] The RDCs have the duty to coordinate local plans, resolving differences among them, and develop bottoms-up regional plans.[129] "Bottoms-up" planning generally refers to a process in which a comprehensive plan is built from constituents' recommendations, rather than coordinated and dictated from a central planning authority. It often refers to plans assembled from recommendations of citizen committees. In this case, the bottoms-up planning synthesizes the concerns of each local government within a region into a regional plan. Although bottoms-up planning is politically attractive, because of the participatory process, it is often difficult to bring such divergent interests together into a meaningful and coordinated plan.

Local governments retain the primary authority to plan and regulate land use and development under the Georgia law. Development of a comprehensive plan, including elements on land use, infrastructure, environmental issues and economic development, became mandatory under the law. However, implementation and enforcement remain entirely matters of local discretion. The mandatory planning requirement will be enforced through denial of Department of Community Affairs grants to local governments that are not "qualifying," meaning they do not adopt plans as required by the law.[130]

The Georgia experience will be interesting for two quite different reasons. First, most of the experience with strong state programs has been in coastal states with relatively high growth rates. Although Georgia has a limited coastline, it is quite different in character from states like California and Florida. Further, its major population center (Atlanta) is not along the coast.

Second, the program is a unique, middle-U.S. blend of local control and regional and state planning. It lacks the strong state controls of Hawaii, Florida and

Oregon, but it includes the same basic goal: to accomplish regional and state co-ordination of diverse local activity.

Washington

Also joining "the second revolution" was the state of Washington, with the adoption of its Growth Management Act in 1990.[131] That act included mandatory planning requirements for the fastest growing counties and cities in the state and a requirement that zoning be brought into conformance with comprehensive plans. Like the Oregon law, it included requirements for the designation of agricultural and forest lands and for the establishment of "urban growth areas."

In September 1990, the Washington State Growth Strategies Commission published its report.[132] The Commission had been appointed by the governor in 1989, before the adoption of the Growth Management Act. Its report provided broad recommendations for planning and growth management in Washington, including proposals for amendments to the just-passed Act.

Many of the commission's recommendations are similar to those cited in discussions of actions in other states. However, a few are worthy of particular note. The Commission recognized the significance of state actions in one of its first recommendations. "All state agencies must plan and carry out actions consistent with the growth strategy goals. The state must develop a coordinated strategy that uses state spending as an incentive to accomplish the goals."[133] Noting that 69 percent of recent growth in Washington had taken place outside cities,[134] the Commission determined that "Cities are the preferred places for urban growth: In areas required to develop comprehensive plans, urban growth areas should be cooperatively identified by counties and the cities within them. Development within the urban growth area should be coordinated and phased through joint county and city planning agreements."[135]

The Commission adopted a philosophy similar to Florida's "concurrency" requirement in determining that "paying for public facilities should be a shared burden between today's citizens and those of the future. New development should pay for its own impacts, and the broad community should fund the cost of improving, over time, existing facilities that are inadequate to meet present needs."[136]

As the system in Washington evolves, it will be interesting to compare its effectiveness with that of neighboring Oregon.

Maryland

Maryland is a small state that includes portions of two major Metropolitan Statistical Areas, Baltimore and Washington, D.C. It also includes such innovative local governments as Montgomery County (see description of program in Chapter 4) and Howard County.

However, at the state level, Maryland's track record on studying issues is better than its record of taking action. As noted in Chapter 3, its legislature failed to adopt an innovative and farsighted development code prepared for it in 1969. More than two decades later, the 1991 session of the legislature rejected legislative recommendations of the Governor's Commission on Growth in the Chesapeake

Bay Region.[137] Among the legislative recommendations of the report were the establishment of a statewide land classification system to designate developed areas for concentrated growth.[138]

Protecting Special Lands

A number of state programs provide special protection for special lands. California's coastal zone management program is a prime example.[139] All coastal states have adopted programs under requirements of a federal law, although not all go as far as California's.

New York has adopted a management program for its Adirondack Park area, which, despite the name, includes 3.7 million acres of private land along with 2.7 million acres of public land.[140] A joint federal-state partnership resulted in a large-scale plan for preservation of New Jersey's Pine Barrens, which also contain a mixture of public and private land.[141]

Other states have adopted mandatory planning requirements. Those include, but are certainly not limited to, Maine, Rhode Island and Delaware.[142] Whether those laws, like one that has long been in effect in Wyoming,[143] will create growth management systems or just better planning is uncertain at best.

SMART GROWTH—THE WAY TO A PLANNED FUTURE?

The term "smart growth" was probably first used in Maryland, which made it the core of a statewide growth management program that arose in substantial part from a report showing that clustering new development around existing communities would save the state substantial amounts of money on infrastructure alone.[144] Maryland set out three simple goals for its program of smart growth:

1. to save our most valuable remaining natural resources before they are forever lost,
2. to support existing communities and neighborhoods by targeting state resources to support development in areas where the infrastructure is already in place or planned to support it, and
3. to save taxpayers millions of dollars in the unnecessary cost of building the infrastructure required to support sprawl.[145]

A key element of the Maryland program from the beginning has been the designation of "priority funding areas," which receive priority for state funding for infrastructure projects. The original priority funding areas were:

Municipalities

Baltimore City

Areas inside the Baltimore and Washington Beltways

Revitalization Areas

Enterprise Zones

Heritage Areas[146]

The state also allows counties to designate the following areas for priority funding:

Areas with industrial zoning.

Areas with employment as the principal use, which are provided with, or planned for, sewer service.

Residential areas that have an average density of two or more units per acre, are within designated growth areas and are served by water or sewer systems.

Rural Villages designated in the comprehensive plan before July 1, 1998.

Other areas within county-designated growth areas that: reflect a long-term policy for promoting an orderly expansion of growth and an efficient use of land and public services, are planned to be served by water and sewer systems, and have a permitted density of 3.5 or more units per acre for new residential development.[147]

Maryland has subsequently expanded the concept of priority funding areas to provide priority for state-sponsored home loan programs.[148] Another innovative portion of the Maryland program is its "smart codes" program, which provides a separate building code for rehabilitating buildings over 1 year old.[149] The state provides this explanation of the code and the reasons for it:

The Maryland Building Rehabilitation Code called "Smart Codes," encourages investment in our existing neighborhoods through the rehabilitation and reuse of existing buildings. The program, a component of Maryland's Smart Growth initiative, centers on the new Maryland Building Rehabilitation Code that establishes the constructions code requirements for work on buildings over 1 year old.

Professionals in the building codes and development fields have raised concerns that the application of the current construction codes can present significant barriers to redevelopment and improvement of existing buildings. The new Maryland Building Rehabilitation Code establishes safety requirements that make sense for rehabilitation work without creating unnecessary regulatory barriers.[150]

The Maryland program now includes a complex array of state-sponsored programs. Many of those predate the "smart growth" concept but are now included within it, in some cases with program modifications.[151]

The catchy phrase, "smart growth," is a politically attractive phrase that has achieved wide notice.[152] It was the subject of a 2002 symposium that examined its "form and consequences."[153] There is a "Smart Growth Network," started with support from the U.S. Environmental Protection Agency; it maintains its own Web site, which is rich with resources.[154] It identifies these essential principles for "smart growth":

Create Range of Housing Opportunities and Choices

Create Walkable Neighborhoods

Encourage Community and Stakeholder Collaboration

Foster Distinctive, Attractive Places with a Strong Sense of Place

Make Development Decisions Predictable, Fair and Cost Effective

Mix Land Uses

Preserve Open Space, Farmland, Natural Beauty and Critical Environmental Areas

Provide a Variety of Transportation Choices

Strengthen and Direct Development Toward Existing Communities

Take Advantage of Compact Building Design.[155]

The National Association of Home Builders supports "smart growth" in concept and gives it this broad definition:

To meet the demands of the ever increasing population and a prosperous economy, smart growth means building a political consensus (a) to support comprehensive local plans employing market-sensitive and innovative land use planning concepts to achieve a wide range of housing choices for all Americans; (b) to fairly and fully finance infrastructure to support necessary new residential, commercial, and industrial growth; and (c) to preserve meaningful open space and protect the environment.[156]

The Urban Land Institute gives it a similarly broad definition. It declares that smart growth is "[D]evelopment that is environmentally sensitive, economically viable, community-oriented, and sustainable" and that it includes the following elements:

Development is economically viable and preserves open space and natural resources.

Land use planning is comprehensive, integrated and regional.

Public, private and nonprofit sectors collaborate on growth and development issues to achieve mutually beneficial outcomes.

Certainty and predictability are inherent to the development process.

Infrastructure is maintained and enhanced to serve existing and new residents.

Redevelopment of infill housing, brownfield sites and obsolete buildings is actively pursued.

Urban centers and neighborhoods are integral components of a healthy regional economy.

Compact suburban development is integrated into existing commercial areas, new town centers, and/or near existing or planned transportation facilities.

Development on the urban fringe integrates a mix of land uses, preserves open space, is fiscally responsible and provides transportation options.[157]

As these excerpts suggest, the term "smart growth" has been broadened in its use to apply to most forms of logical planning, including growth management. There is, of course, benefit in a program that has the National Association of Home Builders publicly committed to public planning; the Urban Land Institute has long demonstrated its commitment to the importance of good planning as a basis for sound development.

It is important, however, not to lose sight of the growth management aspects of the original "smart growth" concept in Maryland. Most development should occur in and around existing communities. That is the opposite of sprawl. It is a program designed to address the issue of revitalization of existing communities, or "the other side of sprawl" (discussed in Chapter 7). It addresses two of the core issues of many growth management programs: ensuring that new development occurs near existing facilities, and minimizing the costs of providing public services. Existing communities typically have sewage systems, water systems, parks, schools and other infrastructure. Often those systems have excess capacity because of the loss of population or the reduced demand placed on many systems by today's smaller families. Where the capacity of the systems is not adequate to handle all of the new development that may occur, updating those existing systems is almost always cheaper than building entirely new ones in new locations. And, as the evidence in Chapter 9 shows clearly, the costs of providing services to sprawling locations is almost always higher than providing the same services in or near an existing community. Smart growth just makes sense.

REGIONAL PLANNING—THE REAL ISSUE?

A metropolitan area in the United States may include a dozen or more counties, 200 or more municipalities, and even more special service districts.[158] There is a strong tradition of local control of land use, local expenditure of funds on capital improvements and, as a corollary, strictly local planning. Overlaid on that is a system of state control of the enormous funding (largely federal) for region-changing highway projects. With a few exceptions, there is little in the way of effective coordination between the steamrollers of state highway builders and the multiplicity of local planners and decision-makers.

A principal advantage of planning at the state level is that it offers the opportunity to control the complexity of the metropolitan regions within the state. The statewide land use planning effort in Oregon is really not about statewide land use planning. It is about providing some order to the regions around Portland, Eugene and a handful of other growing urban areas.

Clawson long ago recommended a regional solution. Under the heading of an "ideal planning process," the first of five recommendations was, "Planning that deals with major land use in the whole of an urban area should be on a metropolitan or SMSA scale since land use planning for only part of an economic area is inevitably only partial in its answers. This does not deny that some problems are local or that planning for their solution cannot be local."[159] In the concluding chapter of his work, Clawson recommended the development of "larger units of government of metropolis-wide scope. Unless some unit of government has the responsibility for planning and action on problems that involve the whole metropolitan area, such problems will simply go unattended."[160]

Several years earlier, the author of a major planning text had recommended a metropolitan regional plan, metropolitan public works policy and an "urban development code" to serve an entire metropolitan region.[161] Writing before the federal government preempted most pollution control activity, he wrote, "The urban development code would reorganize and codify in one metropolitan area instrument the regulations presently scattered through different ordinances in each jurisdiction that relate to land development and the construction, use, and occupancy of structures on the land. Such a code would also include controls in the use of land, water, and air in the larger region."[162]

One participant proposed an interesting approach in an apparently little-noticed paper in a compendium prepared for the report of the 1969 National Committee on Urban Growth Policy.[163] He suggested creation of an "urban development district" as a regional agency in a metropolitan region. His proposed agency would temporarily supersede local land use controls in the region, but it would also actively engage in land development, as well as in economic development activity. In short, it would take a pro-active role in causing the kind of development shown in the regional plan. Ultimately, after the development of its designated region was substantially complete, the agency would be abolished.[164]

Porter later cited the need for regional government, calling it "the missing link in relating transportation and land use."[165] Others have noted that it is virtually impossible to address the issues of decline in the inner-ring suburbs or even downtowns without some form of regional planning and cooperation.[166]

An individual local government can easily implement adequate public facilities standards without the intervention of either the region or the state. However, enforcing such standards may require the cooperation of both. It does little good for a particular community to decide that traffic on its arterials should be at Level of Service "D" (heavy traffic but still moving) or better at rush hour, if adjoining communities allow development to load the same road to LOS "E." Addressing the issues of sprawl and urban form and even the timing of development are issues that can best be accomplished at the regional level.

Bruce Katz of the Brookings Institution reminds us that regionalism "has been around for more than 100 years, ever since the union of Manhattan, Brooklyn, Queens, Staten Island, and the Bronx made New York City a regional metropolis."[167] Despite the lasting effects of that move toward regionalism by a state legislature, it is important to note that the actual metropolitan area of the city now spreads over thirty-one counties with more than 800 municipalities in three states,[168] with the only regional planning conducted by the non-governmental voluntary Regional Plan Association.[169] Harvard Law Professor Gerald Frug has proposed a form of regional governance that would maintain many existing governmental structures but that would open voting to all of the stakeholders in each community, regardless of where they live.[170] Although the scenario that he suggests is not one that is likely to occur in the foreseeable future, his concept provides a useful framework for thinking about regional issues.

Large numbers of mergers of local governments seem likely to be little more common in the 1990s than they were in the 1970s, when Clawson recommended such mergers. However, creating some stronger forms of mandatory regional planning, as Georgia has done, may be more practical and politically realistic in many states than implementing statewide land use planning, as Oregon has also done. The budget problems and resistance to tax increases facing many local governments in the 1990s and 2000s may contribute to increased regional cooperation out of financial necessity. State governments may begin to mandate regional planning or cooperation as a condition of receiving state financial assistance for local projects.

The strong program of state-mandated regional planning in Portland is often cited as a model for regional planning in the United States.[171] A more practical model for much of the country to consider may be that of the Twin Cities region of Minneapolis–St. Paul, Minnesota. Myron Orfield, a long-time participant in the evolution of the Twin Cities model, has written thoughtfully about it in a book for the Brookings Institution.[172] Two thoughtful analysts have contrasted it with the Portland program as a "pragmatic" one that is more consistent with the strong tradition of home-rule and local control in much of the country.[173] Key elements of the Minnesota program include a regional sewage treatment agency, with a regional service area boundary, and a state-adopted system of sharing new tax base among communities in the region.[174] The details of the Minnesota model do not necessarily lend themselves to adoption elsewhere, but the process that has led to their adoption can provide an action model for leaders in other regions.[175]

On the other hand, regional cooperation or even regional planning without strong regional governance may be inadequate. David Rusk, a former mayor of Albuquerque, has argued persuasively—backed by substantial empirical evidence—that *Cities without Suburbs* are healthier than similar cities by many measures. What is striking about Rusk's findings is not just that the central cities are healthier, but that the regions are also stronger where there is one strong central urban government.[176]

Clearly, in some states the problems are statewide. In Hawaii and Vermont, the pressures of tourist and second-home development affect wide areas of the state, many of them outside logical metropolitan regions. In Florida, population growth is occurring throughout the state. In those states, statewide programs seem clearly necessary. However, in other states a modified form of the Oregon approach, with strong, state-mandated regional agencies, may offer a more interesting approach. In that context, it will be interesting to observe the Georgia experience as it implements its mixture of bottoms-up and top-down planning, with a strong regional emphasis.

CONCLUSION

How important is state growth management? It depends on what one is trying to achieve.

Only a state, or a strong regional agency with authority delegated from the state, can use techniques like urban growth boundaries or "state zoning" to control urban form. If the goal is to stop sprawl or to protect certain lands, such as agricultural lands or wetlands, while still accommodating development, only the state can do a fully effective job. If regional efficiency of services is a goal, again only the state, or a regional body empowered by the state, can be effective. Even the adequacy of public facilities can be regulated better at a regional level than at a local one.

Innes argues that state growth management programs are "systems for sharing power."[177] In characterizing state programs in a separate publication, she notes that, "In each state there is some arbiter of conflicts . . ."[178] She also cites as a co-ordination strategy the requirement for planning as applied to state agencies as well as local ones.[179] She notes the significance of the fact that developers, environmentalists and state and local governments have joined to make growth management a reality in most of the states that have adopted programs[180] and remarks that, "These interests have decided they prefer rules of the game to endless controversy."[181]

Regional or statewide planning offers a considerable improvement over the status quo in most states, because it offers some chance of coordinating the diverse activities of the multiple local governments within a typical growing metropolitan area. Although it seems unlikely that a significant number of additional states will, in the foreseeable future, adopt strong statewide programs like those in Vermont and Hawaii, many of the issues addressed in this book are ones that realistically cannot be solved by individual local governments. Encouraging or mandating regional planning may be the most politically practicable form of state role in growth management in most of the United States.

NOTES

1. Bosselman, Callies, and Council on Environmental Quality (U.S.), *The Quiet Revolution in Land Use Control*, 1.
2. American Institute of Planners, Research Office, "Survey of State Land Use Activity" (Washington, D.C.: U.S. Department of Housing and Urban Development, 1976).
3. Council of State Governments, "State Growth Management" (Washington, D.C.: U.S. Department of Housing and Urban Development, 1976).
4. Nelson Rosenbaum, *Land Use and the Legislatures* (Washington, D.C.: Urban Institute, 1976).
5. Healy and Resources for the Future, *Land Use and the States*.
6. Healy, Rosenberg, and Resources for the Future, *Land Use and the States*.
7. Phyllis Myers, "So Goes Vermont" (Washington, D.C.: The Conservation Foundation, 1974).
8. Phyllis Myers, "Zoning Hawaii," *Environmental Comment*, July 1976.
9. Healy, Rosenberg, and Resources for the Future, *Land Use and the States*, 1, 2.
10. De Grove, *Land, Growth & Politics*.
11. Healy, Rosenberg, and Resources for the Future, *Land Use and the States*.
12. De Grove, *Land, Growth & Politics*.
13. Callies, "Dealing with Scarcity: Land Use and Planning"; David L. Callies, *Regulating Paradise: Land Use Controls in Hawaii* (Honolulu: University of Hawaii Press, 1984).
14. Teitz, "California Growth: Hard Questions, Few Answers."

15. Judith Innes, "Group Processes and the Social Construction of Growth Management: The Cases of Florida, Vermont and New Jersey," in *Institute of Urban and Regional Development Working Paper Series* (Berkeley, Calif.: Institute of Urban and Regional Development, 1991); Innes, "Implementing State Growth Management in the U.S.: Strategies for Coordination."

16. John Melvin De Grove, "Growth Management and Governance," in *Understanding Growth Management: Critical Issues and a Research Agenda*, eds. David J. Brower, David R. Godschalk, and Douglas R. Porter (Washington, D.C.: Urban Land Institute, 1989).

17. Myers, "Zoning Hawaii," 16–19.

18. Bosselman, Callies, and Council on Environmental Quality (U.S.), *The Quiet Revolution in Land Use Control*; De Grove, *Land, Growth & Politics*, 9–11; Myers, "Zoning Hawaii," 5–7.

19. Haw. Rev. Stat. Sect. 205-1.

20. Haw. Rev. Stat. Sect. 205-2, 3.

21. Bosselman, Callies, and Council on Environmental Quality (U.S.), *The Quiet Revolution in Land Use Control*, 7–10; Callies, "Dealing with Scarcity: Land Use and Planning," 132–33; De Grove, *Land, Growth & Politics*, 15–17.

22. Bosselman, Callies, and Council on Environmental Quality (U.S.), *The Quiet Revolution in Land Use Control*, 170.

23. Healy, Rosenberg, and Resources for the Future, *Land Use and the States*, 186.

24. De Grove, *Land, Growth & Politics*, 32.

25. George Cooper and Gavan Daws, *Land and Power in Hawaii: The Democratic Years* (Honolulu, Hawaii: Benchmark Books, 1985), 98–99, 110.

26. De Grove, *Land, Growth & Politics*, quotation from p. 32.

27. Cooper and Daws, *Land and Power in Hawaii: The Democratic Years*, 110.

28. City and County of Honolulu, "Development Plan Status Review" (Honolulu, Hawaii: Department of General Planning, 1991).

29. Healy, Rosenberg, and Resources for the Future, *Land Use and the States*, 186.

30. Callies, "Dealing with Scarcity: Land Use and Planning."

31. City and County of Honolulu, "Development Plan Status Review."

32. United States Bureau of the Census, *Quick Tables* (November 2003).

33. Myers, "So Goes Vermont."

34. United States Bureau of the Census, *Quick Tables* (November 2003); "1990 Census of Population and Housing: Summary of Population and Housing Characteristics," in *1990 Census of the Population* (Washington, D.C.: U.S. Department of Commerce, 1991).

35. United States Bureau of the Census, *Quick Tables* (November 2003).

36. De Grove, *Land, Growth & Politics*, 66–67.

37. Healy, Rosenberg, and Resources for the Future, *Land Use and the States*, 41–43.

38. Bosselman, Callies, and Council on Environmental Quality (U.S.), *The Quiet Revolution in Land Use Control*, 54–56; Healy, Rosenberg, and Resources for the Future, *Land Use and the States*, 41.

39. Healy, Rosenberg, and Resources for the Future, *Land Use and the States*, 41.

40. Porter, "Significant Research Needs in the Policy and Practice of Growth Management."

41. 10 Vt. Stat. Ann., Sect. 6081. See also definition of "development" at Sect. 6001(3).

42. 10 Vt. Stat. Ann., Sect. 6086(a).

43. Ibid.

44. De Grove, *Land, Growth & Politics*, 80–94; Healy, Rosenberg, and Resources for the Future, *Land Use and the States*, 61–66; Myers, "So Goes Vermont."
45. Healy, Rosenberg, and Resources for the Future, *Land Use and the States*, 54–56.
46. De Grove, *Land, Growth & Politics*, 94–96.
47. Ibid., 94.
48. Healy, Rosenberg, and Resources for the Future, *Land Use and the States*, 72.
49. Ibid., 73–74.
50. Myers, "So Goes Vermont."
51. Ann L. Strong, "Vermont's Act 250 and Prime Farmland" (Philadelphia: Regional Science Research Institute, University of Pennsylvania, 1977), 25.
52. Ibid.
53. 32 Vt. Stat. Ann., Sect. 10001, et seq.
54. De Grove, *Land, Growth & Politics*, 69–72.
55. Abberger, "Growth Management through Land Acquisition."
56. Governor's Commission on Vermont's Future, "Report of the Governor's Commission on Vermont's Future: Guidelines for Growth" (Montpelier, Vt.: State of Vermont, 1988).
57. 24 Vt. Stat. Ann., Sect. 4302.
58. Ibid.
59. 24 Vt. Stat. Ann., Sect. 4381.
60. 24 Vt. Stat. Ann., Sect. 4382.
61. 24 Vt. Stat. Ann., Sect. 5200.
62. De Grove, "Growth Management and Governance," 38.
63. Vermont Smart Growth Collaborative, "Vermont Smart Growth Progress Report," (Burlington, VT: Vermont Smart Growth Collaborative, 2003).
64. De Grove, *Land, Growth & Politics*, 102.
65. Healy, Rosenberg, and Resources for the Future, *Land Use and the States*, 126–27.
66. Ibid., 128.
67. De Grove, *Land, Growth & Politics*, 105–06.
68. Ibid., 106–14.
69. American Law Institute, *A Model Land Development Code, with Commentary by Alison Dunham, Chief Reporter* (Washington, D.C.: American Law Institute, 1975).
70. Fla. Stat. Sect. 380.05.
71. Fla. Stat. Sects. 380.055, 380.0551, 380.0552, 380.0555, and 380.0558, respectively.
72. Fla. Stat. Sect. 380.06 (1).
73. De Grove, *Land, Growth & Politics*, 126–28.
74. American Law Institute, *A Model Land Development Code, with Commentary by Alison Dunham, Chief Reporter*, art. 7, pt. 2.
75. Ibid., art. 7, pt. 3.
76. Lance de Haven-Smith, *Controlling Florida's Development* (Wakefield, N.H.: Hollowbrook Publishing, 1991), 92–95 and table 4.1 at 74–77.
77. Fla. Stat. Sect. 63.3177.
78. Ibid.
79. Fla. Stat. Sect. 163.3167(1).
80. Fla. Stat. Sect. 163.3202(1).
81. Fla. Stat. Sects. 163.3167, 163.3213.
82. Fla. Stat. Sect. 163.3202(1)(g).

83. De Grove, *Land, Growth & Politics*; Innes, "Implementing State Growth Management in the U.S.: Strategies for Coordination."

84. J. Weitz, "Cpl Bibliography 355/356/357: From Quiet Revolution to Smart Growth: State Growth Management Programs, 1960 to 1999," *Journal of Planning Literature* 14, no. 2 (1999).

85. Paul Ketcham and Scot Siegel, "Managing Growth to Promote Affordable Housing: Revisiting Oregon's Goal 10" (Portland, Oreg.: 1000 Friends of Oregon, 1991).

86. The term "concurrency" does not appear in the statute but rather in the Department of Community Affairs Regulation 9J-5, which provided the regulatory basis for implementing the 1985 act. See Reg. 9-J5.003(19) and (20). The term has subsequently come into relatively wide use. See, for example, Boggs and Apgar, 1991.

87. See, generally, Thomas G Pelham, "Adequate Public Facilities Requirements: Reflections on Florida's Concurrency System for Managing Growth," *Florida State University Law Review* 19, no. 4 (1992).

88. For a general description of this requirement, see H. Glenn Boggs and Robert C. Apgar, "Concurrency and Growth Management: A Lawyer's Primer," *Journal of Land Use and Environmental Law* 7 (1991).

89. Colo. Rev. Stat. 30-28-133(6).

90. Fla. Stat. 132.3202(1)(g).

91. Fla. Stat. 163.3177(3)(a)(1).

92. Advisory Commission on Regulatory Barriers to Affordable Housing, "'Not in My Backyard': Removing Barriers to Affordable Housing."

93. De Grove, *Land, Growth & Politics*, 171; Innes, "Implementing State Growth Management in the U.S.: Strategies for Coordination."

94. William Fulton, "The Second Revolution in Land-Use Planning," in *Balanced Growth: A Planning Guide for Local Government*, ed. John Melvin De Grove (Washington, D.C.: International City Management Association, 1991), 122–23.

95. de Haven-Smith, *Controlling Florida's Development*, 106–08.

96. Ibid., 71–103.

97. Ibid., 109–10.

98. Ibid., 42–43.

99. James Duncan and Associates Inc. et al., "The Search for Efficient Urban Growth Patterns: A Study of the Fiscal Impacts of Development in Florida" (Tallahassee: Florida Department of Community Affairs, 1989), 21.

100. Florida Department of Community Affairs, "Techniques for Discouraging Sprawl," in *Balance Growth: A Planning Guide for Local Government*, ed. John Melvin De Grove (Washington, D.C.: International City Management Association, 1991).

101. James Duncan and Associates Inc. et al., "The Search for Efficient Urban Growth Patterns: A Study of the Fiscal Impacts of Development in Florida"; James Duncan and Associates Inc., et al., "The Search for Efficient Urban Growth Patterns: Technical Appendices" (Tallahassee: Florida Department of Community Affairs, 1989).

102. Fred P. Bosselman et al., *The Taking Issue: A Study of the Constitutional Limits of Governmental Authority to Regulate the Use of Privately-Owned Land without Paying Compensation to the Owners* (Washington, D.C.: For sale by the Supt. of Docs., U.S. Government Printing Office, 1973).

103. De Grove, *Land, Growth & Politics*, 236.

104. Ore. Rev. Stat. Sect. 197.005 et seq.

105. Ore. Rev. Stat. Sects. 197.005k, 197.040, and 197.250.

106. De Grove, *Land, Growth & Politics*, 254.

107. Ibid., 263.

108. Kevin Kasowski, "Oregon: Fifteen Years of Land Use Planning," in *Balance Growth: A Planning Guide for Local Government*, ed. John Melvin De Grove (Washington, D.C.: International City Management Association, 1991), 128.

109. Ketcham and Siegel, "Managing Growth to Promote Affordable Housing: Revisiting Oregon's Goal 10." See also discussion in Chapter 7.

110. De Grove, "Growth Management and Governance"; De Grove, *Land, Growth & Politics*.

111. Kasowski, "Oregon: Fifteen Years of Land Use Planning," 125–26.

112. Carl Abbott, Deborah A. Howe, and Sy Adler, *Planning the Oregon Way: A Twenty-Year Evaluation* (Corvallis, Oreg.: Oregon State University Press, 1994).

113. G. J. Knaap, Arthur C. Nelson, and Lincoln Institute of Land Policy, *The Regulated Landscape: Lessons on State Land Use Planning from Oregon* (Cambridge, Mass.: Lincoln Institute of Land Policy, 1992).

114. Stuart Meck, ed., *Growing Smart Legislative Guidebook: Model Statutes for Planning and the Management of Change* (Chicago, Ill.: American Planning Association, 2002).

115. Stuart Meck, "Growing Smart User's Guide" (Chicago, Ill.: American Planning Association, 2002), 8.

116. American Law Institute, *A Model Land Development Code, with Commentary by Alison Dunham, Chief Reporter.*

117. Meck, ed., *Growing Smart Legislative Guidebook: Model Statutes for Planning and the Management of Change.*

118. Ibid.

119. Johnson, Salkin, and Jordan, "2002 State of the States."

120. Ibid., 6–7.

121. Ibid., 7.

122. Jerry Weitz, *Sprawl Busting: State Programs to Guide Growth* (Chicago: American Planning Association, 1999).

123. Ibid.

124. Fulton, "The Second Revolution in Land-Use Planning."

125. Weitz, *Sprawl Busting: State Programs to Guide Growth.*

126. Code Ga. Ann. Sect. 45-12-201.

127. Code Ga. Ann. Sect. 50-8-4.

128. Code Ga. Ann. Sect. 50-8-33.

129. Code Ga. Ann. Sects. 50-8-34, 35.

130. Code Ga. Ann. Sect. 50-8-2(a)(18).

131. Wash. Code Ann. Sect. 36.70A.010, et seq.

132. Washington State Growth Strategies Commission, "A Growth Strategy for Washington State" (Olympia, Wash.: Washington Department of Community Development, 1990).

133. Ibid., 4.

134. Ibid., 11.

135. Ibid., 10.

136. Ibid., 13.

137. Governor's Commission on Growth in the Chesapeake Bay Region, "Protecting the Future: A Vision for Maryland" (Baltimore, Md.: Maryland Office of Planning, 1991).

138. Ibid., 8.

139. De Grove, "Growth Management and Governance," 26–28; De Grove, *Land, Growth & Politics*, 177–234; Healy, Rosenberg, and Resources for the Future, *Land Use and the States*, 80–125.

140. John S. Banta, "Environmental Protection and Growth Management," in *Understanding Growth Management: Critical Issues and a Research Agenda* (Washington, D.C.: Urban Land Institute, 1989); Bosselman, Callies, and Council on Environmental Quality (U.S.), *The Quiet Revolution in Land Use Control*, 295–98; Healy, Rosenberg, and Resources for the Future, *Land Use and the States*, 178; Frank Popper (1981).

141. Richard F. Babcock, Charles L. Siemon, and Lincoln Institute of Land Policy, *The Zoning Game Revisited* (Cambridge, Mass.: Lincoln Institute of Land Policy, 1985); De Grove, "Growth Management and Governance"; Healy, Rosenberg, and Resources for the Future, *Land Use and the States*, 178.

142. Abberger, "Growth Management through Land Acquisition."

143. J. S. Gilmore and Mary K. Duff, *Boom Town Growth Management: A Case Study of Rock Springs—Green River, Wyoming* (Boulder, Colo.: Westview Press, 1975); William E. Sanborn and Robert Logan, "Wyoming: Meeting Energy Impact Head On," *Environmental Comment*, July 1976.

144. Governor's Commission on Growth in the Chesapeake Bay Region, "Protecting the Future: A Vision for Maryland."

145. Maryland Governor's Office of Smart Growth, *Smart Growth* (Maryland Office of the Governor, 2003 [cited November 2003]); available from www.smartgrowth. state.md.us/.

146. Ibid.

147. Ibid.

148. Maryland Department of Housing and Community Development, *Priority Funding Areas* (Maryland Department of Housing and Community Development, 2003 [cited November 2003]); available from www.dhcd.state.md.us/pfa/index.asp.

149. Maryland Department of Housing and Community Development, *Smart Codes* (Maryland Department of Housing and Community Development, 2003 [cited November 2003]); available from www.dhcd.state.md.us/smartcodes/index.asp.

150. Ibid. (cited).

151. Maryland Governor's Office of Smart Growth, *The Maryland Tool Box* (Maryland Office of the Governor, 2003 [cited November 2003]); available from www.smartgrowth. state.md.us/tool%20box.pdf.

152. International City Management Association and Smart Growth Network, "Getting to Smart Growth II: 100 More Policies For" (Washington, D.C.: Smart Growth Network/International City Management Association, 2003), ii.

153. Terry S. Szold, Armando Carbonell, and Lincoln Institute of Land Policy, *Smart Growth: Form and Consequences* (Cambridge, Mass.: Lincoln Institute of Land Policy, 2002).

154. www.smartgrowth.org/default.asp.

155. Smart Growth Network, *Principles of Smart Growth* (Smart Growth Network, 2003 [cited 2003 November]); available from www.smartgrowth.org/about/principles/default.asp.

156. National Association of Home Builders, *Smart Growth Policy* (National Association of Home Builders, June 13, 2003 [cited 2003 November]); available from www.nahb.org/generic.aspx?sectionID=636&genericContentID=3519.

157. Urban Land Institute, *Smart Growth* (Urban Land Institute, 2003 [cited 2003 November]); available from http://smartgrowth.net/Home/sg_Home_fst.html.
158. Bruce Katz, *Reflections on Regionalism*/Bruce Katz, Editor [Foreword by Al Gore] (Washington, D.C.: Brookings Institution Press, 2000); Rothblatt and Sancton, *Metropolitan Governance: American/Canadian Intergovernmental Perspectives.*
159. Clawson, *Suburban Land Conversion in the United States: An Economic and Governmental Process.*
160. Ibid., 373.
161. Stuart F. Chapin, Jr., "Taking Stock of Techniques for Shaping Urban Growth," *Journal of the American Institute of Planners* 29 (1963).
162. Ibid., 84.
163. Henry Bain, "The Organization of Growth," in *The New City*, ed. Donald Canty (New York: Praeger, 1969).
164. Ibid.
165. Douglas R. Porter, "Regional Governance of Metropolitan Form: The Missing Link in Relating Land Use and Transportation," in *Transportation, Urban Form and the Environment: Proceedings of a Conference, Special Report Series* (Washington, D.C.: Transportation Research Board, 1991).
166. Katz, *Reflections on Regionalism/Bruce Katz, Editor [Foreword by Al Gore]*; William H. Lucy and David L. Phillips, *Confronting Suburban Decline: Strategic Planning for Metropolitan Renewal* (Washington, D.C.: Island Press, 2000).
167. Katz, *Reflections on Regionalism/Bruce Katz, Editor [Foreword by Al Gore]*, 1.
168. Robert Yaro, "Growing and Governing Smart: A Case Study of the New York Region," in *Reflections on Regionalism*, ed. Bruce Katz (Washington, D.C.: Brookings Institution, 2000), 45.
169. Ibid., 53–56.
170. Gerald E. Frug, *City Making: Building Communities without Building Walls* (Princeton, N.J.: Princeton University Press, 1999).
171. Abbott, Howe, and Adler, *Planning the Oregon Way: A Twenty-Year Evaluation;* Nelson, "Oregon's Urban Growth Boundary Policy as a Landmark Planning Tool."
172. Orfield, *Metropolitics: A Regional Agenda for Community and Stability.*
173. Fulton and Mondale, "Managing Metropolitan Growth: Reflections on the Twin Cities Experience."
174. Ibid.
175. Orfield, *Metropolitics: A Regional Agenda for Community and Stability.*
176. David Rusk, *Cities without Suburbs*, 2nd ed., *Woodrow Wilson Center Special Studies* (Washington, D.C., and Baltimore, Md.: Woodrow Wilson Center Press; Distributed by Johns Hopkins University Press, 1995).
177. Innes, "Group Processes and the Social Construction of Growth Management: The Cases of Florida, Vermont and New Jersey," 3.
178. Ibid., 6.
179. Ibid., 6–7.
180. Innes, "Implementing State Growth Management in the U.S.: Strategies for Coordination."
181. Ibid., 3.

CHAPTER 7

Fighting Sprawl: Growth Management and Urban Form

Urban form is a complex subject that can encompass everything from the skyline to the urban landscape to the actual shape of the city. Urban form is both directly and indirectly a concern of growth managing communities. Some communities, such as Boulder and Montgomery County, adopt growth management programs in part to manage the shape of urban growth. Many communities that adopt growth management programs do so hoping to reduce the cost of serving new development. Those costs are, in part, a function of urban form,[1] a topic discussed further in Chapter 9. Finally, urban form can affect housing costs both directly and indirectly. Thus, to understand fully the effects of growth management programs on the land and housing markets and on the public treasury, it is important to understand whether and how such programs affect urban form.

In certain respects, the answer to the question posed here is self-evident. Any conscious attempt to regulate the location of urban growth is bound to affect urban form in some way. An adequate public facilities requirement ensures that most new development will take place reasonably close to existing facilities. That is an effect on urban form. It may or may not be an effect that is consistent with the goals of the community adopting the growth management program, but it is, nevertheless, an effect on urban form.

In discussing urban form, it is important to remember the context in which most growth management programs take place. As the discussion in Chapter 2 indicates, most growth managing communities are parts of metropolitan regions in which dozens, or even hundreds, of local governments and special districts make decisions that influence the patterns of growth (described in Chapter 2). In that typical context, it is very difficult for any one community to make a significant difference in the overall pattern of urban development. It can, of course, make a difference in its own shape, but that is only one small part of the typical metropolitan region.

Dowall describes the competition among communities in the San Francisco metropolitan region, first for each to obtain as much growth as possible and, later, to push as much growth as possible onto other communities.[2] Greenberg documents the very specific competition among communities within the Amador Valley, which includes Livermore. He shows how the willingness of officials of the county and nearby Pleasanton facilitated the continuation of the rapid residential growth that Livermore tried to slow down in the region and created political pressure that threatened the viability of the Livermore program.[3]

URBAN FORM AND SPRAWL

Treatment of the broad subject of urban form goes far beyond this book. However, some growth management programs do address one very significant aspect of urban form: the shape and extent of the urban area.

It is almost a truism among planners and others that sprawl is bad and that the ideal urban form consists of a central city with relatively intense development, surrounded by less intense development, all separated from nearby communities through either public or private open space. In a 1958 piece, William H. Whyte noted that *Fortune* and *Architectural Forum* magazines had recently convened a group of nineteen experts for a "two day conference on urban sprawl," pointing out that the problem was not a shortage of land:

The problem is the pattern of growth, or rather the lack of one. Because of the leapfrog nature of urban growth, even within the limits of most big cities, there is to this day a surprising amount of empty land. But it is scattered; a vacant lot here, a dump there, no one parcel big enough to be of much use. And it is with this same kind of sprawl that we are ruining the whole metropolitan area of the future. . . .

Sprawl is bad aesthetics; it is bad economics. Five acres are being made to do the work of one, and do it very poorly. This is bad for the farmers, it is bad for communities, it is bad for industry, it is bad for utilities, it is bad for the railroads, it is bad for the recreation groups, it is bad even for the developers.[4]

A dozen years later, in his landmark work, *Suburban Land Conversion in the United States*, Marion Clawson noted the inefficiency of sprawl and particularly of what he called "subdivision discontiguity," or "sprawl on the subdivision scale."[5] He also traced the history of sprawl and the role of infrastructure construction, federal policies on housing finance and other governmental influences on creating the sprawling metropolises of the last part of the twentieth century. In 1969, the National Committee on Urban Growth Policy attributed the pattern of sprawl to three factors: "prosperity, automobility, and public policy."[6] The Committee cited two public policies that contributed significantly to sprawl: Federal mortgage policy, which facilitated the purchase of single-family homes; and federal highway policy, which "spread automobility." In 1980, the federally appointed Council on Development Choices for the 80s listed as one of its principal concerns an increase in the consumption of land by urbanization, in part because of a reduction of the intensity of use.[7] The Council made six recommendations for the 80s, two of which directly addressed sprawl:

1. Increase compactness of metropolitan fringe and nonmetropolitan areas;
2. Accelerate the process of infill and redevelopment in existing communities.[8]

More recently, Benjamin Chinitz, in an article challenging some of the premises of those who oppose sprawl, gave this example of "Using Land the Wrong Way."[9] "Urban sprawl that encourages automobile use and results in an inappropriate pattern is illustrative."

Although a number of economists challenge some of the economic basis on which Clawson and others have found sprawl to be "inefficient" (see discussion below), the issue remains an important one in establishing urban development patterns. Thus, to the extent that growth management programs attempt to influence urban form, they are likely to attempt to limit sprawl. Boulder has addressed the issue of contiguous sprawl directly, with its greenbelt. Montgomery County has similarly tackled sprawl, within its focus on preserving "wedges and corridors" of green space as well as large areas of agricultural land, while allowing substantial development in other areas.

The model of a reasonably compact community surrounded by open space (often in the form of agricultural land) is not a modern invention. It finds roots in the independent rural communities that dotted the United States before the automobile facilitated commuting. It resembles the types of compact towns that tended to cluster around commuter railroad stations near nineteenth-century New York and Philadelphia.

That idealized form of development certainly owes some debt to the work of Ebenezer Howard, a British stenographer whose small book, *Garden Cities of Tomorrow*, remains in print more than a century after it was written.[10] Directly or indirectly, it has influenced many planners and accounts directly for the design of Radburn, New Jersey, and Sunnyside, located in the Queens borough of New York City—both built in the 1920s. It also influenced the construction of the federal greenbelt towns of Greenbelt, Maryland, Green Hills, Ohio, and Greendale, Wisconsin, in the 1930s.[11] The same idea underlay the promotion of new towns by the Department of Housing and Urban Development in the 1970s.[12] In creating the new communities program, the Congress made specific findings related to this issue:

The Congress further finds that continuation of established patterns of urban development, together with the anticipated increase in population, will result in: (1) inefficient and wasteful use of land resources which are of national economic and environmental importance; (2) destruction of irreplaceable natural and recreational resources and increasing pollution of air and water; . . . (4) costly and inefficient public facilities and services at all levels of government . . .[13]

One of the reports available to Congress when it adopted the new communities legislation was the 1969 report of the National Committee on Urban Growth Policy.[14] Among its findings, many of which related to inner cities, were these related to suburban growth patterns:

But our concerns extend to the suburbs as well. They are the fastest growing areas of this nation, yet the way they are growing is wasteful and destructive of environmental value. Their residents' taxes increase steadily, yet yield decreasing benefits in terms of the amenities these people came to the suburbs to find. Uncontrolled development is consuming at random the irreplaceable resource of land and steadily polluting the life-giving resources of air and water. Man-made elements of the environment, transportation facilities, water and sewage lines, are being stretched and overburdened by sprawling development. The process is wasteful of money as well: Each extension of these facilities entails a "sprawl tax" of costs that could be reduced by rational planning.[15]

Private developers, operating without federal subsidies, built the original portions of Reston, Virginia, and Columbia, Maryland, in that period. Both are part of a large metropolitan area, but both include concentrated employment centers, relatively high densities, and significant amounts of open space.[16]

Similar concepts of urban form clearly influenced those who developed the programs in Boulder, with its tight urban edge defined by its 35-square-mile greenbelt, and Oregon, with its state-mandated urban growth boundaries.

In the chapter on "General Development Plans" in a standard planning reference book,[17] Barnett outlined four historical periods of urban design as the basis for modern planning ideas.[18] Two relate primarily to the built environment of the inner city and thus do not relate to this discussion. The other two were: garden suburbs and garden cities, distinguishing the free-standing cities proposed by Howard from the garden suburb movement in this country; and "modernist city design," a concept for complete design coordination of a city surrounded by a greenbelt.[19] Bair described a scheme of urban design that he called the "open space net."[20] Not surprisingly, it included nodes of relatively intense development separated by areas of linked open space and surrounded by a greenbelt.

Other ideas of urban form are typically based on concepts of efficiency, minimizing capital or operating costs, or both. Those models also call for relatively compact and contiguous forms of development, although the high-density center and the surrounding greenbelt are not essential to those models.[21]

Of course, one can reach the same type of urban form simply from principles of land preservation. If one believes that the optimal urban development form is one that affects the least total amount of land, clearly a tightly contained, relatively dense urban area best meets that ideal.[22]

In their mid-1970s survey of communities involved in early growth management efforts, a group of researchers at the University of North Carolina found that 78 percent of the communities surveyed listed "reduction of urban sprawl" as an objective of growth management.[23] That objective was second only to "provision of adequate public services" (84 percent). It tied with "environmental protection," and was followed by "preservation of open space" (66 percent), clearly a related topic. A Florida researcher notes, "Redirecting future growth to a more compact urban form has emerged as the all-encompassing vision of Florida's growth management policy."[24]

Whether growth management programs can effectively limit sprawl is the question addressed in the rest of this chapter. The question of whether it makes sense to do so is largely left to Chapters 9 and 10 of this book.

Two Aspects of Sprawl

The relationship between sprawl and efficiency in the use of land raises two separate issues. One is the general density of development. If the growth trends of a community indicate a need for 2,000 additional dwelling units over the next several years, accommodating that growth at eight dwelling units per acre will consume 250 acres of land, whereas accommodating it at more typical suburban densities of three or four dwelling units per acre will consume 500 or more acres of land. Most of the studies of the fiscal impacts of development, the focus of Chapter 9 of this book, compare the relative efficiency of various densities of development.

The other aspect of sprawl, however, is so-called "leapfrog" development, which economists are more likely to call "discontinuous development." As the alternative names suggest, such a pattern of development skips over land next to the community and takes place on land separated from the community by unused or under-used land. Chapter 9 also examines the fiscal impacts of leapfrog development. This chapter contains additional discussion of the debate over other economic effects of leapfrog development.

GROWTH MANAGEMENT AND SPRAWL

Can growth management programs stop sprawl? As a practical matter, yes. Doing so, however, may require more political will than many public officials have.

Effects on Discontinuous Development

Almost any growth management program is likely to limit leapfrog or discontinuous development, at least to the extent of the effective jurisdiction of that community. However, if the jurisdiction of that community adjoins or overlaps the jurisdictions of other communities, which is typically the case in a metropolitan area, a growth management program in one community may simply force the development to leap *further*, beyond the control of that community. Although Boulder limited its growth in housing units to almost exactly 20 percent in the 1980–1990 decade, the number of housing units in Boulder County increased by more than 26 percent (from 74,638 to 94,621) during that period. The figure is even more dramatic when placed in the context of some of the communities that absorbed the growth: the number of housing units in Louisville increased

Table 7-1
Boulder Population as Percentage of County Population, 1960–2000[1]

Population	1960	1970	1980	1990	2000
Boulder	37,718	66,870	76,685	83,312	94,673
Boulder County	74,254	131,899	189,625	225,339	291,288
City population as percentage of county population	50.8	50.7	40.4	37.0	32.5

[1]*Sources:* Actual number of units from Bureau of the Census, 2000, *American Fact Finder, Quick Tables,* http://www.census.gov; Bureau of the Census, 1991, *Census of Population and Housing: Summary Population and Housing Characteristics,* Part 6, Table 18; Bureau of the Census, 1982, *Summary Characteristics by Governmental Units and Standard Metropolitan Statistical Areas,* Part 6, Table 2; Bureau of the Census, 1972, *City and County Data Book,* Table B-2; Bureau of the Census, 1972, *Census of Population, Vol. 1, Characteristics of the Population,* Part 7, Table 10 (includes 1960); percentages computed by author.

111 percent (2,264 to 4,785); the number in Lafayette increased by 55 percent (3,703 to 5,775); and Longmont, with a much larger base, increased its housing stock by 25 percent (16,346 to 20,480)[25] (to see the same issue treated in people, rather than dwelling units, through 2000, see Table 11-2 in Chapter 11). Because household size decreased over that decade, Boulder's rate of population increase was only about 1 percent. Further, its share of the county population has decreased consistently under its growth management program (see Table 7-1).

Fischel cites an unpublished study of Fairfax County by George Peterson for data showing that even within a jurisdiction, restrictive controls in one area can force development further out within the same jurisdiction.[26]

Clearly, a regional urban growth boundary, such as those imposed by the states of Hawaii and Oregon, can minimize the problem of forcing discontinuous development to leap further out. However, even such techniques have their limitations. A 1991 study found that, based on development patterns to date, there would not be enough land within Portland's urban growth boundary to absorb all projected growth under current zoning over the planning period.[27] Relying on new population projections and land-use data gathered since 1992, in 2002 the metropolitan government approved the expansion of the urban growth boundary by nearly 19,000 acres; that decision was largely affirmed by the state Land Conservation Commission in early 2003.[28]

Furthermore, if a growth boundary of any sort is as impermanent as a line on a zoning map, it is likely to have little effect on leapfrogging. Bair describes the difficulty faced by Montgomery County in adhering to the strong open space component of a 1965 plan when the county faced massive urban development pressure around the nation's capital.[29] Interestingly, a study on the price effects of Portland's urban growth boundary found that the outer boundary significantly affected land prices but that an inner, interim boundary had little discernible effect.[30] He concluded that the reason for the difference was that the outer boundary was viewed as a relatively permanent constraint on the market. The corollary of that conclusion is, of course, that those involved in the market apparently did not take the inner boundary very seriously.[31] A state agency controlled the ability of the region and local governments to change the more permanent, outer, boundary in Portland. It is thus both procedurally and politically more difficult to change than the inner boundary, which remains under regional control. If a growth boundary is not permanent enough to affect land prices, it probably will not be permanent enough to make much difference in the shape of the community. Clearly, the Boulder approach of owning the greenbelt is the only technique most to ensure the preservation of that part of Ebenezer Howard's "garden city" concept.

Subsidizing Leapfrogging?

If the installation of such public improvements as freeways and interceptor sewer lines to or through an area makes leapfrogging possible, arguably the public sector subsidizes leapfrog, or discontinuous, development. That is probably true regarding freeways, which are typically constructed with federal and state funds. A researcher has calculated the substantial direct and indirect subsidies to automobile use in one community in Wisconsin.[32] Because of widespread policies of "making growth pay its own way" through exactions,[33] communities clearly subsidized sprawl less in the 1980s and early 1990s than in earlier periods. A participant in a program on transportation and urban form noted that by the early 1990s it was not uncommon for developers to participate in financing even major freeway improvements.[34]

Nevertheless, there are circumstances in which a community still subsidizes sprawl, whether it intends to or not. New freeway and other major road construction, carried out for a variety of community purposes, will certainly encourage development along them. When a community builds such a road away from existing urban areas, something that it may do simply because of the lower cost of right-of-way, it is likely to encourage sprawl. A road or interceptor sewer line to a new industrial park outside town will attract development along it. As the conclusion to Chapter 5 urges, the point of understanding that phenomenon is not to stop building public works with public money but simply to do so with a full understanding of the secondary impacts.

A hidden form of subsidy to sprawl often occurs after the fact. Many leapfrog developments are built under county jurisdiction, under regulations designed primarily for small, rural subdivisions. When exurban development moves into such areas, it often creates demands that overwhelm available systems. Schools buses that once served primarily young people living on farms now pick up large numbers of exurbanites, with the costs buried in the school budget. Fire fighters and EMTs make more and longer runs in rural areas, and county sheriffs increasingly find themselves running full-fledged police departments.

Another form of subsidy arises when systems serving exurban development fail. In wet states such a failure is most likely to occur when the effluent from the aggregation of septic tanks in a subdivision contaminates the water from which individuals or even the entire subdivision may draw their water. Such a situation is, of course, a public health crisis of sorts. A nearby city or other service provider often agrees to provide water service, thus supporting after the fact what it had not approved in the first place. Although in many such situations, the service provider requires that the exurbanites pay the costs of the line extensions, the provider rarely recovers a pro-rata share of the costs of the treatment plans and central system that make the service possible. A similar crisis can arise in dry states when the community well serving the subdivision goes bad and the residents petition the nearby local government for water service. The primary difference between the two scenarios is that, in the dry state, the provision of water service may solve the problem for some time. In the wet states, the extension of public water service may mask the symptoms (by eliminating use of the contaminated water in the subdivision), but the real problem—the contamination—remains and must ultimately be solved with a sewer system.

Effect of Growth Management on the Intensity of Development

Can growth management make a community more dense? Although Downs, Audirac and others argue that creating greater density conflicts with consumer desires (see discussion and citations in the last section of this chapter), there is evidence that at least one program has done so.

A major study of the Portland program found, among other things, that:

- The *volume* of multiple family and attached single family development increased dramatically;
- The *proportion* of multiple family and attached single family housing increased dramatically; and
- The *proportion* of smaller and more affordable developed single family lots increased.[35]

The study was a joint project of 1000 Friends of Oregon, widely viewed as an environmental organization, and The Home Builders Association of Metropolitan Portland, a trade group.

The Oregon program, however, consists of more than the simple urban growth boundary. Under the Oregon growth management law, local jurisdictions must develop plans to meet state goals (see program description in Chapter 6). One of the state goals, Goal 10, requires that local governments plan and implement affordable housing programs.[36] Further, because the urban growth boundary was a long-term limit on urban growth, state policy required that local governments accommodate long-term housing needs within that boundary.

One of the other findings of the 1000 Friends/Home Builders study was, "In providing the 'opportunity' for development to occur at targeted densities, most local governments predicated Housing Rule compliance on the assumption that maximum allowable densities (under comprehensive plan designations) could be achieved."[37] In other words, local governments assumed that an area planned for development of multi-family units at "not more than" 12 units per acre would develop at exactly 12 units per acre. That did not happen, for a couple of reasons, according to the study. The first was that some of the land was "underzoned." In other words, some local governments had left the zoning on land in more restrictive categories than the new plan required. That is a surprising finding, because it means that the local governments were ignoring their own new plans in preparing their regulations. The Oregon growth management law clearly requires consistency between local plans and local rules. Even before adoption of that law, the Oregon Supreme Court had upheld the application of a developer to build a project at a density greater than that permitted by the zoning but within the density range suggested by a newly adopted plan.[38] Note that Florida is the one state that has addressed the issue of implementation of mandatory state plans, by requiring review of not only the plans but also the implementing regulations (see Chapter 6).

The second reason that development fell short of that planned in some parts of the Portland region, according to the study, was "underbuilding," in which developers built less intense projects than local plans and zoning would have permitted. For example, 12 percent of single family subdivisions developed during the study period were built on lands zoned for multi-family housing.[39] The study found that the principal causes of "underbuilding" were market demand factors and both natural and human-made site constraints. The primary market demand factor influencing decisions to build at less than planned density was the continued demand for single-family detached homes on relatively large lots.[40] Site constraints ranged from power line easements to wetlands and floodplains.[41] Surprisingly, the study found citizen opposition to the increased density to be a relatively minor factor in underbuilding.[42]

Perhaps the most interesting of eight major recommendations of the 1991 Portland report was that local governments be required to include *minimum* densities in their zoning ordinances.[43] Zoning ordinances have always contained density standards, but those have been *maximum* density standards. As the Portland study discovered, it is not unusual for actual development to fall below the maximum permitted density.

Specific recommendations for implementing the minimum density rule in Oregon include a prohibition of single family homes on land zoned for apartments, rather than the more typical "cumulative" approach, which permits in each residential zone any type of residential development up to and including the primary intensity for that zone.[44] The Portland study also proposed limiting the subdivision of higher density single-family zones into large lots and a requirement that, in multi-family zones, development occur at no less than 75 percent of the maximum permitted intensity.[45] Presumably the authors of the report would also recommend that, in determining the size of a 20-year growth boundary, planners should calculate the development capacity of the area within the urban growth boundary at 75 percent of the permitted density rather than at 100 percent.

A minimum density requirement attacks directly one of the concerns about sprawl: the low intensity use of land. That might seem to limit the range of housing opportunities available. The Portland study found that it has done so (that aspect of the study is discussed in Chapter 10 of this book). However, a University of Wisconsin study found a surprising amount of overlap in the types of dwelling units theoretically buildable at various densities.[46] The authors determined that single-family detached residences could be built at as many as 12 units per acre, while attached dwelling units (townhouses) could be built up to 57 units per acre.[47] Target density ranges for communities in the Portland area range from six to ten units per net buildable acre.[48] Thus, according to the Wisconsin study, it would be possible for the communities to meet their *density* goals with a mix that included few apartment units. Because Goal 10 primarily addresses affordability, Oregon would probably not permit that. However, where the reduction in the consumption of land is the primary concern, it would be possible to implement similar density goals without significantly disturbing the diversity of housing types in the market.

THE OTHER SIDE OF SPRAWL

There is increasing recognition that sprawl is an issue that must be addressed from the center as well as from the edges. Some of the original popular literature attacking the failures of planning today focused on the perceived problems of the suburbs.[49] The Brookings Institution's Bruce Katz frames the issue this way:

On the one hand, many cities and older suburbs are either not growing or are in decline. . . . They are now home to increasing concentrations of poor people and lack the resources to deal with the problems of concentrated poverty: joblessness, family fragmentation, failing schools and decrepit commercial districts. Older suburbs have found that so-called urban problems easily cross urban borders, and these communities are often even less able to cope than cities. Meanwhile, newly developing suburbs find that they are growing too fast. Traffic congestion increases, schools become overcrowded, and the open space that residents prize disappears under an onslaught of new construction.[50]

To try to solve the problem of sprawl on the fringe is like squeezing a balloon—pushing it in one place has the direct result of making it pop out elsewhere. To the extent that some development can be attracted back to the urban core, however, it is like removing some of the air from the balloon—the outward pressure decreases or stops. David Rusk, former mayor of Albuquerque and now of the Brookings Institution, frames it as an *Inside Game/Outside Game*—one that must be played from both sides at once.[51]

Jonathan Barnett argues that one of the keys to revitalization of the urban core is creating an "entrepreneurial center." He notes, "an urban downtown these days is a high-risk entrepreneurial business, and cities are in it whether they like it or not."[52] Some of the leading examples of how to accomplish that come from parts of the Midwest sometimes called "the rust belt." Much-maligned Cleveland boasts of I.M. Pei's Rock and Roll Museum as a key element of its successful downtown revitalization. William Hudnut, III, and Richard Lugar as mayors of Indianapolis displayed the kind of entrepreneurial attitude that Barnett advocates. Two visible results in that city's downtown are the Circle Center Mall, a vibrant public-private partnership, and a plethora of athletic centers, including the new home of the National Collegiate Athletic Association. Hudnut has shared his vision in an upbeat book entitled *Cities on the Rebound.*[53] Hudnut calls for local leadership, civic involvement and regional cooperation. He also notes the need for "community capitalism."[54] Subsequent to the publication of his book, a trio of scholars produced a thoughtful examination of community issues that focused in significant part on the need for "place-based capital."[55]

Success leads to success and, two decades after Hudnut last served as mayor, Indianapolis is seeing a resurgence of interest in in-town housing, ranging from subsidized and moderately priced housing in a "Hope VI" project that will replace a public housing project, to high-end townhouses and condominiums, built and sold entirely in the free market.[56]

The National Trust for Historic Preservation's Richard Moe argues that a critical element to revitalization of older communities is creating a character that identifies a place.[57] He extends his argument beyond the major cities to the many quiescent or dying small towns in the United States. Redeveloping around in and around such places is a core element of the "Smart Growth" program in Maryland, discussed in Chapter 6.

In this context, former government and foundation leader Paul Grogan finds that, "The American inner city is rebounding—not just here and there, not just cosmetically, but fundamentally. It is the result of a fragile but palpable change in both the economics and the politics of poor urban neighborhoods."[58] A remarkable case study set out in Grogan's book is that of the troubled South Bronx in New York City.

Every young couple, retiree or even family that is attracted to live in a revitalized downtown is a household that will not seek housing on the fringe. Although the topic of urban revitalization it largely beyond the scope of this book, it is critical that the reader understand that those who would manage growth in the suburbs have a substantial stake in the success of the core.

IS SPRAWL ALL BAD?

There remains the question of whether the influences of growth management on urban form are beneficial. Advocates of compact, contiguous patterns of development argue that higher densities combined with contiguity result in lower housing costs for consumers and lower service costs for the public. The arguments and their critiques are contained in Chapters 9 and 10. However, it is important to consider here another aspect of the issue. Is a compact, contiguous development pattern generally beneficial?

Some persuasive voices argue that it is not, for somewhat different reasons. Richard Peiser, a California researcher, raised one of the most interesting arguments in favor of leapfrog development, although he criticized low-density urban development as ". . . inefficient. It increases transportation costs, consumes excessive amounts of land, and adds to the cost of providing and operating public utilities and public services."[59] Nevertheless, in the same article, Peiser builds a theoretical and empirical argument *favoring* leapfrog, or discontinuous, development. His argument is that, over the long-run, discontinuous development will encourage greater densities. He hypothesized that land prices on the omitted parcels (the land over which the early development leaps) will increase faster than those at the urban fringe. That is a perfectly logical argument, because that land, being surrounded by development (the original community and the "leaped" area), would presumably have most or all urban services. The very fact that it would be surrounded by development would increase its market value. Peiser next argued that the higher land prices would force developers to build higher densities on the omitted parcels, resulting in higher infill densities on the omitted parcels than would have occurred with continuous patterns of development. In other words, in order to recover the higher land costs, developers would find ways to increase the intensities of use on those parcels omitted by the leap of early development.

Peiser tested the hypothesis with data from Fairfax County, Virginia; Dallas, Texas; and Montgomery County, Maryland. Montgomery County's regulations thwarted his hypothesis by prohibiting higher densities on the omitted parcels. However, he found that the data from Fairfax County, which had permitted increased densities on infill parcels, generally supported his theory. The data from Dallas was mixed. Despite the limited relevant data, he concludes, "The regressions indicate that, for cities which allow higher densities on infill parcels, discontinuous development may lead to higher densities than are likely to occur where discontinuous development is prevented."[60]

Peiser ignores an important variable in this process—the political process. In a careful study of Sacramento County, a University of California–Davis team found that implementation of an urban services boundary was easier than encouragement of infill development.[61] Citizens involved in the plan implementation process forced the reduction of infill densities below those projected by planners in Sacramento County. Peiser's model would permit the ultimate infill site to be surrounded by neighbors, who, as developers know, frequently become opponents of intense development. Thus, although Peiser's economics appear to be sound, it is essential to account for the political aspect of the process.

Interestingly, in a separate article, Peiser acknowledges exactly such concerns, although in a different context.[62] He acknowledges the logical corollary of his argument regarding land prices and densities: if urban growth boundaries increase land prices, then they should lead to increased densities. He would presumably support minimum density requirements, such as those included in the urban growth boundary program in Portland. He argues in favor of exactions and adequate public facilities requirements. "New residents should bear their fair share of costs associated with urban growth."[63] He continues, in the same article:

While sprawl may be unjustly maligned for generating low density development, the potential benefits of discontinuous growth nevertheless depend on the full-cost pricing of development. If discontinuous development is subsidized by utility companies, highway programs, or municipal contributions, sprawl patterns of development may be spread over so large an area that inefficiencies associated with sprawl would outweigh any potential benefits from higher density infill development.[64]

Some studies have argued that the best way to reduce sprawl is to encourage the development of higher density, mixed-use projects, often called "planned unit developments"[65] or simply "planned developments." In a separate and earlier article, Peiser argued that there are institutional reasons why there is not more construction of planned (unit) developments in the United States. His analysis tacitly recognized that construction of "planned development" typically requires one developer willing to undertake an entire, large-scale project. He cited the risks inherent in large projects with long build-out times, including the risk of market changes, the difficulty in obtaining financing, and regulatory barriers in the community. Finally, he noted the significant risk that with a long-term building project, new residents who move in may begin to exercise political power to oppose completion of the project as planned.[66] In short, although Peiser acknowledged some advantages to planned development rather than sprawl, he has not been optimistic about achieving such patterns on a large scale.

Ohls and Pines, whose earlier work was cited by Peiser, made two arguments consistent with those of Peiser, although one of them is quite different in nature.[67] Ohls and Pines argued that commercial development is typically not financially feasible at the urban fringe when residential development first takes place there. Thus, omitted tracts (land over which earlier development leaps) provide opportunities for later construction of convenient and accessible commercial development, leading to a more efficient development pattern than if commercial development is forced further out on the expanding urban fringe. That argument is entirely consistent with Peiser's hypothesis of higher values and the need for more valuable uses on omitted land, because commercial development is typically a higher value and more profitable use than residential development. However, that portion of the Ohls and Pines argument is also subject to the same limitation that Peiser acknowledged for his own work. If the sprawl is so great that it skips over large land areas, those areas may never develop efficiently. Ohls and Pines' argument for essentially using sprawl to "reserve" tracts for convenient commercial development is more persuasive as to individual tracts of land than it is toward large tracts of land around a community.

Ohls and Pines' other argument is that "if people prefer lower densities (or if lower costs are associated with lower densities) it may make sense initially to

build lower-density housing relatively further from the city center to accommodate this desire for low density as much as possible, while at the same time reserving the central land for its ultimate high-density development."[68] Their
model is "based on a trade-off between living space and accessibility."[69] It uses a
combination of transportation costs and housing costs to determine the housing
options available to a family. It thus shared a philosophical base with Alonso's
early work and Wingo's integrative model of transportation and land use (see
discussion in Chapter 5), although they do not cite either of those works.

One difficulty in assessing the efficiency or desirability of a particular growth
pattern is the increased complexity of the urban fabric. As two researchers have
separately noted, an increasing number (and proportion) of employment opportunities are in the suburbs.[70] Planners in Montgomery County and elsewhere seek a
"jobs-housing balance" within local planning areas to reduce commuting.[71]
However, Cervero found in a study of San Francisco and Chicago suburbs that,
even where such a balance exists, commuting distances and times are greater
than ever.[72] Adding even more complexity to the model is the fact that the service
patterns of commercial centers have changed and no longer follow traditional,
somewhat hierarchical models used by planners.[73]

One area that has been successful in attracting more jobs to the central city is
the Boulder Valley in Colorado. Ironically, policies of the City of Boulder limit
population growth within the city. The growth of jobs thus in the 1990s out-
stripped the growth of population in the city, with a population increase in the city
averaging 1.2 percent per year from 1990 to 2000 and job growth in the city averaging 2.4 percent over a 30-year period.[74] This trend, at least statistically, will
increase the need for commuting in a city that remains heavily dependent on automobiles. The 2001 plan for the valley projects the city reaching "build-out" at
121,000 people, while the number of jobs within the city continues to increase.[75]

Despite these largely theoretical arguments, data presented in Chapter 9 suggests that the fiscal impacts of sprawl on a community may be significant, at least
over the short-run. That finding is not inconsistent with Peiser's argument, given
above. His argument is that, over the long-run, infill development will make
leapfrog development become efficient. Over the short-run, his argument would
acknowledge the inefficiency.

Land as a Scarce Resource

The economic discussion above disregards a key point, which is that land is a
finite resource. The recognition of land as a scarce resource clearly led to the
adoption of the original system of statewide zoning in Hawaii and the similar
system of establishing urban growth boundaries in Oregon.

Increasing population threatens the land resource. Although the rate of population increase in the United States has slowed, the rate of growth in new households
continues to be significant. The combination of these factors, plus some need for
replacement housing stock, drives the residential portion of the development economy. An economist who is a purist will argue that the market will efficiently

account for the value of land as the demand for it increases (or shrinks or stays stable). Society, however, may make a different determination. The current market may suggest that the value of non-urban land is not very great, but state or local officials may decide, as they have in Oregon and Hawaii, that the public sector has a stake in protecting that finite resource until society needs it. As long as it remains relatively cheap (and non-urban land is usually relatively cheap when compared to urban land), the market system will not provide that long-term protection.

Note that this issue is different from the issue of protecting particular lands, an issue addressed in the next chapter. The point of this brief discussion is that society may decide to encourage relatively compact development simply to minimize the consumption of land and to reserve as much undeveloped land as possible for long-term use, regardless of the operation of the current market.

CONCLUSION

Many growth management programs affect urban form. Adequate public facilities requirements tend to encourage contiguous, rather than leapfrog, development, except where the community has extended adequate public facilities to some non-contiguous location such as a public airport. Growth phasing systems that emphasize the location of growth also tend to promote contiguous development. A tightly drawn urban growth boundary creates a clear urban edge and increases the density of development within the boundary, but it is also likely to force some leapfrog development into other communities. A widely drawn urban growth boundary should create a clear urban edge in the long run and may increase densities somewhat in the short run.

Despite the disdain in which "sprawl" is held by most planners and many citizens, it is not clear that efforts to control it through growth management will yield more benefits than costs. Urban growth boundaries in particular may stop one form of sprawl (low-density, contiguous development) while causing another (leapfrog development) that is arguably worse. As the discussion in Chapter 10 indicates, such programs also create significant shifts in the housing supply. The costs and benefits of those shifts must be carefully considered in analyzing the desirability of adopting such a program for a particular community.

Some economists argue that sprawl is actually efficient over the long run. As the discussion in Chapter 9 suggests, one problem with that argument is that the long run may not come, or it may come much farther in the future than anyone expects. That is, a community may permit leapfrog development in one year, anticipating that the omitted parcels will develop over the next decade or so. However, if growth suddenly slows, the omitted parcels may not develop for 20, 40, 50 or more years. In that case, the short run, during which the leapfrog development pattern is clearly in many ways inefficient, become much longer than most planners (or economists) would anticipate.

Nevertheless, the fact remains that sprawl is not a desirable form of development. Or is it?

AFTERWORD: SPRAWL AND THE INTERESTED CITIZEN

Downs analyzes the relationship of housing consumers and sprawl with a twist on the old adage that "in a democracy, people get the government that they deserve." He argues that, "In reality the major causes of increased suburban traffic lie in the behavior patterns of the same households who are now complaining about it."[76] He cites as those causes three specific sets of desires and resulting behavior patterns:

• Living at low densities;
• Having access to a wide choice of places both to work and to live; and
• Commuting by private automobile.[77]

This argument is, of course, entirely consistent with the conclusions of Fuguitt and Zuiches, who found that people want to live in a small community with access to a big city.[78] It is also consistent with Dubbink's detailed study of two growth management communities in California, San Juan Capistrano and Bolinas.[79] He found that what the communities sought through growth management was the maintenance of a "rural illusion," or the creation of a "disguised" or "anti-suburban suburb."[80] He noted that both communities had been rural market centers that had suffered, but also enjoyed, years of economic doldrums. During the times of limited economic activity, the communities by default retained older houses, small town character and expanses of agricultural land around them. He found that the growth management movement in each community was an effort, led by recent arrivals, to retain and/or recapture that small town character.

Similarly, in an assessment of residential preferences among Florida residents, Audirac and two colleagues, found that "while there is a small clientele for compact downtown environments in large metropolitan cities, there is a stronger preference for single family homes and rural and semi-rural residence, as well as a willingness to make longer commutes in order to live in such places."[81] Although they did not provide demographic detail sufficient to determine whether one should believe that this preference represents the general population or just the middle class, it is entirely consistent with the findings of several other studies cited here. There is little reason to believe that the dream homes of the urban poor are significantly different from those of the middle class, even if their chance of achieving their dreams is smaller.

Yet it is noteworthy that many of those interviewed by Dubbink in his study of the two California communities were commuters, clearly dependent on the larger metropolitan area. That fact confirms Downs' hypothesis and Fuguitt and Zuiches' earlier findings.[82] In his conclusion, Dubbink noted that Bolinas, located in Marin County with some of San Francisco's richest suburbs, and San Juan, located north of San Diego along a booming strip of seaside communities, are "private islands, awash in nostalgia for something they can never be."[83]

One of the attractions of exurban homesites is often the apparent cost advantage. It is usually cheaper to buy a tract of vacant land in the country than to buy a finished lot in town. That evaluation is a short-term and superficial one, however, because it ignores the many hidden costs—the cash costs of installing a well and septic tank, as well as the lifestyle costs of reduced services. After accounting for everything, including a lower initial housing price, a study at Rutgers University published in 2003 found that occupancy costs were 8 percent higher in such locations than in communities with managed growth.[84]

Suburban residents have a love–hate relationship with sprawl. Most do not like the idea of sprawl, nor do they like the increased traffic or higher taxes that they perceive as side effects of sprawl. On the other hand, those same suburban residents want to live in single-family detached homes with large yards in a quiet, "semi-rural" community from which they can easily commute by private automobile to a nearby metropolitan center that offers a greater variety of shopping, services and employment opportunities than residents may find in their "anti-suburb suburbs". That pattern of development essentially defines "sprawl". The scenario reminds the author of Walt Kelly's "Pogo" comic strip character, who would occasionally remark, "We have met the enemy and he is us."

NOTES

1. James Duncan and Associates Inc. et al., "The Search for Efficient Urban Growth Patterns: A Study of the Fiscal Impacts of Development in Florida"; Real Estate Research Corp., "The Costs of Sprawl: Environmental and Economic Costs of Alternative Residential Development Patterns at the Urban Fringe."
2. Dowall, *The Suburban Squeeze: Land Conversion and Regulation in the San Francisco Bay Area*, 14–33.
3. Greenberg, "Growth and Conflict at the Surburban Fringe: The Case of the Livermore-Amador Valley."
4. William Hollingsworth Whyte, "Urban Sprawl," in *The Exploding Metropolis*, the Editors of Fortune Magazine (New York: Doubleday & Co., 1958), 116–17.
5. Clawson, *Suburban Land Conversion in the United States: An Economic and Governmental Process.* Quoting from p. 320, but see generally Chapters 8 and 9.
6. Published in Canty, Urban America (Organization), and National Committee on Urban Growth Policy, *The New City*, 18.
7. Council on Development Choices for the 80s, "Interim Report," (Washington, D.C.: U.S. Department of Housing and Urban Development, 1980), 10–13.
8. Ibid.
9. Chinitz, "Growth Management: Good for the Town, Bard for the Nation?" Emphasis in the original.
10. Ebenezer Howard and Frederic James Osborn, *Garden Cities of Tomorrow* (Cambridge, Mass.: M.I.T. Press, 1965). Originally published in 1898 under the title *Tomorrow: A Peaceful Path to Real Reform.*
11. Hugh Mields, Jr., "Federally Assisted New Communities: New Dimensions in Urban Development," in *ULI Landmark* (Washington, D.C.: Urban Land Institute, 1973); K.C. Parsons, "Clarence Stein and the Greenbelt Towns: Settling for Less," *Journal of the American Planning Association* 56 (1990).
12. Mields, "Federally Assisted New Communities: New Dimensions in Urban Development."

13. *Housing and Urban Development Act of 1970*, Sect.710(a).
14. Published in Canty, Urban America (Organization), and National Committee on Urban Growth Policy, *The New City*.
15. Ibid., 169.
16. Mields, "Federally Assisted New Communities: New Dimensions in Urban Development."
17. So and Getzels, eds., *The Practice of Local Government Planning*.
18. Jonathan Barnett, "Urban Design," in *The Practice of Local Government Planning*, eds. Frank So and Judith Getzels (Washington D.C.: International City Management Association, 1988).
19. Ibid., 178–85.
20. Fred Bair and Virginia Curtis, eds., *Planning Cities* (Chicago: Planners Press, 1979), 161–88.
21. James Duncan and Associates Inc. et al., "The Search for Efficient Urban Growth Patterns: A Study of the Fiscal Impacts of Development in Florida"; Real Estate Research Corp., "The Costs of Sprawl: Environmental and Economic Costs of Alternative Residential Development Patterns at the Urban Fringe."
22. Whyte, "Urban Sprawl."
23. Brower, *Urban Growth Management through Development Timing*, 109, Table 5.
24. Ivonne Audirac, Anne H. Shermyen, and Marc T. Smith, "Ideal Urban Form and Visions of the Good Life: Florida's Growth Management Dilemma," *Journal of the American Planning Association* 56 (1990): 477.
25. United States Bureau of the Census, "1990 Census of Population and Housing: Summary of Population and Housing Characteristics."
26. Fischel, *Do Growth Controls Matter? A Review of Empirical Evidence on the Effectiveness and Efficiency of Local Government Land Use Regulation*.
27. Ketcham and Siegel, "Managing Growth to Promote Affordable Housing: Revisiting Oregon's Goal 10," 8.
28. In the matter of the periodic review of the urban growth boundary for metro, partial approval and remand order, 03-WKTASK-001524, Land Conservation and Commission (2003), available at http://www.lcd.state.or.us/pdfs/MetroFinalOrder.pdf
29. Bair and Curtis, *Planning Cities*, 108–19.
30. Knaap, "The Price Effects of Urban Growth Boundaries in Metropolitan Portland, Oregon."
31. Fischel, *Do Growth Controls Matter? A Review of Empirical Evidence on the Effectiveness and Efficiency of Local Government Land Use Regulation*.
32. Mark E. Hanson, "Automobile Subsidies and Land Use: Estimates and Policy Responses," *Journal of the American Planning Association* 58 (1991).
33. Frank and Rhodes, eds., *Development Exactions*; Robinson, ed., *Financing Growth: Who Benefits? Who Pays? And How Much*; John W. Witt and Janis Sammartino, "Facility Financing in the 1990s: The Second Step in Urban Growth Management," *Washington University Journal of Urban and Contemporary Law* 38 (1990). See also discussion in Chapter 3.
34. Jeffrey A. Parker, "Does Transportation Finance Influence Urban Form" (paper presented at the Transportation, urban form and the environment, Washington, D.C., 1991).
35. Ketcham and Siegel, "Managing Growth to Promote Affordable Housing: Revisiting Oregon's Goal 10," 6–8.

36. See discussion in Nohad A. Toulan, "Housing as a State Planning Goal," in *Planning the Oregon Way: A Twenty-Year Evaluation*, eds. Carl Abbott, Deborah A. Howe, and Sy Adler (Corvallis, Oreg.: Oregon State University Press, 1994).
37. Ketcham and Siegel, "Managing Growth to Promote Affordable Housing: Revisiting Oregon's Goal 10," 48–49 and Appendix E.
38. *Baker v. City of Milwaukie*, 533 P.2d 772 (1975).
39. Ketcham and Siegel, "Managing Growth to Promote Affordable Housing: Revisiting Oregon's Goal 10," 9.
40. Ibid., 52–53.
41. Ibid., 57–58.
42. Ibid., 59–60.
43. Ibid., 69.
44. For a discussion of cumulative zoning, see Kelly, "Zoning," 269.
45. Ketcham and Siegel, "Managing Growth to Promote Affordable Housing: Revisiting Oregon's Goal 10," 69.
46. Ernest R. Alexander, K. David Reed, and Peter Murphy, "Density Measures and Their Relation to Urban Form," (Madison, Wis.: Center for Architecture and Urban Planning Research, University of Wisconsin, 1988).
47. Ibid., 34–40.
48. Ore. Admin. Rules, Sec. 660-07-035.
49. Joel Garreau, *Edge City: Life on the New Frontier*, 1st ed. (New York: Doubleday, 1991); Richard Harris and Center for American Places, *Unplanned Suburbs: Toronto's American Tragedy, 1900 to 1950, Creating the North American Landscape* (Baltimore, Md.: Johns Hopkins University Press, 1996); James Howard Kunstler, *The Geography of Nowhere: The Rise and Decline of America's Man-Made Landscape* (New York: Simon & Schuster, 1993).
50. Katz, *Reflections on Regionalism, ed.*, Bruce Katz, [Foreword by Al Gore], 3.
51. David Rusk, *Inside Game/Outside Game: Winning Strategies for Saving Urban America* (Washington, D.C.: Brookings Institution, 1999).
52. Barnett, *The Fractured Metropolis: Improving the New City, Restoring the Old City, Reshaping the Region*, 119. See also E. Terrence Jones, *The Metropolitan Chase: Politics and Policies in Urban American* (Upper Saddle River, N.J.: Prentice-Hall, 2003), 34–36.
53. William H. Hudnut and Urban Land Institute, *Cities on the Rebound: A Vision for Urban America* (Washington, D.C.: ULI—The Urban Land Institute, 1998).
54. Ibid., 27.
55. Thad Williamson, David Imbroscio, and Gar Alperovitz, *Making a Place for Community: Local Democracy in a Global Era* (New York and London: Routledge, 2002).
56. Chris Palladino, "If Redevelopment Can Occur on the Northside of Indianapolis, It Can Occur Anywhere," *Planning* 2003.
57. Richard Moe and Carter Wilkie, *Changing Places: Rebuilding Community in the Age of Sprawl*, 1st ed. (New York: Henry Holt & Co., 1997).
58. Paul S. Grogan and Tony Proscio, *Comeback Cities: A Blueprint for Urban Neighborhood Revival* (Boulder, Colo.: Westview Press, 2000).
59. Peiser, "Density and Urban Sprawl," 193.
60. Ibid., 201.
61. Robert A. Johnston, Seymour I. Schwartz, and Steve Tracy, "Growth Phasing and Resistance to Infill Development in Sacramento County," *Journal of the American Planning Association* 50 (1984).

62. Richard B Peiser, "Does It Pay to Plan Suburban Growth," *Journal of the American Planning Association* 50 (1984).

63. Peiser, "Density and Urban Sprawl," 202.

64. Ibid., 203.

65. Council on Development Choices for the 80s, "Interim Report"; Sachs Rahenkamp, Wells & Associates and American Society of Planning Officials, "Innovative Zoning: A Digest of the Literature," (Washington, D.C.: U.S. Department of Housing and Urban Development, 1977); Real Estate Research Corp., "The Costs of Sprawl: Environmental and Economic Costs of Alternative Residential Development Patterns at the Urban Fringe."

66. Peiser, "Does It Pay to Plan Suburban Growth," see especially p. 430.

67. James C. Ohls and David Pines, "Discontinuous Urban Development and Economic Efficiency," *Land Economics* 51 (1975).

68. Ibid., 228.

69. Ibid., 225.

70. Cervero, "Jobs-Housing Balance and Regional Mobility"; Gary Pivo, "The Net of Mixed Beads: Suburban Office Development in Six Metropolitan Regions," *Journal of the American Planning Association* 56 (1990).

71. Montgomery County Planning Board, "Annual Growth Policy for Montgomery County, 2003." The policy is not new, as shown by its inclusion in Montgomery County Planning Board, "Fy 1991."

72. Cervero, "Jobs-Housing Balance and Regional Mobility."

73. Deborah A. Howe and William A. Rabiega, "Beyond Strips and Centers: The Ideal Commercial Form," *Journal of the American Planning Association* 58 (1992).

74. Boulder and Department, "Boulder Valley Comprehensive Plan," 117–18.

75. Ibid.

76. Anthony Downs, "The Real Problem with Suburban Anti-Growth Policies," *The Brookings Review* (1988): 24.

77. Ibid.

78. Fuguitt and Zuiches, "Residential Preferences and Population Distribution."

79. David Dubbink, "I'll Have My Town Medium Rural, Please," *Journal of the American Planning Association* 50 (1984).

80. Dubbink, "Cosmopolitan Villages: Growth Management Planning and the Vision of Small Town Society," 135–39.

81. Audirac, Shermyen, and Smith, "Ideal Urban Form and Visions of the Good Life: Florida's Growth Management Dilemma," 477.

82. Anthony Downs, *New Visions for Metropolitan America* (Washington, D.C., and Cambridge, Mass.: Brookings Institution; Lincoln Institute of Land Policy, 1994); Fuguitt and Zuiches, "Residential Preferences and Population Distribution."

83. Dubbink, "Cosmopolitan Villages: Growth Management Planning and the Vision of Small Town Society," 199.

84. Robert W. Burchell and Sanan Mukherji, "Conventional Development Versus the Costs of Sprawl," *American Journal of Public Health* 93, no. 9 (2003).

CHAPTER 8

Growth Management and the Natural Environment

This chapter examines the effect of growth management programs on environmentally sensitive lands. Floodplains, wetlands, steep slopes, prime agricultural lands and forests are some of the kinds of lands that environmentalists, planners and many interested citizens today seek to preserve.[1] Such lands are sensitive in the sense of being particularly vulnerable to harm from development, or their development represents a vulnerability to the development or to the community at large. For example, development of a floodplain may not particularly hurt that piece of soil, but it may increase flooding in the community as a whole and it will subject the buildings on the land and the people in them to an increased risk of damage from flooding.

The issue of protecting such lands is partly, but not wholly, a question of urban form. Concerns with sprawl lead logically to concerns about the efficient use of land and the preservation of the maximum practicable amount of land for non-urban uses. Protecting particular lands is a related but quite different subject.

Environmental issues rank behind issues related to public facilities and more general concern about "sprawl" and community character in the reasons for adopting growth management programs, but protecting such lands is certainly a factor in the adoption of some growth management programs.[2] A 1975 study of early growth management programs found, in part, "Concern for environmental damage was a motivating factor in most of the thirteen case studies and second only to concern for provision of public services."[3]

All the designated areas of state concern in Florida are environmentally sensitive lands (see Chapter 6). Vermont based its original development-control program on the objective of preserving agricultural lands (see Chapter 6). The joint state–federal effort to preserve the Pinelands in New Jersey was based completely on ecological concerns.[4] New York State also based its program to protect the Adirondack Park area on environmental concerns.[5] Thus, although environmental issues are not at the forefront of some of the most famous growth management programs, protection of the natural environment is a growth management concern in a few large and significant areas. Further, a growth management program that sets priorities for growth patterns without regard to sensitive lands would verge on being irresponsible, because it would ignore a valuable and often irreplaceable resource of the community. Thus, the protection of sensitive lands is, or should be, a concern in all communities that are serious about managing growth.

THE CHARACTER OF SENSITIVE LANDS

Like the porcupine, sensitive lands contain some built-in protection. Development on such lands is often difficult and expensive. The only type of sensitive land on which development is easy is agricultural land. The flat, well-drained character of good farmland lends itself easily to development in patterns required by engineering-driven subdivision regulations and makes solving drainage problems easy. Prime agricultural soils are typically stable for building.[6]

Any type of development on steep slopes, wetlands or other sensitive lands typically involves extra engineering, earth-moving and other costs. Developers often skip over parcels of sensitive lands in sprawling metropolitan areas, just because of the cost of developing those parcels. In the 1000 Friends/Home Builders study of the effects of growth management on housing costs, cited in the previous chapter, the authors found that among the principal reasons for "underbuilding" (building less than planned densities) were "site constraints," such as floodplains, creeks and wetlands,[7] and "site amenities" such as "hilltop views" and "wooded surroundings."[8] In one sense, the example demonstrated bad planning, because the original Portland plans should have excluded such lands from density calculations. The combination of state pressure to increase density (see discussion in Chapter 7) and the lack of apparent protection for such lands could be devastating to sensitive lands within the urban growth boundary. It is somewhat remarkable that market forces were sufficient to protect some of them in the face of the public pressure to increase densities.

Although both the consumer interest in living on hilltops and in woods and the costs of developing such sites offer some protection to sensitive lands, that protection is not perfect. In the context of today's wide interest in protecting wetlands,[9] it is noteworthy that vast areas of Chicago, Boston, Miami, San Francisco and other cities sit on fill in what were once wetlands or even parts of bodies of water. Filling those areas was clearly expensive. The fact that it occurred reflected not only a lack of understanding of, or a lack of concern with, the environmental consequences. Those early earth-moving activities also demonstrated a significant perceived need for the land for urbanization.

SENSITIVE LANDS AND THE URBAN REGION

There are serious and unavoidable conflicts in any attempt to preserve sensitive lands from urbanization. Those conflicts are more complex than the straightforward ones between local governments and landowners or developers. Many sensitive lands stand squarely in the path of development and some can be developed easily.

Programs that attempt to preserve prime agricultural land face immediate conflicts because of the location of most cities near rivers. Early settlers in this country, as in others, located towns near rivers because they provided a source of water to support the population and a means of transportation. As settlement moved west, it remained along rivers, even where those rivers were too small to offer a form of transportation. Construction of the railroads and, later, highways, typically served established population centers, which were generally located along rivers, and thus reinforced the importance of those centers. For a graphic illustration of the effects of those patterns, note the inverted "L" around which virtually all the population centers in New York State form. That L-shape follows the Hudson River north from New York City to Albany and then the route of the Erie Canal west to Buffalo. It later became the route of the railroad and then of the New York State Thruway.

What is the character of the river bottoms around which so many cities focus? It is generally very rich soil deposited by the river. In dry climates where irrigation is necessary for successful agriculture, water is readily available in the river bottom. The land is typically flat and well-drained. Those are predominant characteristics of prime agricultural land. River bottoms typically provide such lands. Many communities of significant size sit in or surround such river bottoms. Thus, any random development pattern of the city will consume at least some good agricultural land.

Planners often characterize these river bottoms around which so many cities form in another way. They refer to them as "floodplains." The founders of these cities sought locations where water would be readily accessible. Sometimes it is entirely too accessible. Attempts to limit sprawl and encourage infill development puts increased development pressure on undeveloped lands within the urban area, including floodplains. Thus, a growth boundary may increase development pressure on floodplains and other sensitive lands within the urban area.

Many floodplains contain growth magnets, making the problem worse. Public works engineers typically design sewer systems to use gravity flow (see discussion in Chapter 5). That design leads to the installation of interceptor sewer lines in floodplains, because the river represents the lowest point in the community. The installation of such a growth magnet in the floodplain reinforces the development pressures on the floodplains. Further, in areas in which floodplains remained relatively undeveloped or developed only in marginal economic activities in the 1960s and 1970s, land prices in the floodplains were often relatively low. The low land costs and the continuity of the riverbed made the floodplains attractive routes for those seeking land for new interstate highways, which are themselves significant growth magnets. If built in the floodplain, they are likely to attract development to the floodplain.

Metropolitan areas often include wetlands, steep slopes and other sensitive lands within them. Often those lands remained undeveloped during early community building because of the higher cost of developing such lands. Efforts to reduce sprawl or to promote development near existing public facilities may encourage the development of omitted parcels that happen to include wetlands or steep slopes. Thus, growth management programs do not necessarily protect sensitive lands, regardless of the intentions of their creators. They may have quite the opposite effect, encouraging the development of sensitive lands that market forces have essentially protected.

METHODS OF PROTECTING SENSITIVE LANDS

The best way to protect sensitive lands, such as floodplains, steep slopes, wetlands and prime agricultural lands, is to preclude development on them. McHarg argued cogently and influentially that in many cases it is possible to *Design with Nature*, or, typically, to design around sensitive lands.[10] He suggested, and used, natural resource analysis as the basis for developing plans for particular developments and for entire communities. Others have made similar recommendations, in large part based on McHarg's work.[11] For legal and political reasons, it is often difficult to prohibit all development on private property. In such cases, it is desirable to minimize the amount of development on sensitive lands such as hillsides.[12] Another approach suggests that development regulations require that a proposed project be designed in such a way as to mitigate the environmental problem. Such mitigation techniques can range from special foundation designs in difficult soils to rock-diversion barriers in landslide-prone areas.[13] Lane Kendig and Susan Connor, based in part on experience in Lake County, Illinois, proposed a system of zoning based essentially on McHarg's techniques.[14]

In an article assessing Florida's attempts to control urban form by limiting sprawl, Audirac and her colleagues argues that sensitive lands should be protected directly by local and state laws, rather than indirectly through limits on urban development. "Regulating development to be more dense and compact delays confronting the real environmental impact of rapid population growth and unplanned conversion of land to urban use. . . . Ian McHarg's organic conception of urban development designed for the carrying capacity of the land[15] seems a more appropriate vision for the future good life in Florida than abstract notions of ideal urban form."[16]

Similarly, in a relatively early work on growth management, Finkler and Peterson argued that local planning should be based on carrying capacity analyses that include the capacity of public facilities, the natural environment and less tangible human systems.[17] They noted that a carrying capacity approach would best be implemented at a regional level, coincident with regional air and water basins.[18]

Although they did not cite McHarg, their carrying capacity concept alluded clearly to the ideas that McHarg had set forth in his book five years earlier.

One community that used the carrying capacity approach in its comprehensive plan was Hilton Head Island, South Carolina.[19] That island community that in one sense constitutes a region by itself, because its environment is quite separate from the nearby mainland. On the basis of a carrying capacity analysis, the plan allocated development to various parts of the island based on a combination of environmental and infrastructure capacities.[20] Initial work on the plan was developed by John Rahenkamp, who, like McHarg, is a Philadelphia-based landscape architect and whose firm, like McHarg's, had ties to the University of Pennsylvania.

In proposing the use of a carrying capacity approach to environmental protection, Peterson and Finkler included the concept in a list of alternative approaches to growth management.[21] The list also included growth phasing systems, development moratoriums (*sic*) and other techniques. Thus, they recognized that the protection of sensitive lands was, in a sense, a separate issue from controlling the timing and location of growth, although the two issues are certainly related.

THE EFFECTS OF GROWTH MANAGEMENT

{TX}Growth management programs may make the problem of sensitive lands better or worse, or they make no difference whatsoever. The same 1975 study that found environmental concerns second only to those about public facilities in communities adopting growth management programs noted, "None of the case studies evaluated the environmental impact of the proposed systems, nor were such studies done in any other location."[22] The report later continued, "Environmental studies used as a basis for the design of growth management systems are weak or nonexistent. . . ."[23]

Little has changed from that early assessment. In 1989, Porter noted, "Environmental concerns sparked much of the early development of growth management systems, but the environmental effects of growth are still not well understood."[24]

The nature and location of the sensitive lands and the type of growth management program determines the effect. For sensitive lands within the primary development area or inside an urban growth boundary, a growth management program is unlikely to protect sensitive lands and may increase development pressure on them. If one effect of a growth management program is, directly or indirectly, to discourage sprawl, the pressure to develop vacant, infill parcels will increase. If land becomes scarce through such a program, the extra costs of developing a hillside or a wetland may become comparatively insignificant in the market. Thus, an urban growth boundary program or an adequate public facilities program in an area in which outlying facilities are limited is likely to increase the development pressure on sensitive lands within the primary development area.

A rate-of-growth program that uses qualitative criteria to rate developments (for reasons explained in Chapter 3, both Boulder and Petaluma have abandoned such criteria) could certainly provide a lower priority to projects that propose the development of sensitive lands. Otherwise, a rate-of-growth program is unlikely to have any particular effect on sensitive lands. A phased growth program could protect sensitive lands if it phased most growth in other directions. However, as Chapter 4 indicates, most communities with phased growth programs base them on the availability of public facilities. The likelihood that the geographical pattern of development most likely to preserve sensitive lands and the one most likely to optimize use of existing facilities will coincide is small. Thus, such programs also are not likely to have a significant impact on sensitive lands.

The best protection for sensitive lands within the primary urban development area, other than outright purchase, is through local land use controls such as performance standards.[25] Design regulations requiring that such areas be preserved in the development process can work well where the sensitive land amounts to a small part of a large parcel.[26] With such a site, it is possible to "cluster" development on developable land, thus preserving the sensitive land at little or no net economic cost to the developer.[27] Communities can implement such controls through zoning and subdivision regulations. Those effective tools are quite separate from a growth management strategy.

Growth management techniques can limit the development pressure on sensitive lands outside the primary development area. Considering the development suitability of lands within the metropolitan area in deciding how to phase growth or where to draw the urban grown boundary can make an enormous difference in the development pressure on sensitive lands.

Non-structural techniques are also important. Where it is possible to omit environmentally sensitive lands from annexation plans, a community should do so. A community should certainly avoid sensitive lands to the maximum extent practicable in deciding where to locate new roadways, interceptor sewer lines, and other growth-inducing public investments. If there is a large and sensitive area outside a community, such as the steep mountain backdrop west of Boulder, urban growth boundaries and a long-range refusal to annex territory or to provide public services can provide significant protection. It is also important to remember that Boulder has not relied solely on refusing to annex and serve such lands. In addition, it has bought many acres of them (see discussion in last section of Chapter 5).

Insofar as sensitive lands fall within the logical area of urban growth, as they often do, growth management techniques simply increase the development pressure on them. Protecting those lands adequately over time requires a combination of strategic public acquisition, performance and other development standards and incentives to "cluster" development on less sensitive land under common ownership.[28] Montgomery County[29] and a few other communities have used transferable development rights as a method to encourage the preservation of sensitive lands. However, there are major legal and practical difficulties with implementing such a program, and a discussion of it is far beyond the scope of this work.

It is difficult to overemphasize the value of purchasing sensitive lands when possible. Boulder's greenbelt will be green long after sensitive lands in other communities that simply planned or designated those lands for preservation have turned into shopping centers.

CONCLUSION

The growth management proposal rejected by the 1991 Maryland legislature included a program of "visioned growth." Visioned growth was a plan for more compact and contiguous development that would:

I. concentrate development in suitable areas;

II. protect sensitive areas;

III. establish rural centers;

IV. preserve the Chesapeake Bay;

V. conserve natural and economic resources; and

VI. do this in a way that allows appropriate financial resources to be directed to appropriate acts and actors.[30]

The Maryland proposal represented an interesting and responsible combination of growth management and environmental protection. It is unfortunate that the Maryland legislature again lost the opportunity to be a national leader.

The careful reader will note the lack of absolutes in the analysis in this chapter—"The community should consider. . ." and ". . . avoid . . . to the maximum extent practicable." Although there are some who take an absolutist view on the protection of certain sensitive lands, public officials implementing a growth management program must consider many other factors in deciding where and how to direct growth. If a community must choose between permitting development on prime farmland, or forcing new development five miles further from town to avoid a large belt of prime agricultural soils, its leaders face a difficult choice. They must choose between immediate damage to the agricultural resource and sprawl, with its potential for other types of long-term degradation. It is the kind of choice that politicians dread, but it is exactly the type of public policy choice that a representative democracy asks its leaders to make. A professional planner or a book author cannot tell officials facing such a decision what the "right" answer is. All that the professional can do is to provide the basis for the public officials to make a well-informed choice.

The worst results will occur when public officials in a community decide to manage growth without regard to the issues of sensitive lands. In such a community, the growth management program may increase the growth pressure on sensitive lands omitted from development through market forces. In such a community, highway and sewer construction without regard to sensitive lands will provide magnets to development that affect such lands. Only by considering the role of sensitive lands in a community can public officials develop a growth management program that provides a degree of protection to such lands that is appropriate to the community. Some states now mandate minimum levels of protection for some lands (see Chapter 6), but in others each community must decide for itself what is appropriate. Some people will undoubtedly disagree with any particular choice, finding it too restrictive or not protective enough. By making an express and carefully considered decision on the subject, a community can reach a reasonable and appropriate policy regarding the protection of sensitive lands and the priority of that goal in relation to other goals such as those encouraging efficient, contiguous development patterns.

NOTES

1. See, generally, Ian L. McHarg, *Design with Nature*, 25th anniversary ed. (New York: J. Wiley, 1994); "National Agricultural Lands Study: Final Report," (Washington: National Agricultural Lands Study, 1981); Charles Thurow, William J. Toner, and Duncan Erley, "Performance Controls for Sensitive Lands," in *Planning Advisory Service* (Chicago, Ill.: American Society of Planning Officials, 1975).
2. Brower, *Urban Growth Management through Development Timing*, 108–12; Greenberg, "Growth and Conflict at the Surburban Fringe: The Case of the Livermore-Amador Valley," 260–71.
3. Gleeson, "Effects of an Urban Growth Management System on Land Values," 109.
4. Babcock, Siemon, and Lincoln Institute of Land Policy, *The Zoning Game Revisited*; Terence Moore, "Saving the Pinelands," in *Growth Management: Keeping on Target?*, ed. Douglas R. Porter (Washington, D.C.: Urban Land Institute, 1986).
5. Thomas A. Ulasewicz, "Adirondack Park: Successful State Management," in *Growth Management: Keeping on Target?*, ed. Douglas R. Porter (Washington, D.C.: Urban Land Institute, 1986).
6. See Gerald Olson, *Soils and the Environment: A Guide to Soil Surveys and Their Applications* (New York: Chapman & Hall, 1981). Or see the descriptions of soil suitability in the tables in any local soil survey; for more information, see http://soils.usda.gov/.
7. Ketcham and Siegel, "Managing Growth to Promote Affordable Housing: Revisiting Oregon's Goal 10," 57–60.
8. Ibid., 56.
9. David Salvesen, *Wetlands: Mitigating and Regulating Development Impacts*, 2nd ed. (Washington, D.C.: Urban Land Institute, 1994).
10. McHarg, *Design with Nature*.
11. Edward John Kaiser et al., "Promoting Environmental Quality through Urban Planning and Controls," in *Washington University Journal of Urban and Contemporary Law* (Washington, D.C.: U.S. Environmental Protection Agency, 1974); Thurow, Toner, and Erley, "Performance Controls for Sensitive Lands."
12. Thurow, Toner, and Erley, "Performance Controls for Sensitive Lands," 570–84.
13. Bruce Hendler, *Caring for the Land: Environmental Principles for Site Design and Review* (Chicago, Ill.: American Society of Planning Officials, 1977); David C. Shelton and Dick Prouty, "Nature's Building Codes: Geology and Construction in Colorado," (Denver, Colo.: Colorado Department of Natural Resources, 1979).
14. Lane Kendig and Susan Connor, *Performance Zoning* (Washington, D.C.: Planners Press American Planning Association, 1980).

15. See McHarg, *Design with Nature.*
16. Audirac, Shermyen, and Smith, "Ideal Urban Form and Visions of the Good Life: Florida's Growth Management Dilemma," 477.
17. Finkler and Peterson, *Nongrowth Planning Strategies: The Developing Power of Towns, Cities, and Regions,* 89–92.
18. Ibid., 92.
19. Town of Hilton Head Island, "Executive Summary: Comprehensive Plan for the Town of Hilton Head Island," in *Growth Management: Keeping on Target?,* ed. Douglas R. Porter (Washington, D.C.: Urban Land Institute, 1986); John Rahenkamp & Associates, "Comprehensive Plan for the Town of Hilton Head Island, South Carolina," (Hilton Head Island, S.C.: Town of Hilton Head Island, 1985).
20. Hilton Head Island, "Executive Summary: Comprehensive Plan for the Town of Hilton Head Island."
21. Finkler and Peterson, *Nongrowth Planning Strategies: The Developing Power of Towns, Cities, and Regions.*
22. Gleeson, "Effects of an Urban Growth Management System on Land Values," 109.
23. Ibid., 113.
24. Porter, "Significant Research Needs in the Policy and Practice of Growth Management."
25. Thurow, Toner, and Erley, "Performance Controls for Sensitive Lands."
26. Hendler, *Caring for the Land: Environmental Principles for Site Design and Review*; Kaiser et al., "Promoting Environmental Quality through Urban Planning and Controls"; Kendig and Connor, *Performance Zoning,* Land Use Planning Committee, ed., *Planning and Zoning for Better Resource Use* (Ankeny, Iowa: Soil Conservation Society of America, 1971).
27. See illustrated examples in Hendler, *Caring for the Land: Environmental Principles for Site Design and Review,* 14–65; Salvesen, *Wetlands: Mitigating and Regulating Development Impacts,* 69–77. See also Gary Pivo, Robert Small, and Charles R. Wolfe, "Rural Cluster Zoning: Survey and Guidelines," *Land Use Law & Zoning Digest* 42, no. 9 (1990); Sachs Rahenkamp, Wells & Associates and American Society of Planning Officials, "Innovative Zoning: A Local Official's Guidebook," (Washington, D.C.: U.S. Department of Housing and Urban Development, 1977).
28. Pivo, Small, and Wolfe, "Rural Cluster Zoning: Survey and Guidelines"; Rahenkamp and Officials, "Innovative Zoning: A Local Official's Guidebook."
29. Hamblen, "Montgomery County at the Crossroads."
30. Governor's Commission on Growth in the Chesapeake Bay Region, "Protecting the Future: A Vision for Maryland," 73.

CHAPTER 9

Growth Management and the Cost and Availability of Public Services

This chapter refers to a number of statistical studies that compare the costs of public service for different patterns and types of growth. In considering those studies, it is important to retain a common sense approach to the issue and not to get lost in the numbers. With little analysis (and the analysis will support these assertions), it is safe to assert that:

- Any growth management program that limits the approval of new development to an amount that can be served by available public services will, by definition, ensure the availability of public services and will do so better than a program that does not contain such requirements.

- On the other hand, a rate-of-growth program, growth phasing program or urban growth boundary program that establishes the growth rate, phases or boundaries based on criteria other than the availability of public services may or may not ensure the availability of public services.

- Over the long run and with good planning, an urban growth boundary program should result in the full availability of services throughout the growth area concurrently with the full development of the area. However, there may be localized or even area-wide imbalances in the short run.

- Any growth management program that requires or encourages new development to take place in areas with existing services (which will typically, but not always, be adjacent to existing development) will result in a lower cost of services than would result if there are no limitations on the location of development.

- Increased capital costs resulting from increased distance, for example for longer roads or larger pumps, will usually mean increased operating and maintenance costs.

Nothing in the studies cited below contradicts these common sense principles. Some of the studies confirm them. Like most studies with large numbers of figures, however, the ones cited below can become confusing.

EFFECT ON PUBLIC SERVICE AVAILABILITY

A properly administered adequate public facilities program should result in a balance between the demands on public facilities and the capacities of those facilities, or in a surplus of capacity.

When Westminster, Colorado, established its growth management program, based largely on the availability of public facilities, it was issuing permits at the rate of 1,000 dwelling units per calendar quarter. It then had more than 3,600 "permit-ready" lots in the city, an additional 1,000 lots approved for single-family development and thousands of additional units approved through early stages of the development review process. In contrast, the city had enough sewer and water capacity to serve about 2,600 additional dwelling units.[1] By the early 1980s, capacity available in Westminster's infrastructure systems exceeded development demand, and the city has had no difficulty in accommodating growth since that time. Thus, the growth management system initially restored the balance between service capacities and demands and then maintained it during and after the peak years of building.[2]

In Livermore, growth management began as a citizen initiative to limit new development to the amount that did not create demand exceeding the capacities of the schools and sewer and water systems. A researcher found that the Livermore program, like the one in Westminster, served its purpose. "All approved residential projects were thoroughly reviewed, and the availability of infrastructure was assured in advance. By 1980, water supply, wastewater treatment and overcrowding in schools ceased to be major civic concerns."[3]

Montgomery County provides a different example. As the description in Chapter 4 indicates, Montgomery County is one managed-growth community where development pressures continued at a high level in the 1980s (see Chapter 4). When the county first established a growth management system in 1974, sewers were the critical limitation on development there and throughout the Washington, D.C., metropolitan area.[4] Nearly three decades later, relative capacities has changed. Although the availability of sewer service remained one of the criteria in the growth management program, the critical link was traffic,[5] which became such a concern that the county used it in two levels of development regulation. First, the general traffic loads of each of the policy areas of the county play a role in establishing the "staging ceilings," or growth capacities of each of those areas. Second, the county requires that larger projects provide site-specific traffic impact analyses through a Local Area Transportation Review Process and that the developers then mitigate any unacceptable impacts.[6]

Other types of programs may not be as effective at ensuring a balance between the capacity of public facilities and the demands placed on them. Boulder's determination that it would accept growth of 2 percent each year and Petaluma's decision that it would permit 500 new dwelling units each year (plus a number of exemptions in each community) clearly bore no particular relationship to the capacities of public facilities. The programs reflected that fact in their terms, because both limited their controls to residential development. Clearly, commercial and industrial uses also consume water and generate sewage. It is noteworthy in this context that the federal district court considering the Petaluma program found that the city had adequate capacities in both its sewer and water systems to absorb development beyond that permitted by the regulatory system in its early years.[7] It is similarly noteworthy that Boulder lost a lawsuit with a developer when it refused to provide service to a developer when the city controlled lines that ran near the development site and had available capacity[8] (see discussion of both cases in Chapter 4).

However, these different types of programs differ both in effect and in purpose. Snyder contrasted the "basic motivation" of Boulder, "To limit growth in terms of both rate and magnitude," and Westminster, "To insure that the city maintains the service and fiscal capacity necessary to accommodate growth."[9] In his study of the growth management program in San Juan Capistrano, Dubbink concluded that technical capacity issues were not the basis for the program there. He commented, "My impression was that the technical findings of the [staff] report had long been eclipsed by the hours of public hearings associated with setting San Juan's yearly growth quota. This seemed to be an essentially political event where the unrest of the protectionists was balanced against the unrest of those with land to develop and the costs of extending services was balanced against the cost of litigation for withholding them."[10]

Perhaps the most dramatic illustration of the lack of relationship between some growth management programs and the availability of public facilities came from Ramapo, New York. Its initial point system allocated development "points" to a project based on the relative availability of sewer service, access, park and school sites, fire protection and drainage. The Ramapo program was a phased growth system tied to an eighteen-year capital budget. Under the program and the capital budget, the community presumably provided for the complete eighteen-year build-out of the town limits. However, when the regional sewer district failed to construct the sewer improvements as scheduled, "the Town Council decided to automatically award the maximum number of points (five) to special permit requests since that time."[11]

One could argue, of course, that Ramapo officials were simply trying to be fair to developers by not penalizing them for the fact that a regional entity had fallen behind in its own commitment. On the other hand, if the town had been serious about ensuring the availability of public facilities, there was no excuse for essentially exempting a significant number of projects from the sewer criterion under the point system.

The conclusion of this section is not complicated; it is, in fact, as the introduction to the chapter suggests, a common sense result. Growth management programs that directly regulate the adequacy of public facilities succeed in ensuring the availability of public facilities as new development takes place. Other types of growth management systems do not ensure that availability.

Certainly a program that slows the growth rate or limits the geographic area within which growth may take place may reduce the likelihood and/or the extent of any service problems, but that is quite different from ensuring that services are available as development takes place. Livermore imposed an adequate public facilities requirement early in its growth management history, although it later replaced that requirement with a residential rate-of-growth program. Westminster and Montgomery County have always based their growth management programs in part on the adequacy of public facilities. A Florida law passed in 1985 and phased into effect over the next several years requires that all local governments within it ensure the "concurrent" availability of adequate public facilities before approving new development (see discussion in Chapter 6). The 1990 state growth management law in Washington tied land development approvals to the availability of transportation facilities, but the state Growth Studies Commission recommended, "The Act should be revised to link land use planning and development approvals with other public facilities such as parks, schools, sewers, stormwater drainage, fire protection, and water supply and distribution."[12]

In short, if one of the goals of a community in adopting a growth management program is to ensure the adequacy of public facilities, it should include adequate public facility requirements in its program.

A Different Issue of Timing

Just having an adequate public facilities requirement on the books is not enough to ensure the availability of public facilities. Many projects are not built when the community initially approves them. It is important to include such projects in the growth management equation.

Westminster did not intentionally overcommit its sewer and water capacities by 400 percent. Its city officials were not unconscious of its capacity limitations. A sudden acceleration in building permit applications in early 1977 surprised public officials there. Many of those applications were not for new projects. They were for revivals of projects that the city had approved years earlier but that developers had apparently abandoned. Of four lawsuits brought against the city's growth management program, three were brought by foreclosing lenders who wanted to revive dormant projects. Westminster, like most communities, then had no system for tracking developments that had received various stages of approval but that had not been built.

Although the situation in Westminster in 1977 may have been extreme, it was not unique. Old, unbuilt subdivisions dot the countryside around most major metropolitan areas. Site plans for shopping centers and apartment houses that were never built sit fading in planning offices. Scattered vacant lots in an urban area may not seem significant when viewed individually, but the total of them can be quite significant. In a vital economy, buildings will gradually occupy most of the subdivided lots. While many unbuilt projects may remain permanently dormant, some may be revived. That is more likely in a booming economy and in a context in which an old project approval may offer the developer the possibility of relief from more rigorous requirements under current rules.

Controlling the problem of unbuilt projects is not particularly difficult if a community is conscious of the issue. One key element in such a process is a provision for various approvals to lapse if they are not used within a specified period of time. For example, Westminster's city code provides that a preliminary plan lapses if a final plan application is not submitted within one year, and that the final plan lapses if a subdivision plat or building permit application is not submitted within one year after its approval.[13] A 1991 New Hampshire law permits local governments to revoke approved subdivisions under certain circumstances. Among those circumstances is the failure of the developer to conduct sufficient construction to vest development rights during a specified time.[14]

That does not totally address the issue, however. One question is how far the project can get in the system before the adequate public facilities review affects it. Both Westminster and Montgomery County consider adequate public facilities availability at all stages of development review. In contrast, Boulder, Livermore and Petaluma do not implement their housing permit review processes until the subdivision stage.[15] Thus, a project in one of those communities could presumably obtain zoning and other preliminary planning approvals with no assurance that the community would permit actual building of the project. That not only creates additional risk for the developer, it creates the risk of the city granting some form of approval to a project that it may not be able, or willing, to serve. Although the legal significance of that kind of action varies from state to state, it represents poor public policy anywhere.

In most states, local governments cannot provide for the lapse or reversion of zoning approvals. It is also very difficult in most states to vacate a final subdivision plat without the consent of the property owner(s). Many growth management communities overcome that difficulty by requiring a separate development permit that controls the issuance of an actual building permit. Westminster requires the issuance of a "service commitment" before it will approve a final (site) plan, but that service commitment then serves as the basis for the issuance of subdivision approvals and building permits.

Westminster and Montgomery County essentially "encumber" the capacity to serve a project for a limited time, during which the development approval permits construction in the project. If the developer does not build the project within that time, the approval lapses, the encumbered capacity reverts to the system and the developer must get back in line. The developer may still build the project when it wants to, but it runs the risk of delay due to future capacity problems if the project is not built during the initial approval period, when capacity is reserved for it.

This discussion may seem somewhat esoteric. However, in the boom-and-bust real estate markets of high growth communities, it is not at all unusual for a community to continue to approve development projects right up to the peak of a real estate market. When the market turns down, many developers abandon those projects.

Whether the community then forgets those project approvals or, like Montgomery County and Westminster, tracks them, will determine the success or failure of an adequate public facilities program when the market again revives.

FISCAL IMPACTS OF GROWTH AND GROWTH MANAGEMENT

Growth generally increases both revenues and expenses for local governments. Snyder found that, between 1970 and 1979, as Westminster's growth accelerated, revenues grew more quickly (707 percent) than expenses (462 percent). However, a dramatic increase in capital expenditures absorbed the difference.[16] One of the reasons for the concern about the fiscal impacts of growth is that growth is not always profitable.[17] On the other hand, a statewide study in Colorado found that growth counties were better off by all fiscal measures than non-growth counties.[18] Interestingly, in the Colorado study, per capita expenditures were generally lower in the growth counties.[19] A New Jersey study found that residential development generally created a fiscal surplus when school costs and revenues were removed from the equation.[20]

Although methods of fiscal impact analysis, such as those described in the studies just cited, examine both costs and revenues, the emphasis of the examination here is on the expenditure side. There are several reasons for that, but there is one basic one. An $80,000 home with a typical family that can afford such home should yield, in theory, the same amount of revenue to the local government in 1999 regardless of whether it is built in 1993 or 1997 and regardless of whether it is built on the west side, on the east side or in some other part of town. That will not always be true. For example, the nearest shopping for the house on the west side may lie within the community and generate sales tax for that community, while the shopping nearest the east side location may be in another community that will thus receive the sales tax from new residents there. Addressing such issues goes somewhat beyond the scope of most growth management programs, which deal with timing and location issues on a fairly gross basis. It also overcomplicates the task presented here.

Thus, the examination below proceeds largely on the assumption of stable per-unit revenues with an examination of potential cost savings from alternative development patterns. Note also that rate-of-growth and growth phasing programs may delay construction of a particular home or other building. Such delays will affect both revenues and expenditures and are thus disregarded in this analysis.

The landmark study on the relationship between growth and the fiscal impacts of development is *The Costs of Sprawl*.[21] It compared the capital and operating costs of communities of 10,000 units and neighborhoods of 1,000 units with six different development patterns:

I. Planned Mix. Housing mix 20 percent single-family conventional, 20 percent single-family clustered; 20 percent townhouses; 20 percent walk-up apartments; 20 percent high-rise apartments. "Neighborhoods are contiguous and large areas of open space preserved."

II. Combination Mix. Housing mix the same as for I. Assumes development pattern is 50 percent planned (same as I) and 50 percent sprawl.

III. Sprawl Mix. Housing mix the same as I. Sprawl, leapfrog development pattern.

IV. Low Density Planned. Housing mix is 75 percent single-family clustered, 25 percent single-family conventional. Lower densities than I.

V. Low Density Sprawl. Housing mix is 25 percent single-family clustered and 75 percent conventional single-family.

VI. High-Density Planned. Housing mix is 10 percent single-family clustered, 20 percent townhouse, 30 percent walk-up apartments, 40 percent high-rise. High densities with lots of open space.[22]

The study found significant differences in capital and operating costs, as illustrated in Table 9-1.

The differences between Type VI (high density planned) and Type V (low density sprawl) are, of course, quite significant. The high density project incurs only 68 percent of the capital costs of traditional, low density sprawl and 89 percent of the comparable operating costs.

However, that often-cited comparison is a deceptive one. The two represented radically different lifestyles.[23] Type VI assumed that 40 percent of the residents would inhabit 900-square-foot high-rise apartments, whereas Type V assumed that all residents would inhabit 1,600-square-foot single-family residences. The study acknowledged that the same people would not inhabit both projects, because it acknowledged that the average occupancy projected for the high-rise units was 2.8 persons and the average occupancy for the detached units was 3.5.[24]

Table 9-1
Public Service Costs for Different Patterns of Development[1]

	Development Type	Capital Costs	Operating Costs
I.	Planned mix	$124,870	$19,373
II.	Combination mix	$130,459	$19,516
III.	Sprawl mix	$135,556	$19,652
IV.	Low-density planned	$145,823	$20,672
V.	Low-density-sprawl	$164,620	$21,109
VI.	High-density planned	$109,948	$18,731

[1]*Table Sources:* Real Estate Research Corp. 1974, *The Costs of Sprawl: Environmental and Economic Costs of Alternative Residential Development Patterns at the Urban Fringe*; capital costs are from sub-total on Table 44, p. 97; operating and maintenance costs are from Table 45, p. 98; this table by author from cited data.

However, the figures used here project the expenses for all housing types based on assumed constant population; otherwise, the costs for the higher-density projects, with fewer children, would be dramatically lower because of the reduction in school-related costs.

The cost difference between the two types of projects that consist entirely of single-family dwelling units (Types IV, low-density planned and V, low-density sprawl) is small, with a 3 percent saving in capital costs and a 2 percent saving in operating costs. The reason for the differences in the two comparisons is quite straightforward. Virtually all the public capital cost savings of the high density project over the sprawling one result from the need to construct fewer linear feet of roads and the utility lines that lie under them. The clustering of single-family dwellings similarly generates most of the saving between those two types of projects, but the saving is much smaller because each house is still on its own lot; some of the lots are simply narrower and thus require fewer feet of street. The authors acknowledged the significance of these differences. "Thus, while planning results in cost savings, density is a much more influential cost determinant. Clearly, the greatest cost advantages occur when higher density planned developments are contrasted with low density sprawl."[25]

Real Estate Research Corporation, a reputable Chicago-based consulting firm, prepared *The Costs of Sprawl* under contract to the Council on Environmental Quality, the Department of Housing and Urban Development and the Environmental Protection Agency. Although the study relied on projections, entirely hypothetical data, the figures used above were all objectively determinable at the time. The data cited here was entirely reliable and remains reliable, if deflated, for analytical purposes. The important question is not whether it is accurate. The important question is, "What does it mean?" A careful analysis indicates that simply planning better for the same types of housing results in some saving, but it is very small. The real saving comes from persuading people to move from single-family homes to high-rise apartments or attracting a different demographic group that will. That is not a realistic policy option for most local governments, although the regional government in Portland has implemented such a program.

Interestingly, in a 1984 comparison of "planned development" or "unplanned development" on a 7,500-acre site in Houston, Peiser found that the planned development approach yielded savings of approximately 1.6 percent in construction of utilities. The primary cost difference in Peiser's comparison resulted from the assumption that the unplanned development would require multiple package water and sewer plants. Peiser's comparison of road construction costs in the two is not useful for purposes of this chapter, because he made different assumptions about who would pay for different roads in the two models and then calculated the costs only for those to be constructed by the principal developer. Peiser's comparison held the dwelling unit mix and population constant, thus making the two types of projects reasonably competitive in the market.

The Costs of Sprawl was the subject of two contemporaneous critiques, one a review by Alan Altshuler and the other a longer article specifically labeled a "critique." Altshuler challenged many of the assumptions of the report, most of those relating to its analysis of energy consumption, air pollution and other items beyond the scope of this book. One of his grounds for dissent, however, does affect the fiscal analysis. He argued, "The key question, it appears, is whether density per se affects the demand level for community service. The authors of *The Costs of Sprawl* explicitly assumed that it did not. Numerous other analyses have judged that the residents of high density communities do seem to require and/or demand more expensive packages of community services than those who live at low densities."[26]

Altshuler cited examples ranging from the likelihood that suburban residents might be willing to live without sidewalks to the greater need and political demand for police and fire services when people live at higher densities. Altshuler argued that if the study were "calibrated against the experience of real communities," the result might be quite different.[27] A government finance expert had previously cited a study from Fairfax County, Virginia, that supported an argument such as the one made by Altshuler.[28]

In a review, Windsor challenged *The Cost of Sprawl*'s conclusions on similar grounds and others. He was particularly critical of the variations in floor areas of the different dwelling units and the resulting population differences. He also noted that the report failed to account for what would happen to the unused land saved through the higher density project and that any use of that land would also have fiscal implications.

Windsor recalculated some of the figures from *The Costs of Sprawl*. Although in general he found smaller cost differences among housing types than did the original report, he actually found a greater savings in infrastructure costs when comparing the low density planned and low density sprawl development patterns; he computed a savings of about 11 percent for the planned development. He found a far smaller savings than did the original, however, for infrastructure in the high density planned development; there he computed a savings of approximately 20 percent.[29]

One issue neither Windsor nor Altshuler addresses, and which is pertinent here, is the revenue side. Although this chapter makes no attempt to examine differences in revenues that may result from alternative development locations, *The Costs of Sprawl* examined alternative development *types*. The smaller apartment units in the study would clearly generate lower property taxes than the larger and more expensive single-family homes. As the study acknowledged, they would contain fewer residents, which would thus reduce sales tax revenues. Furthermore, the lower cost might attract residents with lower incomes than those who would inhabit the single-family dwellings. Thus, reduced revenues would clearly offset, at least in part, the reduced costs of the "most efficient" development type in the study. That would presumably not be true of the same-cost, same-size single-family dwelling units in the planned and sprawl projects. Thus, the 3 percent capital cost and 1 percent operating cost savings of the planned project should pass through to the bottom line.

Professor James Frank synthesized data from nine major studies involving the costs of infrastructure and different development patterns and adjusted the data

Table 9-2
**Capital Costs of Streets and Utilities for Different Development Types,
per Dwelling Unit[2]**

Development Type	Streets	Utilities	Total
Single-family 1 unit per acre	$12,308	$19,789	$32,097
Single-family 3 units per acre	$7,083	$11,388	$18,461
Single-family cluster 5 units per acre	$7,526	$8,843	$16,369
Townhouses 10 units per acre	$6,785	$6,019	$12,804
Mixed 12 units per acre*	$6,229	$6,865	$13,184
Multi-family 15 units per acre	$5,297	$3,384	$8,691
Multi-family 30 units per acre	$3,773	$3,096	$6,869

*Mix of 20 percent of single-family clustered, single-family conventional, townhouses, garden apartments, and high-rise apartments (comparable to "planned mix" in the *Costs of Sprawl* data in Table 9-1.

[2]James E. Frank, *The Costs of Alternative Development Patterns: A Review of the Literature* (Washington, D.C.: Urban Land Institute, 1989) extracted from tbl. 8, p. 40.

from all of them to 1987 dollars. He noted that the principal variables in the equations are the costs of streets, sewers, water systems, storm drainage and schools.[30] Because the capital cost of schools varies primarily with the number of pupils, that factor is disregarded here. However, Frank found the potential for enormous saving in streets and utilities. Table 9-2 summarizes part of his data.

Note that the differences shown in Table 9-2 represent the differences based on the pattern of development. Frank noted that most of these cost differences were assessed to developers in the form of subdivision improvement requirements and, ultimately, passed on to the home buyer, who gains the enjoyment of the larger lot.[31] That assertion is undoubtedly valid, as the requirement that developers pay all on-site subdivision costs was almost universal in the early 1990s. However, it disregarded the significance of the operating costs that the local government absorbs. Seventy-five feet of street costs more to maintain than sixty feet of street.

Table 9-3 gives additional figures from the Frank report. He computed these additional costs based on the *location* of development, costs that he says are

Table 9-3

Capital Costs for Different Development Patterns in Leapfrog and Remote Locations per Dwelling Unit[3]

Development Type	Distance**		
	Leapfrog	5 Miles	10 Miles
Single-family 1 unit per acre	No Data	$7,300	$14,600
Single-family 3 units per acre	$3,297	$7,300	$14,600
Single-family cluster 5 units per acre	No Data	$7,300	$14,600
Townhouses 10 units per acre	$5,019	$6,875	$13,750
Mixed 12 units per acre*	$3,870	$6,875	$9,400
Multi-family 15 units per acre	$5,019	$6,875	$13,750
Multi-family 30 units per acre	$5,019	$5,840	$11,680

*Mix of 20 percent of single-family clustered, single-family conventional, townhouses, garden apartments, and high-rise apartments (comparable to "planned mix" in the *Costs of Sprawl* data in Table 9-1.

**Distance to employment, sewage plant, water plant, receiving body of water.

[3]James E. Frank, *The Costs of Alternative Development Patterns: A Review of the Literature* (Washington, D.C.: Urban Land Institute, 1989) extracted from tbl. 8, p. 40.

generally not fully passed through to the developer and are thus subsidized by the community.[32]

Frank's findings were dramatic. However, it is risky to accept them at their apparent face value. Peiser would argue that the leapfrog and distance figures are simply short-term cash flow figures and that, over the long-run, infill development would use that infrastructure, resulting in a reallocation of the cost over a much larger number of units and a resulting reduction in the per-unit cost (see discussion in Chapter 7). Frank acknowledged similar economic arguments in his conclusion, in which he discussed who should bear the cost of excess capacity: whether it should be allocated evenly among ultimate users, acknowledging that some of them will not pay their share for many years, or whether it should be allocated fully to present users. However, he did not apply that economic logic to the figures given in Table 9-3.[33]

In 1989, a team of consulting firms, led by James Duncan of Austin, Texas, conducted a major fiscal impact study for the Florida Governor's Task Force on Urban Growth Patterns.[34] It is the only major study based on actual case studies of developed areas. The Duncan team made no attempt to examine internal development costs, which, as this chapter has suggested and as that study noted, "have been widely studied and shown to be strongly related to density, as well as typically borne by developers and passed on to consumers."[35] The study also controlled for location and thus did not test the factors that Frank assigned for developments located at a long distance from existing development, although the study did cite Frank's work on that type of cost.

The Florida study findings confirmed the substantial cost savings from contiguous development patterns. The study examined eight case study areas and assigned them to five categories:

- **Scattered**: A pattern of urban growth which is generally characterized by low density development that has prematurely located ("leapfrogged") past vacant land into relatively undeveloped areas. Other factors usually characterizing this urban form are extended distances to urban employment centers and central public facilities, minimal nonresidential support services and lower levels of services. . . .

- **Contiguous**: A pattern of urban growth which is generally characterized by moderate density development and is located adjacent to or near established urban areas. Other factors usually characterizing this urban development form are mixed land uses, proximity to nonresidential support services and satisfactory levels of public services. . . .

- **Linear**: A pattern of urban growth which is generally characterized by relatively low densities and intensities of mixed use development extending outward from established urban areas along one or more major transportation corridors. Other factors usually characterizing this urban development form are decreasing land use intensities along the corridors and heavy dependence upon vehicular access. . . .

- **Satellite**: A pattern of urban growth which is generally characterized by moderate to high intensity mixed use development that occurs primarily within discrete outlying suburban or exurban areas. Other factors usually characterizing this urban development form are a cultural and economic relationship to, but a physical separation from, established major urban centers. . . .

- **Compact**: A pattern of urban growth which is generally characterized by higher intensity development that occurs within an established urban area. Other factors characterizing this urban development pattern include more vertical development, redevelopment of underutilized parcels and undercapacity public facilities. . . .[36]

The Duncan team's Florida findings regarding capital costs are presented in Table 9-4.

Landis performed a paired-community comparison of communities that manage growth and those that do not. All the communities were in California and the paired communities were near each other. He found that "the various growth control communities slightly outperformed their respective pro-growth counterparts. That is, revenue growth outpaced expenditure growth by a greater margin in the

Table 9-4
Capital Costs for Different Types of Existing Development[4]

Area	Urban Form	Unit Cost
Downtown Orlando	Compact	$9,208
Southpoint	Contiguous	$10,560
Countryside	Contiguous	$12,707
Tampa Palms	Satellite	$14,816
Cantonment	Scattered	$15,102
University	Linear	$16,628
Kendall	Linear	$16,628
Wellington	Scattered	$23,639
AVERAGE		$14,773

[4]*Source:* James Duncan and Associates Inc. et al., "The Search for Efficient Urban Growth Patterns: A Study of the Fiscal Impacts of Development in Florida." (Tallahassee: Florida Department of Community Affairs, 1989), fig. 2.2, p. 15.

slow-growth cities than in the pro-growth cities."[37] Landis did not attribute great significance to his findings. He suggested that:

Overall, it appears that growth-control communities have been better able to manage spending than their pro-growth counterparts while not suffering undue revenue declines. This does not necessarily mean that growth control is good for city budgets, however. What is more likely is that city finances are in better shape than those communities with traditions of good government, good management, good planning, and higher levels of citizen involvement, exactly the types of communities most likely to try to control growth.[38]

The Maryland Governor's Commission on Growth in the Chesapeake Bay Region applied Duncan's cost model to two alternative statewide growth scenarios.[39] Again excluding education costs, under the "trend" growth scenario of continuing sprawl, the commission projected capital infrastructure costs for roads and utilities totaling $9,191 per single-family unit and under a more compact and contiguous scenario of $4,104 per single-family unit.[40] When the Commission aggregated all costs for all development (not just residential) statewide, the fiscal impact figures were particularly interesting. It showed a reduction of capital costs from $7,701,686 under "trend" development to $6,519,701 under "vision" development, a 15 percent cost savings. However, the revenue side showed less than a 1 percent

Table 9-5
Comparison of Infrastructure (Capital) Costs for Alternative Development Patterns, U.S., 2000–2025 (all figures in millions)[5]

	Conventional Development	Managed Growth	Savings	Percentage Savings
Water and sewer infrastructure	$189,767	$177,160	$12,609	6.6
Local road infrastructure	$927,000	$817,310	$109,700	11.8

[5]*Source:* Robert W. Burchell and Sanan Mukherji, "Conventional Development Versus the Costs of Sprawl," *American Journal of Public Health* 93, no. 9 (2003): tbl. 3, p. 1537, tbl. 4, p. 38.

reduction from "trend" development at $5,311,370 to "vision" development at $5,272,394.[41]

A later study at Rutgers University took an approach similar to that of the Maryland study in that it dealt with aggregate costs, based on two alternative development patterns. It was a more ambitious study, attempting to deal with the costs of development in the nation over 25 years under two different development patterns, "sprawl" and "managed growth."[42] The researchers' definition of "managed growth" was similar to the concept of "smart growth" discussed in Chapter 6; specifically:

Managed growth is defined as limiting a significant share of development to already-developed counties or to areas as close to already developed locations as possible.[43]

The Rutgers team calculated that the "managed growth" scenario would redirect 11 percent of new households and 6 percent of new jobs "away from counties that are sprawling."[44] The team's findings showed substantial savings in capital costs (see Table 9-5).

The Rutgers researchers also found that there would be significant savings in operating costs, although neither scenario generated enough costs for new development to offset fully its own operating costs.[45] Not surprisingly, the researchers also found that the compact and contiguous growth patterns suggested by "managed growth" resulted in lower development costs, some 7.8 percent lower for residential development.[46]

The researchers took into account the fact that land costs and even some public service costs are lower in more remote locations.[47] Even after accounting for those savings, the Rutgers team found a substantial "cost of sprawl" for the occupant— occupancy costs some 8 percent higher in the sprawl scenario than under managed growth.[48]

Researchers at Virginia Tech focused on water and sewer utility costs for sixty different development scenarios, which varied both lot size, tract dispersion and over-all distance from existing sewer and water systems.[49] They found that all three factors helped to explain cost differences. Some specific examples include:

- When other factors were held constant, it was nearly twice as expensive to provide sewer and water service to .25-acre lots than to 1-acre lots;
- Although they found that the effects of tract dispersion (essentially scattered development) were "more modest" than those from the other factors, they nevertheless found that "in all cases, cost increases as tract dispersion increases due to increases in pipe lengths and pump capital costs;" and
- Increasing the distance of a development from .25 mile from the nearest service system to 4 miles from such a system (leapfrog development) resulted in a substantial capital cost increase and a net cost increase of 30 percent. [50]

In a separate study, a New Zealand researcher, drawing on experience and studies in the United States, tested a model for examining the fiscal impacts of variations in density. He generally found that the "divergence of costs from revenues" increased as density went down, but he hypothesized that there may be an optimum density for each community.[51]

MARGINAL VS. AVERAGE COSTS

The Maryland study noted candidly that much of the cost savings under "vision" growth resulted from "targeting much of the projected growth to previously developed and/or adjacent growth areas."[52] In other words, the Maryland planners proposed to limit *marginal* costs by using existing capital plant to the maximum extent practicable. Savings on short-run costs may be only short-run savings, deferring the need for the community to extend the interceptor sewer line or freeway. On the other hand, in a typical community, the practice of over-designing facilities extending in several directions while growth may only go in one results in significant excess capacity in many systems. Insofar as a "vision growth" pattern or other adequate public facilities requirement takes advantage of capital plant capacities that might otherwise be wasted, marginal cost savings can result in long-term savings and significantly reduce long-term average costs.

Frank analyzed this issue differently.[53] He referred to the marginal or incremental costs actually incurred (such as the cost of extending a new sewer line to the site) as "precipitated" costs. He contrasted those with "inherited" costs, which are the average cost factors for facilities with excess capacity that is used by the new development.

In purely economic terms, with perfect foresight and perfect planning, so that all capacity is ultimately used, it should make little difference whether costs are "precipitated" or "inherited". In the operation of a particular local government, it can make the difference between building a new school for several million dollars or just adding a few students (and some new tax revenues) to a school that already exists. A school is a particularly dramatic example to many people, because the handful of new students who suddenly push the existing school(s) past capacity generate an enormous (and highly visible) marginal cost per student to the district that must then build the new school. However, the new development that requires a major expansion of the sewer plant or the water treatment plant may have an even greater "precipitated" cost effect on a particular local government at a particular time.

Average cost information is important over the long run, but marginal, or "precipitated," cost information is critical over the short run. Whether the marginal cost involves buying a police car for a small town or a new sewer plant for a large one, a community that approves a development that pushes it past the threshold at which that expenditure becomes necessary must be certain that it has a way to pay the cost.

TIME AND FISCAL IMPACTS

Careful fiscal impact studies discount future costs and revenues using a reasonable rate of return and thus compute the present value of a future stream of income or costs. They also discount future capital expenditures, recognizing that a dollar spent next year is cheaper, in today's money, than one spent today, because of the interest income. Thus, they attempt to account for the effects of time on the computations. Most such studies disregard inflation and project both costs and revenues in present dollars. There are three reasons for that approach. First, inflation is notoriously difficult to predict. Second, inflation will presumably affect both costs and revenues. Third, the comparisons conducted in fiscal impacts make more sense if presented in "constant," or uninflated, dollars.

However, there are two other aspects to the issue of time and fiscal impacts. One is lead-time. Although state laws on the subject vary enormously, in most cases, revenues from new development will lag behind costs. A new home is typically assessed during the first year construction is complete, resulting in a tax bill the following January 1. In the meantime, residents may have occupied the house for eighteen months or more, certainly for at least twelve months. Residents new to the area will begin using services the day they move into the house, and yet their first tax bill to the state will not come due until sometime in the following spring. Commercial development included in the fiscal impact analysis of a mixed-use project may not be built until one of the later years of the project.

The State of Colorado commissioned a detailed study of the lag involved in tax revenues, based on projected development in a mining region. The study found that revenues would lag behind cost "needs" for nearly seven years in a tri-county area, although revenues would then exceed costs over the long run.[54] Much of the deficiency was attributable to capital costs that might be financed through bonds or through developer (or, in this case, industry) exactions. The point is not that the lag-time problem is insurmountable, but that it must be addressed. Obviously, the lag time issue in suburban development is most severe for non-contiguous development that generates the need for major off-site capital expenditures, which that community cannot fully exact from the developer. Certainly, a thorough fiscal impact analysis accounts for such factors. However, most of the fiscal impact literature focuses on average costs, figures that will be entirely valid after a few years but that do not recognize the lead time problem.[55]

There is still another aspect of time that the fiscal impact literature does not address at all. Time brings market risks. Virtually all fiscal impact projections are based on full build-out of the project analyzed. Those are, in turn, based on the developer's projections, which are usually the same optimistic projections that the developer gave to the bank that financed the project. The chance that they will be wrong is great, and time increases that risk significantly.

The worst case circumstance occurs when the developer installs most of the public facilities but completes few of the tax-generating homes and commercial buildings before the economy turns sour and halts the project. The local government then finds itself with virtually the full operating costs (and, for non-contiguous development, some measure of off-site capital costs) and only a fraction of the projected revenues. Because school costs vary with the number of pupils, this problem is not as great with schools as with other facilities. However, with roads, sewer lines, water lines and drainage facilities, the maintenance costs are nearly as great with only a few families using them as with them operating at capacity. If the developer completes absolutely *no* private (taxable) buildings, the community may have the option of simply abandoning the public facilities to the elements, but that is not a likely scenario.

Westminster provides a useful illustration. In the early 1970s, the city aggressively annexed land. Acknowledging willingly the need to serve the new territory, the city then borrowed heavily to construct the major trunk water lines and interceptor sewer lines necessary to serve the city's expansion to the north and west. It was an early user of this type of exaction. The city thus counted on large fees from developers, to be paid at the time of sewer or water connection but in addition to traditional "tap" fees, which basically reimbursed the city for the costs of inspecting new connections, or "taps." Then the real estate market turned down in 1973. By the time the city faced the growth crunch in 1977, the city confronted two conflicting problems. Although it had serious limitations on its capacity to serve new development, it needed the revenue from sewer and water connection fees from such development to meet existing bonded debt.[56] The Westminster story has a reasonably happy ending in its successful implementation of a growth management program, but the story could have ended differently. Had growth not revived, the city would have faced a continued fiscal crisis due to the commitment to service facilities that essentially facilitated the leapfrogging of growth far into its new territory.

The figures can be staggering. In some Colorado special districts, in which developers completed most of the public facilities but few of the taxable private improvements, tax bills for individual homeowners went from $500 to $10,000 per year.[57] A number of such districts in Colorado have taken bankruptcy, thus leaving bondholders with substantial losses.[58] The problem would not appear so dramatic if the project had simply been included within the financial operations of a municipal government, so that the negative fiscal impact would be averaged out over the gross operations of the community. However, that would just mask the numbers, not change them.

Peiser's argument that sprawl is efficient over the long run because it ultimately encourages more intensive use of the omitted parcels must be considered in this context.[59] If a community permits discontiguous (leapfrog) development based on Peiser's argument and the infill occurs rapidly, then Peiser's argument can hold and the community may be in good fiscal shape. However, if the same community approves leapfrog development based on Peiser's advice and the economy then turns sour for several years, or, worse yet, the largest employer in town pulls out or lays off a few thousand workers, then the community will be left with an inefficient and fiscally costly pattern of development with which it must live for many years, if not for the long term.

GROWTH PHASING AND EXACTIONS

Landis identifies another potential concern for growth managing communities, although his data neither supports nor denies his hypothesis. "By slowing the pace of development, growth controls limit the financial leverage cities have over developers. In particular, developers may be less willing to build or finance large capital projects for cities unless they can be assured of a long-term development entitlement, the types of assurances yearly growth caps make impossible."[60] He goes on to suggest that the result would be that growth-managing communities would have to pay a larger proportion of the costs of new infrastructure than pro-growth communities.

His assertion, although undocumented, is worth considering because it is so logical. Note that there are two separate issues inherent in this hypothesis. One is the short-term issue of cash flow. If a community cannot exact a major public improvement from a developer, the community may have to advance the cost of that improvement. However, Landis suggests that this is not just a short-term cost-shifting from the developer back to the community, but a long-term one. If a particular community can advance the costs of improvements and then recover most or all of the costs through impact fees, there will be only a short-term shift. However, if Landis' hypothesis is fully correct, communities that establish some types of growth management systems may find themselves paying a larger share of the costs of growth than in the recent past.

Peiser's issue is one of concern only for communities with competitive rate-of-growth programs or highly restrictive phased growth programs. Both of those create uncertainty for a developer. Such a program typically requires annual applications for development approvals, leaving the developer with no assurance of being able to complete the kind of long-term, large-scale project that justifies advancing the cost of a major capital improvement.[61] Other types of growth management programs do not create any greater uncertainty than do other land use controls. With an urban growth boundary, a developer knows that a proposed project is either inside or outside the boundary. A responsible developer (and the developer's banker) should know whether a proposed project has "adequate public facilities." Those types of programs simply do not create the uncertainty that a competitive program does.

CONCLUSION

Growth management clearly affects the fiscal position of a local government. Any program that encourages or requires growth to occur closer to existing development and existing facilities will reduce costs to some extent, without affecting revenues. Over the long run, in a steadily growing community, the savings will not be very significant. However, in a particular year when new development takes place in a remote or underserved location, the fiscal impacts can be significant. Further, if economic forces change and the growth rate slows (or even halts) shortly after that development occurs, the community may suffer for many years. Growth phasing programs, adequate public facilities requirements and urban growth boundaries all tend to encourage development in more efficient *locations*, although adequate public facilities requirements are the most effective in doing so. Growth management programs can also encourage more efficient *patterns* of development, but the cost savings of doing so do not appear to be significant.

NOTES

1. Westminster, "[Untitled Working Documents on Growth Management] A, B, C and D," charts 78(C)(1) through 78(C)(4), Report B, p. 13.
2. James Duncan and Associates Inc. and Kelly, "Adequate Public Facilities Study for Montgomery County, Maryland"; Snyder, "An Evaluation of Colorado's Attempts to Cope with Rapid Growth."
3. Greenberg, "Growth and Conflict at the Surburban Fringe: The Case of the Livermore-Amador Valley."
4. Montgomery County Planning Board, "First Annual Growth Policy Report: Framework for Action."
5. Montgomery County Planning Board, "Annual Growth Policy for Montgomery County, 2003."
6. Ibid.
7. *Construction Industry Association of Sonoma County v. City of Petaluma,* 375 F. Supp. 574 (1974).
8. *Robinson v. Boulder,* 547 P.2d 228 (Colo. 1976).
9. Snyder, "An Evaluation of Colorado's Attempts to Cope with Rapid Growth," 259.
10. Dubbink, "Cosmopolitan Villages: Growth Management Planning and the Vision of Small Town Society," 129.
11. Hammer Siler George Associates, "Unpublished; Prepared for National Association of Homebuilders; Cited Copy Hand-Labeled 'Draft'." 11.
12. Washington State Growth Strategies Commission, "A Growth Strategy for Washington State," 13.

13. Code of Westminster, Title 11, Chaps 4 and 5.

14. N. H. 1991 New Laws, H.B. No. 434, p. 781.

15. James Duncan and Associates Inc. and Kelly, "Adequate Public Facilities Study for Montgomery County, Maryland."

16. Snyder, "An Evaluation of Colorado's Attempts to Cope with Rapid Growth," 234.

17. Eleanor Breen, Frank Costa, and William S. Hendon, "Annexation: An Economic Analysis: Whether a Small Village or Town Should Annex Adjacent Land Is a Cost/Revenue Problem," *American Journal of Economics and Sociology* 45, no. 2 (1986); Robert W. Burchell and David Listokin, *The Fiscal Impact Handbook: Estimating Local Costs and Revenues of Land Development* (New Brunswick, N.J.: Center for Urban Policy Research, 1978); Coe, "Costs and Benefits of Municipal Annexation"; Gonzalez and Mehay, "Municipal Annexation and Local Monopoly Power"; Mehay, "The Expenditure Effects of Municipal Annexation."

18. Therese E. Lucas, "The Direct Costs of Growth: A Comparison of Changes in Local Government Expenditure in Growth and Non-Growth Counties in Colorado," (Denver, Colo.: Colorado Land Use Commission, 1974).

19. Ibid., 18–27.

20. New Jersey County and Municipal Government Study Commission, "Housing & Suburbs: Fiscal & Social Impact of Multifamily Development," (Trenton, N.J.: County and Municipal Government Study Commission, 1974), 12–13.

21. Real Estate Research Corp., "The Costs of Sprawl: Environmental and Economic Costs of Alternative Residential Development Patterns at the Urban Fringe."

22. Ibid., 90.

23. For one critique on this issue, see Gabriel P. Dekel, "Housing Density: A Neglected Dimension of Fiscal Impact Analysis," *Urban Studies* 32, no. 6 (1995).

24. Real Estate Research Corp., "The Costs of Sprawl: Environmental and Economic Costs of Alternative Residential Development Patterns at the Urban Fringe," 37.

25. Ibid., 21.

26. Alan Altshuler, "Review of *the Costs of Sprawl*," *Journal of the American Planning Association* 43 (1977): 208.

27. Ibid.

28. Thomas Muller, *Fiscal Impacts of Land Development: A Critique of Methods and Review of Issues* (Washington, D.C.: The Urban Institute, 1975), 5.

29. Duane Windsor, "A Critique of *The Costs of Sprawl*," *Journal of the American Planning Association* 45 (1979): 288.

30. James E. Frank, *The Costs of Alternative Development Patterns: A Review of the Literature* (Washington, D.C.: Urban Land Institute, 1989), 39.

31. Ibid., 41–42.

32. Ibid.

33. Ibid., 44.

34. James Duncan and Associates Inc. et al., "The Search for Efficient Urban Growth Patterns: A Study of the Fiscal Impacts of Development in Florida."

35. Ibid., 4.

36. Ibid., 8.

37. Landis, "Do Growth Controls Work? A New Assessment," 30.

38. Ibid., 36.

39. Governor's Commission on Growth in the Chesapeake Bay Region, "Protecting the Future: A Vision for Maryland."

40. Ibid., 78, exh. 19.
41. Ibid., 108, fig. 1.; the differences between the development types are explained briefly near the end of Chapter 7).
42. Burchell and Mukherji, "Conventional Development Versus the Costs of Sprawl."
43. Ibid., 1536.
44. Ibid.
45. Ibid., Table 5, p. 1539.
46. Ibid.,Table 6, p. 1539.
47. Ibid., 1534.
48. Ibid.
49. Cameron Speir and Kurt Stephenson, "Does Sprawl Cost Us All? Isolating the Effects of Housing Patterns on Public Water and Sewer Costs," *Journal of the American Planning Association* 68, no. 1 (2002): 57.
50. Ibid., 60.
51. Dekel, "Housing Density: A Neglected Dimension of Fiscal Impact Analysis."
52. Governor's Commission on Growth in the Chesapeake Bay Region, "Protecting the Future: A Vision for Maryland," 109.
53. Frank, *The Costs of Alternative Development Patterns: A Review of the Literature.*
54. "Tax Lead Time Study: The Colorado Oil Shale Region," (Denver, Colo.: Colorado Department of Natural Resources, 1974), 1–13.
55. See, for example, Robert W. Burchell, "Fiscal Impact Analysis: State of the Art and State of the Practice," in *Financing Growth: Who Benefits? Who Pays? And How Much?*, ed. Susan G. Robinson (Washington, D.C.: Government Finance Research Center, 1990).
56. Kelly, "Comment on Westminster Growth Control Cases"; Westminster, "Growth Management Plan: Phase II Report."
57. "Colorado's Special District Woes," *Public Investment*, June 1991; Michael Mehle, "Districts' Losses Cost Investors," *Rocky Mountain News,* 1991.
58. Mehle, "Districts' Losses Cost Investors."
59. Peiser, "Density and Urban Sprawl."
60. Landis, "Do Growth Controls Work? A New Assessment," 33.
61. On this issue, generally, see Peiser, "Does It Pay to Plan Suburban Growth."

CHAPTER 10

Growth Management and the Diversity of Housing Opportunities

All land use controls affect the cost and availability of housing in some way. A growth management program, as part of the larger system, may mitigate or aggravate the problems that have led a number of study commissions to determine that there is a serious problem in the cost and availability of housing in the United States.[1] It is important to understand how growth management programs relate to this larger regulatory system.

GOVERNMENT REGULATION AND HOUSING COST

Government regulation affects housing costs in many different ways.[2] Most or all of those fall in one of the following seven categories:

- **Quality Improvements.** Government frequently establishes regulations to improve the quality of housing. Smoke detectors, substantial insulation and "egress windows" in bedrooms are all examples of requirements that most communities impose on new housing today but that few communities imposed thirty years ago. These are "quality improvements" in the sense that the consumer who pays more for the house with such a feature also gets something more. Whether all of those quality improvements are things that the consumer needs or wants is a topic that goes far beyond the scope of this chapter.[3]

- **Cost Shifting.** "Make growth pay its own way" is a rallying cry of growth-control advocates in many communities. Today, through impact fees, requirements for land dedication and negotiated deals, communities require developers to pay for improvements that the community at large once financed from general revenues, bonded debt or intergovernmental aid programs. New parks, fire stations and arterial (major) roads fall in this category in many communities today. Economists debate the extent to which these costs are passed on to consumers.[4] If they are passed on, they clearly represent a form of cost shifting from the public sector to the consumer. The consumer who buys a new house today is unlikely to get any better quality access to parks or fire stations than a consumer who bought a comparable house thirty years ago; it just costs more, because of the cost shift.

- **Over-specification.** Sometimes government imposes requirements that are unreasonable. Without entering the endless debate over what is "reasonable," it is useful to note that most building codes prohibited flexible electrical cable and PVC (a plastic plumbing pipe) for a decade or more after they had been thoroughly tested and approved by federal agencies. Both are cost saving because of the ease of installation and reduced labor cost. Most local governments have acknowledged their safety by permitting them in most residential installations today. Thus, they provide easy examples of "over-specification" that increased housing costs for a number of years (see, generally, Seidel 1978, Chap. 5, pp. 71–100). Clearly, there are other examples of unreasonable requirements still on the books in many communities.

- **Regulatory Overhead.** Time is money, or so most business people in the United States think. There is evidence for their position. A developer who suffers project delays from government red tape pays interest on borrowed money or loses interest on capital while the land and other capital investments languish, pending regulatory approval. If approvals take longer than is necessary for a thorough review, the system imposes unnecessary regulatory overhead on development projects.

- **Market Impacts.** The law of supply and demand dictates that prices will rise in the face of steady demand and a restricted supply. Some regulatory systems restrict the land supply, while others restrict the housing supply. Either type of program will affect the cost of housing through market impacts.

- **Stifling Innovation.** It is remarkable that over the last century, during which humankind has witnessed the use of technology to change the way that humans communicate and travel, there has been little if any innovation in housing technology. Over the last century, humans have witnessed the invention of flight and its implementation as a primary method of long-range transportation, the development of radio and the implementation of sophisticated audio and video communication systems over-the-air, and the invention of many labor-saving devices using high technology. Despite a number of proposals for technological innovation,[5] during that time the way that humans construct housing, particularly in the United States, has changed little. Because the homebuilding market in particular and the construction market in general are highly competitive markets that, economists would argue, should be both efficient and innovative, one suspects that the lack of innovation can be traced to other factors. Highly prescriptive building codes look like a good target.

- **Exclusionary Effects.** By "protecting" single-family neighborhoods, many communities limit or preclude the construction of townhouses, apartments and other forms of housing that clearly cost less than single-family detached homes and that provide important housing alternatives for significant numbers of housing consumers.[6]

Many of the issues suggested in the list above go far beyond the scope of this book. Nevertheless, it seems useful to have a conceptual framework against which to review the impacts of growth management programs to housing costs.

How Growth Management Programs Relate to These Categories

Of the seven categories above, three are most pertinent to growth management: regulatory overhead; market impacts; and exclusionary barriers. Quality improvements are typically building code issues, as the examples used above suggest. Some land use controls, such as requirements for street trees or sod in the front yard, may arguably amount to "quality improvements," but those controls are usually separate from growth management programs.

Chapter 4 suggests briefly that increased cost-shifting through the imposition of exactions has paralleled the evolution of growth management in the United States. Those concerned about the impacts of growth are often the ones who seek to "make growth pay its own way" through exactions. However, the issues of cost-shifting and exactions are very separate in the sense that a community can choose to manage growth without shifting development costs, and many communities that shift development costs have not adopted any sort of growth management program. Thus, the complex issues related to cost-shifting and exactions remain for consideration in other works (see sources cited in the first section of Chapter 5).

Over-specification affects both requirements for housing and for public improvements. Many communities require that every street in town be wide enough for their widest fire trucks to turn around, regardless of whether the department will ever need the large trucks on a particular street (has anyone ever seen a hook and ladder truck on a cul-de-sac?), and regardless of whether the truck may have a reverse gear to use in leaving a fire. Thus, although this issue relates to land use controls, like cost-shifting, it is quite separate from the adoption of growth management programs.

Stifling innovation appears to be largely a building-code issue. To the extent that zoning requires single-family detached homes in too many neighborhoods and thus precludes the development of more townhouses and apartments, it may stifle creative design. However, that is not the same as restricting the type of technological innovation that might revolutionize the production of housing.

The rest of this chapter thus addresses the remaining issues and, in particular, the market impacts of some growth management systems.

THE EFFECTS OF REGULATORY OVERHEAD

"'Not in My Back Yard': Removing Barriers to Affordable Housing," prepared by the Advisory Commission on Regulatory Barriers to Affordable Housing, was the 1991 version of a federal study commission on housing costs (see citations to other recent ones in the first paragraph of this chapter). Because Secretary Jack Kemp of the U.S. Department of Housing and Urban Development appointed the Commission, it is often called, and is called here, "the Kemp Commission Report."[7] The report was a conceptual one. Although it provided anecdotal evidence of particular impacts, it made no attempt to quantify the impacts of regulatory barriers on the market. It did list the ways in which regulatory barriers affect the market.

That Commission noted in 1991 that "burdensome and uncoordinated approval and permitting systems" were a significant barrier to affordable housing in many jurisdictions.[8] It cited the problem of multiple and potentially conflicting reviews by separate jurisdictions, a problem addressed 15 years earlier in a report published by the Urban Land Institute.[9] It also addressed the issue of procedural delays. In a sidebar, it gave two anecdotal examples: a housing development on Staten Island, New York, for which it took two developers more than 12 years to get approvals and permits from 28 government agencies; and a project for which a developer, who was clearly once both optimistic and rich, had spent $95 million for "carrying costs and regulatory costs" over a 16-year period of seeking permits, without constructing anything.[10]

There are three excellent, earlier studies of the delay issue. All are somewhat dated, making the numbers of little interest. However, the principles are applicable today, and the Kemp report certainly provided evidence that the problem continued long after these studies were prepared.

A 1978 study by Rice University found that the average processing time for a typical development had increased by 5 months over the previous decade, from 8 months to 13 months.[11] The study determined that the additional 5-month delay cost the individual home buyer a minimum of $560 to $840. That amount was between 1 percent and 1.5 percent of the cost of an average house in Houston then.[12] The principal element in the increase was interest on capital invested in the project, although overhead and inflation each played a role.

A Center for Urban Policy Research study of projects in several states at about the same time reached similar conclusions.[13] The survey of homebuilders included in that study found that the average processing time for a project had increased from five months in 1970 to more than thirteen months in 1975.[14] The authors computed the average carrying cost at $38 per month for a quarter-acre lot, implying a lot cost increase of $404 from the 8-month increase in processing time.[15] Those findings were remarkably consistent with the findings of the Rice study in Houston. It is interesting that the delay costs were somewhat higher in Houston, which long prided itself on its limited regulation and which had yet to adopt zoning, as of mid-1992.

As both the CUPR and Rice studies noted, builders generally try to maintain a consistent ratio between house price and lot cost and consequently are likely to increase the cost price and/or cost of the house placed on a lot by a multiple of four or five times the cost increase in the lot.

On the basis of nine case studies in Colorado, a Bickert, Browne & Coddington team reached similar conclusions in another 1970s study.[16] The team found somewhat shorter processing times there (6 and 7 months were typical), but those also represented significant increases. Those numbers were probably misleading, because it does not appear that the Colorado study team included all steps in the development review process in its calculations. It nevertheless found regulation-induced cost increases of $1,500 to $2,000 per dwelling unit over the 1970–1975 study period. Arvada, the only case-study breaking out delay costs as a separate item, showed delay costs (presumably resulting only from the increased processing time) amounting to about $245 per lot. That was a little more than three-quarters of one percent of the price of a "modest house" used as a benchmark in the study.

Analysis

Delay costs are a major irritant to homebuilders and frequently surface in surveys such as those described above. At less than one percent of the price of a house, delay cost is probably not a significant item in the issue of affordable housing. On an $80,000 house with interest at 9 percent, an increase of one 1 percent, or $800, in the price of a house would increase monthly payments by about $7, if fully financed. If, as some of the studies suggest, builders actually increase the cost and/or price of the house by a multiple of the lot cost, the implication could be a cost increase of $3000 to $4000 and an increase in payments of $30 or so per month, obviously more significant numbers. On the other hand, no one gains from the delay, and it is difficult to justify any cost increase resulting from it.

With quality increases, the consumer presumably gets a better house. With cost-shifting, the local government saves some amount of money as a trade-off to the increased cost imposed on the consumer. In those cases, there are at least two sides to the cost-benefit analysis. There is no economic or other basis for a similar argument regarding delay costs when the delay exceeds the reasonable processing time necessary for a thorough project review.

Do growth management programs result in unnecessary delay? Many of them are administered as additional steps in the development review process, with each additional step adding an incremental period to the review process.[17] It is noteworthy that both Boulder and Petaluma took steps in the mid-1980s to reduce the complexity of their review processes by eliminating the qualitative review of each project and substituting a first-come, first-served system of allocating permits in years when demand exceeds supply.[18]

A community can minimize delay costs by integrating the growth management review with the rest of the development process, so that there is no extra step. The establishment of an urban growth boundary does not imply any changes in the regulatory process and thus should not affect the processing time or costs of development. With an adequate public facilities requirement, it is easy to add the public facilities standards to the various, existing steps of development review, thus eliminating the need for any additional review.

For a growth phasing system or rate-of-growth system, the problem is more difficult. Montgomery County integrates its development phasing review with the first stage of subdivision review, which is procedurally efficient.[19] However, uncertainty is another major concern of developers,[20] who may prefer a system in which they can obtain the "go/no-go" decision on growth phasing before investing in the substantial engineering costs involved in a preliminary subdivision plat. One approach to that is simply to place the coordination of the reviews at the developer's option. Thus, a developer may choose to expedite the process by including the application for a growth management allocation with the first application otherwise required, taking the risk that the denial of one may moot the other. Alternatively, the developer has the choice of reducing the risk by making the first round of applications in two stages.

MARKET IMPACTS OF GROWTH MANAGEMENT PROGRAMS

Clearly, growth management programs have significant potential to affect both the land and housing markets. The Kemp Commission listed "growth controls" at the top of the list of suburban regulatory barriers to affordable housing.[21] The law of supply and demand dictates that, when supply is constrained in the face of constant demand, price will increase. Rate-of-growth programs may constrict housing supply. Phased-growth, adequate public facilities and urban growth boundary programs will affect the supply of developable land over the short-run.

It is important to understand clearly the principles at work before examining some numbers related to them. First, as it is impossible to remind the reader too often, most communities that adopt growth management programs are part of larger metropolitan areas. Thus, a Ramapo, a Livermore or a Petaluma does not control enough of the market for its actions to affect prices of land very significantly, at least in theory. However, these communities were high-growth communities because location, amenities or other factors caused them to attract growth. Those factors may allow such communities to command a premium, even if there is a significant supply of competing land in the area.

A community may adopt a growth management program that does not significantly affect supply, even if the community intended for it to do so. For example, applications for building permits in both Boulder and Petaluma fell far short of the numbers that the two cities were willing to issue during most of the 1980s and the early 1990s. The number of dwelling units built in Petaluma fell far short of the number allowed by the plan (see Figure 10.1). Because of annexations and program exemptions, the rate of increase in the number of dwelling units in Boulder far exceeded the two percent per year permitted by the plan. That number nearly doubled from 21,632 in 1970 to 40,726 in 2000.[22] In Boulder, the actual population growth rate in the 1980s was only one percent per year. See discussion in Chapter 4 and compare Table 4-2 there with Figure 10.2 here. A community might adopt an urban growth boundary that extends out so far from the city that it would have little if any impact on the land market. Under those circumstances, the actions of the cities should not, in principle, have much of an affect on price, because there is no apparent affect on practicable supply.

However, the very existence of the restrictions may create a psychological form of shortage rather like the reactions of consumers several years ago when the rumor of a toilet paper shortage spread through the country. Although the

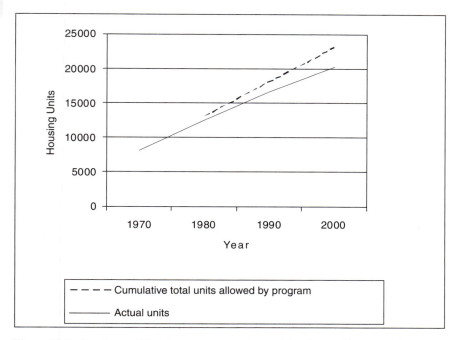

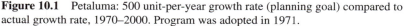

Figure 10.1 Petaluma: 500 unit-per-year growth rate (planning goal) compared to actual growth rate, 1970–2000. Program was adopted in 1971.

Sources: Actual number of units from Bureau of the Census, 2000, *American Fact Finder, Quick Tables,* http://www.census.gov; Bureau of the Census, 1991, *Census of Population and Housing: Summary Population and Housing Characteristics,* Part 6, Table 18; Bureau of the Census, 1982, *Summary Characteristics by Governmental Units and Standard Metropolitan Statistical Areas,* Part 6, Table 2; Bureau of the Census, 1972, *City and County Data Book,* Table B-2; other figures computed by author; graph by author.

facts later demonstrated that there was no shortage, one can easily imagine the short-term reaction of the average consumer. More than a century and a half ago in *Extraordinary Popular Delusions and the Madness of Crowds,* Charles Mackay documented how the psychological effects of apparent scarcities can create wild speculations in markets.[23] The book remains in print and on the assignment lists at business schools. Thus, just as perceived scarcity once created inordinate value for tulip bulbs, the mere perception of a shortage of land (or housing) caused by a growth management program may affect the price of land and housing beyond the market effects that an economist might expect.

An economist would anticipate the greatest effects of growth management programs on land prices to occur in areas in which there is a measurable, relatively short-range limitation placed on the supply of land or housing.[24] In a study using 1970s data from California, Elliott confirmed that hypothesis.[25] He found that growth management programs have a far greater effect on housing prices in

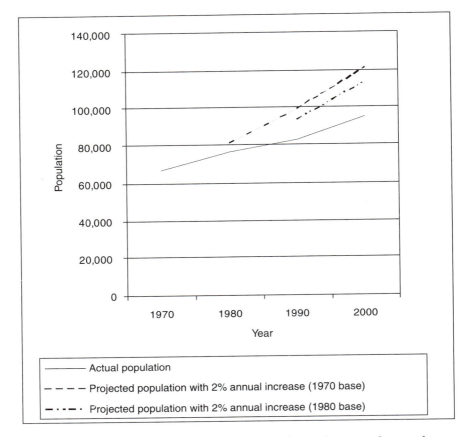

Figure 10.2   Boulder: Two percent growth rate (planning goal) compared to actual growth rate, 1970–2000.

Sources: Actual number of units from Bureau of the Census, 2000, *American Fact Finder, Quick Tables,* http://www.census.gov; Bureau of the Census, 1991, *Census of Population and Housing: Summary Population and Housing Characteristics,* Part 6, Table 18; Bureau of the Census, 1982, *Summary Characteristics by Governmental Units and Standard Metropolitan Statistical Areas,* Part 6, Table 2; Bureau of the Census, 1972, *City and County Data Book,* Table B-2; other figures computed by author; graph by author.

a county in which most communities had adopted relatively stringent growth controls. That is consistent with the findings of two economists (one from Harvard and the other from Wharton) who concluded that "America is not facing a nationwide housing affordability crisis. . . . [but] the bulk of evidence marshaled for this paper suggests that zoning, and other land use controls, are more responsible for higher prices where we see them."[26] That finding is consistent with another contemporary study that found that zoning tends to raise the "value" of residential land.[27]

The effects of a single growth management program in a county were far less significant.[28] Based on a literature review, two Colorado researchers concluded, "[W]here growth control measures are ubiquitous and where controls may grant monopoly power to builders, average housing prices may be as much as 35 to 40 percent higher than similar communities without growth control. In cities located in metropolitan areas where growth controls are largely absent, growth controls may have little or no effect on housing prices, but they increase building activity in surrounding communities. Most growth control communities exist between these two extremes, with typical price effects between 10 and 20 percent."[29]

Similarly, based on a very comprehensive review of the literature, Fischel concluded that, "Land use controls, especially overall growth control programs, are important constraints on the land market. This in turn affects housing values, especially in suburban and exurban communities."[30] In citing Fischel's work, it is important to note that he is an economist who clearly believes that the free market works better than most government regulations. He has been as critical of zoning as he is of growth management programs.[31] Regardless of whether one agrees with Fischel's view of government regulation, his economic analysis is straightforward and generally consistent with that of other researchers in the field.

Economists from the University of California–Davis criticized many of the published studies on the price effects of urban growth management systems in an important 1986 article.[32] Subjects of their criticism included several studies cited here. Their basic argument, however, was not that the studies were wrong. They simply regretted the inability of researchers to conduct a growth management analysis in a laboratory, in which they could constrain the number of variables. To prove their point, they tested the apparent price effects of the growth management system in Davis, California, using some of the methods from the published studies. Their analyses showed significantly different levels of impact on price, depending on the research method, but all confirmed that growth controls increase housing prices. The authors concluded that the careful researcher ought to use multiple methods to test the effects of a particular growth management system.[33]

The Davis research team made a good scientific argument but a poor public policy one. It is rarely possible to have a complete set of data to make a public policy decision, and students in the field typically learn about the necessity of "muddling through."[34] Public officials still must make decisions. When existing studies provide consistent conclusions, as they do on this subject, that is useful information. It is useful for public officials who must make decisions about growth management programs and for others in society who are interested in those decisions. Because of the possible inconsistencies resulting from different methods and different assumptions, it would be risky to rely very heavily on the particular numbers (or percentages) reflected in the studies cited here.

In a generalized study involving thirty metropolitan areas, two other researchers examined the causes of the differences in price increases in land among those metropolitan areas.[35] Over the study period, 1975–1980, price increases for a standard residential lot increased by as little as thirty-one percent in one area and as much as 176 percent, or five times as much, in another. The authors found that a four-factor model explained 80 percent of the differences. An index of regulatory restriction was the only supply factor in the model; the other three factors all affected demand. Not surprisingly, the high-priced, high-increase market was one already cited repeatedly in this book as a growth managing community—San Jose.[36] Also among the communities with the highest rate of increase were Boulder and Portland. The Black and Hoben study is widely cited, probably because it illustrated clearly the fundamental principles of supply and demand as applied to the land market.

Case Studies

In 1977, Gruen Gruen + Associates, a consulting firm well regarded for its work in the economics side of planning, joined with the Urban Land Institute to perform two major case studies of housing cost increases induced by regulations. One of the case studies focused on San Jose, California (its growth management program is described in Chapter 4). San Jose had adopted a three-tiered urban growth boundary in 1970 and later simplified it to two tiers. According to the study, the lines in the tiers were relatively rigid. Demand was relatively inelastic due to the lack of comparable, constraint-free land in other communities in the area.[37]

The study covered the period 1967–1976. The consultants did not have to rely on regression analyses. They had access to primary data, the developers' books. The researchers compared the actual cost and price increases affecting a particular model of house offered over that period. The study found that the sales price of Builder A's homes increased by 80.2 percent over the study period and that the sales price of Builder B's home increased by 121.3 percent over the study period. Of those increases, some were clearly inflationary and unrelated to local policies. However, the study found that 32 percent of Builder A's price increase and 43.4 percent of Builder B's price increase were attributable to "public policy costs," or the impacts of various taxes and regulations. Builder A's land price increased by 29.5 percent, while Builder B's increased by 168.9 percent. It is the story behind those figures that is also the story behind the difference in the overall price increases. In building homes in 1976, Builder A used land acquired in 1972, thus avoiding a significant portion of the cost impact of the urban growth boundary. Builder B clearly felt the brunt of that. Table 10-1 presents selected figures from the study, adjusted to 1976 dollars.

It is interesting to note that Builder B reduced the portion of the price attributable to land cost, presumably by restraining the extent of price increase that otherwise might have been taken.

Using totally different methods, Knaap tested the effects of the Portland urban growth boundary on land price.[38] Knaap analyzed "every 'arms-length' residential land transaction recorded in fiscal year 1980" in a defined portion of the Portland area.[39] Among the fifteen variables included in the regression analysis, besides the critical one related to the urban growth boundary, were variables for zoning, access and location in relation to a sewer line. Knaap tested both the

Table 10-1
Price Effects of Urban Growth Boundary in San Jose, California

	Builder A			Builder B		
Item	1967	1976	Change	1968	1976	Change
Sales price	$42,440	$44,950	+5.9%	$37,874	$49,250	+30.1%
Land cost	$5,432	$4,151	−23.9%	$4,778	$5,973	+58.1%
Land cost as percentage of house price	12.7%	9.3%	N.A.	10.0%	12.1%	N.A.

Source: Research Division. Urban Land Institute and Gruen Gruen & Associates, "Effects of Regulation on Housing Costs: Two Case Studies," in *ULI Research Reports*, ed. Donald E. Priest (Washington, D.C.: Urban Land Institute, 1977), tbls. 5 and 6, pp. 17–18.

effects of the principal urban growth boundary and of the intermediate growth boundary. Although he found inconsistent results in testing the intermediate growth boundary, he found that "land values were approximately 50 percent lower outside the urban growth boundary in Washington County and 60 percent lower outside the urban growth boundary in Clackamas County."[40] Chapter 7 explains the differences between the effects of the two types of boundaries. The state exerts significant control over the urban growth boundary, making it difficult to change. Local governments, through the regional council that governs the growth management program, can change the intermediate growth boundary. Thus, the outer urban growth boundary is a long-term constraint, whereas the intermediate boundary is, at most, a short-term constraint and may amount to little constraint at all.

Landis found that the woes of San Jose builders and home buyers continued well past the date of the Gruen study.[41] He examined growth management programs in Fresno, Sacramento and San Jose, noting some significant differences among the programs and the markets, although he noted that the "growth management systems of San Jose, Fresno and Sacramento County differed not in intent or broad purpose, but in degree, timing and style of implementation."[42] According to Landis, county officials in Sacramento were "flexible" in implementing a growth phasing system and constantly made new land available as it appeared to be needed, at one time providing enough land subject to current development to accommodate an additional 100,000 residents. The focus of the Sacramento system was on the availability of public facilities. Fresno adopted a variable fee system, through which the city held developers financially accountable for decisions to develop in relatively remote locations. San Jose maintained its urban growth boundary program.

Landis also found significant differences among the three housing markets. He characterized Sacramento as a "competitive market" in economic terms, in which there were few if any barriers to entry by new players. He found San Jose to be a "contestable" market, in which new players can enter the market, subject to paying significant entry costs. Among the entry costs cited by Landis are high land costs and substantial impact and other public fees imposed on development. He cited Fresno as a "noncontestable" or "closed market," resulting primarily from a dual land market in which existing players controlled most of the land at the urban fringe that could most easily be developed under the local growth management system. Landis then compared developer costs, profits and housing prices in the three markets, using 1980 figures.[43] Table 10-2 presents part of his findings.

Although Landis did not have access to the builders' books, as Gruen, Gruen + Associates did for their study, he interviewed a number of builders in each of the communities and thus appeared to have a solid basis for his comparison. It is important to understand that he made no attempt to compare the types of units in the three markets nor to compare other factors that influenced the market. Thus, the $129,000 mean price in San Jose may (or may not) buy a substantially different home than $83,000 in Sacramento. However, the significant difference in mean prices is clearly attributable to more than coincidence. The fact that the combination of land cost, profit and overhead ranges from 28 percent in Sacramento

Table 10-2
Housing Prices, Land Costs, and Builder Profits in Three California Communities

Item	Fresno	Sacramento	San Jose
Mean 1980 sales price, single-family unit	$99,300	$83,000	$129,000
Development and building costs	$66,100	$56,800	$80,150
Profit and overhead	$28,200	$14,700	$29,850
Raw land cost	$5,000	$8,500	$20,000
Profit and overhead as percentage of mean house price	28.4	17.8	23.1
Land cost as percentage of mean house price	5.0	10.2	15.5

Source: John D. Landis, "Land Regulation and the Price of New Housing," *Journal of the American Planning Association* 52 (1986): tbl. 4, p. 19; percentages in fifth and sixty rows of this table developed by author from data in the original.

(the competitive market) to 38.6 percent in San Jose tells part of the story. Note that the low land cost and high profit in Fresno compared to the high land cost and lower profit in San Jose are direct functions of one another. The long-time developers in Fresno profit handsomely from their low-cost, long-held land, while developers in San Jose must dip into future profits to pay one of the market's "entry costs," high land acquisition costs. Developers in both markets, however, profit substantially more than those in the highly competitive Sacramento market.

Gleeson tested the effects of a different type of growth management program on land prices in and around a Minneapolis suburb.[44] The Brooklyn Park program examined by Gleeson combined an adequate public facilities requirement with a public policy decision not to extend public services into agricultural areas. Knaap criticized Gleeson's study as a study of the price differences of urban and nonurban land.[45] The criticism was valid, but that in no way detracts from the value of Gleeson's study. Using a very practical system of planning, Brooklyn Park determined what land should be urban and then made it that way. It did so through a combination of planned infrastructure investment in some areas and significant development restrictions in others. Thus, rather than establishing an arbitrary urban growth boundary, it reinforced and guided normal market forces with public investment and regulation. Gleeson's findings were interesting, but hardly surprising. He found significant differences between the prices of farmland that was not currently developable under Brooklyn Park policies and urban land that was developable. He then disaggregated the factors in his analysis and assigned a dollar value to various factors, including: access, availability of storm sewer, availability of trunk water line and lateral (local) water line, and availability of sanitary sewer trunk and lateral lines.[46] Predictably, each of those items contributed a portion of the land value; some were, of course, negative factors. Because trunk water and sewer lines were generally available in the developable area, they did not influence land values within the urban area; however, the availability of those trunk lines did affect the values of land in farm areas. Studies cited earlier in this book indicate that the factors tested by Gleeson generally affect land developability and thus land values (see discussion in Chapter 5).

There was also some residual difference in values between land in the urban area and the farm area in Gleeson's study. That difference could not be explained by anything except the general categorization of urban or rural. That categorization amounted to a type of urban growth boundary.[47] That residual difference is somewhat surprising, because Brooklyn Park appears to be too small to have a significant impact on the housing market of the Twin Cities region.[48] Without comparing Gleeson's findings to land values for the entire region, it is impossible to know why the program in Brooklyn Park appears to have had that effect.

A team of economists from the University of California–Davis compared Petaluma to nearby Santa Rosa to determine the "effect of growth control on the price of moderate-priced housing."[49] Table 10-3 presents some of their findings.

The original authors interpreted the data summarized in Table 10-3 as follows. "These data provide strong evidence of the shift in Petaluma's housing away

Table 10-3
Percentage of Houses by Price Range, Petaluma and Santa Rosa, California

	Petaluma		Santa Rosa	
Sale Price	1970	1976	1970	1976
Less than $25,000	9.1	0.0	26.2	10.7
$25,001–$35,000	90.8	74.7	52.3	63.4
More than $35,000	0.1	25.3	21.5	25.9

Source: Seymour I. Schwartz, David E. Hansen, and Richard Green, "The Effect of Growth Control on the Production of Moderate-Priced Housing," *Land Economics* 60 (1984): tbl. 1, p. 112.

from the low end of the market after growth control. The data for floor area document the disappearance of the small house from Petaluma."[50] The authors attributed the elimination of the small house to the competitive aspects of the growth management program (that aspect of the program was later abandoned; see history in Chapter 3) and to the governing body's public statements that it wanted "high quality" projects.[51] To keep their data in perspective, however, it is important to note that Petaluma had less low-priced housing even before it adopted its growth management program (see Table 10-3). Whether growth management was thus a symptom of other factors tending to make development and housing both more expensive in the community, or whether it was the cause of some of the later price increases is not clear. The correlation is clear, but, as with any correlation, that does not explain the cause. The alternative scenario, that the adoption of growth management is more a symptom than a cause, is analogous to Landis' suggestion that the relatively healthy fiscal condition of growth managing communities might be explained by the fact that they are better governed communities rather than by the fiscal impacts of growth management.[52]

Paul Niebanck, a long-time advocate for affordable housing, used a different method to compare housing prices in Santa Cruz County, which has had growth controls, to those in nearby jurisdictions that did not. Niebanck compared sales of specific houses in Santa Cruz County with sales of comparable houses in the other jurisdictions. He concluded, "It is safe to say that, after 10 years of growth control, the prices of owner-occupied houses, across the board, are at least 10 percent higher than they would have been in the absence of controls."[53]

In a study quite different from his 1986 one, Landis provided a conceptual context in which to consider the effects of growth controls in California communities in particular. In a working paper entitled *Do Growth Controls Work?* he compared the rate of increase in median house prices in selected pairs of communities; each pair included one community that managed growth and one or more that did not.[54] He found that "median single-family home prices did not rise any faster or to higher levels in the seven case-study communities than in their counterpart pro-growth cities."[55] He acknowledged that there may be a number of reasons why these results seem to contradict the law of supply and demand. Among explanations that he suggested were, "the controls, as implemented, may not really be all that effective. Second, there may be adequate spill-over opportunities in other nearby communities, so that growth displaced from one city can easily and cost-lessly be accommodated in nearby or adjacent communities. . . . [T]he price effects of localized growth controls may be quite small in relation to other, region-wide forces which are acting to raise or depress housing prices."[56] He also noted that there may be other forms of growth limits in the control communities. Landis did not acknowledge the problems inherent in using median home sale prices. Such a comparison, used in several of the studies because the figures are usually readily available, compares the sales of whatever houses happen to sell in particular communities at particular times. Whether those homes are at the high-end, at the low-end or in fact representative of the middle of the market depends on many factors that such a comparison does not reflect.

However, the next section of the same report provided a better explanation of his results. He projected housing need for selected metropolitan counties in California, using 1980 as a base. His apparent intent was to compare counties in which there were strong growth controls with those in which there were not. What he found was that, "Throughout California, but especially in the state's coastal markets, housing supply failed to keep pace with housing demand. . . . [T]he problem of insufficient housing production was (and still is) systemic throughout California, and not limited to cities and counties that have enacted formal growth controls."[57] Independently and without reference to any of Landis' work, Fischel took this argument one step further. He argued that "the disparity between the growth of California's housing values in the 1970s and that of housing values in the rest of the United States was caused by growth controls."[58]

Fischel identified California's coastal zone program and stringent environmental regulations as being among its state regulatory programs that have exclusionary effects Fischel argued in depth and Landis essentially implied that California has adopted a statewide package of growth-limiting land use and environmental regulations. Thus, comparisons of communities within California probably understate the nature of the problem. In the later study, Landis concluded that, "Compared to such regional shortfalls, the growth-limiting effects of local growth-controls programs are but a drop in the bucket. These findings should not be viewed as an exoneration of local growth-control programs, however. To the extent that such programs contribute to regional housing shortfalls, they directly contribute to rising housing prices and declining affordability."[59]

Two researchers conducted an interesting study in Montgomery County, Maryland. They compared changes in housing prices among different planning areas of the county, based on the relative restrictiveness of each area.[60] The Montgomery County system is relatively rare in providing different sets of controls in different planning areas and thus may be one of few for which such a study could be conducted. Although the researchers used aggregate market data, they created a housing index and then tested their model for a "standard-quality house" rather than for mean or median house prices. Using those methods, they, as all the other studies cited here, found a strong correlation between restrictive land-use controls and increases in housing prices.[61]

Another researcher examined the effect of the Pinelands growth management program on land and housing prices in South Jersey. He found a substantial increase in the prices of houses within the protected areas of the Pinelands, probably reflecting amenity value.[62] He also found increases in land prices, including those lands that are most restricted under the New Jersey program. He speculated that over the long run, some of those values may drop. However, the conclusions regarding the housing prices unequivocally showed the costs of restrictive growth control in the market.

A 1991 study of the implementation of a housing choice policy in conjunction with Portland's urban growth boundary concluded that, "the Portland region's 'pro-housing' policies have helped to manage regional growth while promoting affordable housing."[63] However, the conclusion was based on a significant increase in the proportion of multi-family units in the new housing stock and an increase in the number of single-family homes on small lots.[64] The study's findings may have some meaning for housing costs if the single-family homes built on the smaller lots are comparable in size and quality to those formerly built on larger lots and if the homes on the smaller lots are in fact less expensive. If builders have simply built smaller houses on smaller lots, what the Portland program has done is to shift the housing supply. The Portland study indicated that the homes on the smaller lots (5,000–7,001 square feet) were about twelve percent cheaper than homes on medium lots (7,001–9,000 square feet) and about half the price of homes on large lots (9,001-plus square feet).[65] However, the authors acknowledged that the price differences reflect changes in the home cost by builders to maintain a house price-to-lot cost ratio of 4:1 or more. The house on the smaller lot is cheaper, but it is probably smaller (some of the homes on 5,000 square foot lots are undoubtedly townhouses) and may be of lesser quality. Thus, the increase in the number of cheaper homes on smaller lots, like the increase in the proportion of apartments, illustrates a regulatory shift in the supply side of the market, not a real reduction in the cost of delivering a particular housing product.

The Costs of Sprawl illustrated clearly how a community could reduce average housing costs by shifting from a mix of single-family homes in unplanned development patterns to a high-density mix including a large number of apartments and townhouses (development types are described above). However, such a regulatory shift in the housing supply with no adjustment in demand may simply lead to further increases in prices of the most desirable types of housing and to higher levels of frustration in the market among those who do not obtain their preferred form of housing. Thus, the Portland study leads logically to the next section of this chapter, which discusses how growth management affects housing opportunities and choices.

Analysis

Any growth management program that significantly restricts the supply of housing or the supply of land on which developers can build housing is likely to affect the price of housing in the community. A rate-of-growth system that establishes a rate below market demand most clearly illustrates such a system. An urban growth boundary that reserves too little land for urban development may have that effect. A phased-growth system that restricts land supply below market demand may have a similar effect.

An adequate public facilities program, in contrast, appears simply to limit the ability of a developer or outlying landowner to profit from leapfrog development. Studies cited in Chapter 5 that showed significant land price differences for land located near public facilities, as well as the Gleeson study and others cited in this chapter, illustrate that builders will pay more for land with services than for land without them. In Gleeson's study, which involved an adequate public facilities requirement, the value differences were substantial. Only if a community quits expanding its critical infrastructure systems will an adequate public facilities requirement unduly constrain the land market.

GROWTH MANAGEMENT AND DIVERSITY OF HOUSING OPPORTUNITIES

The problem of exclusion is in part a matter of economics. Given enough money, most families could overcome the most exclusionary of local land use control systems. However, some systems simply limit the total number of housing opportunities or the type of opportunities available in a particular community. Although the market will allocate the available units among competing users, there may simply not be enough units to satisfy the reasonable demand, and the allocation may or may not be consistent with public policy goals.

There appear to be two, quite different, exclusionary trends occurring in growth management communities. The effect of growth management in some communities appears to be the elimination of the lower end of the housing market, with continued vitality of the single-family home on a larger lot. In others, it is the single-family home on a large lot that the community is driving away. These alternative scenarios have very different demographic and public policy implications.

In Petaluma[66] and Davis, growth management appears to have erased the low-end of the housing market. As shown in Table 10-3, Petaluma housing costs increased significantly more than those in Santa Rosa, a nearby and somewhat comparable community. Economists who found the difference attributed much of it to the elimination of lower cost houses.[67] The earlier-cited University of California–Davis study of that community found that not only the price but the quality of older housing in the community increased after the adoption of growth controls.[68] Fischel interpreted data from the study as showing that "older housing in Davis was filtering up rather than down."[69] The cost increases in other communities, discussed in the previous section of this chapter, would suggest comparable results. A thorough literature review in 1987 found similar results from a number of studies.[70] They concluded that, while growth management efforts "may have helped maintain the desired community character, housing prices have increased and in many cases the availability of low- or moderate-priced housing has declined substantially or even disappeared."[71]

Where the effect of a growth management program is to preserve opportunities for single-family homes on large lots while precluding or limiting the construction of apartments, townhouses and other affordable alternatives, that growth management program is similar in its effect to various schemes of exclusionary zoning. Courts in New Jersey, Pennsylvania, Virginia, New Hampshire and elsewhere have struck down exclusionary zoning schemes under which very large lot sizes, prohibitions on apartments, excess improvement requirements and undue development delays, among other techniques, limited the availability of housing for the lower end of the market.[72] Regardless of the good intentions behind a growth management program, its effects may run up against bans on exclusionary zoning. Part of the New Jersey remedy is the requirement that each community absorb a "fair share" of the region's growth.[73] As figures discussed below show, a major effect of some growth management programs, at least over the short-run, has been to reduce the share of the region's growth that the growth managing city accommodates. That is also typically the apparent intention of rate-of-growth programs and some growth-phasing and urban growth boundary programs.

The Portland study illustrated a very different trend. Of new housing units approved from 1985 through 1989, 54 percent were multi-family and only 46 percent single-family.[74] That was a radical shift in the housing supply in a metropolitan region in which 66.4 percent of the 489,470 housing units counted in the 1990 census were single-family units.[75] Only 13,036 of the single-family units, or 2.7 percent of the total, were attached (townhouse) units. Even in Portland itself, more than 64 percent of the housing units were single-family, of which only 1.8 percent were attached units, meaning that more than 62 percent of the city's housing stock consisted of single-family detached units. By 2000, the share of dwelling units in Portland that were single-family had dropped to 60.4 percent.[76]

The changes in housing mix significantly assisted Portland in meeting its housing goal, because the study found that 77 percent of households could afford a two-bedroom apartment, while only 25 percent could afford to purchase a new home on a small lot with a 5 percent down payment. The percentage who could afford to purchase increased to 31 percent with an increase in down payment to 20 percent of the price; the increased down payment reduces the monthly payments, thus increasing the portion who can "afford" the units with the increased down payment, based on ordinary income-ratio lending criteria. As a practical matter, down payments are often more difficult for families to find than slight increases in monthly payments, so that aspect of the study is questionable.

Boulder, which also has adopted goals to improve the availability of affordable housing, has also changed its housing mix over the last decade, as Table 10-4

Table 10-4
Boulder Housing Mix, 1970–2000 (in Percentages)

Unit Type	1970	1980	1990	2000
Single-family detached	58.1	50.8	41.7	43.8
Townhouse			6.8	6.3
Mobile home		2.4	3.2	3.6
Duplex, triplex, fourplex	12.1	10.7	10.1	9.7
Multi-family, 5 or more units	29.9	36.0	38.2	36.5

Sources: Raw data from Bureau of the Census, 2000, *American Fact Finder, Quick Tables*, www.census.gov; Bureau of the Census, 1991, *Census of Population and Housing: Summary Population and Housing Characteristics*, Part 7, Table 8; Bureau of the Census, 1983, *Census of Population and Housing, Census Tracts, No. 138, Denver-Boulder Standard Metropolitan Statistical Area*, Table H-7; Bureau of the Census, 1972, *Census of Population and Housing, Census Tracts, Denver, Colorado, Standard Metropolitan Statistical Area*, Table H-2; percentages computed by author.

shows. Another researcher documented an earlier change in the mix, but not the resulting demographic change shown in the table.[77]

Anthony Downs has argued that exclusion of multi-family housing through restrictive zoning is one of the most serious obstacles to development of affordable housing in this country.[78] A program such as that in Portland responds directly to that criticism. If the effect of the change is to provide increased housing opportunities for those who otherwise might lack them, an action for which Downs argued in *Opening Up the Suburbs*, clearly the region will benefit.[79] If the effect of the change is to force families accustomed to (or hoping to become accustomed to) living in single-family homes into apartments, the benefits are less clear and the social costs are significant.

The Costs of Sprawl illustrated how a community could reduce housing costs, energy costs and municipal costs by encouraging more compact forms of development, containing smaller dwelling units.[80] Much of the criticism of the report has centered on the apparently unrealistic assumption that the same people who would otherwise live in single-family detached units would live in the high-rise, high-density model that optimized benefits in that early 1970s study (critiques are discussed in Chapter 9). As the following discussion of the effects of the Boulder program shows, implementing such a program in a single community in a larger region may simply force people to live in other communities. However, where a state or regional entity implements a region-wide program that significantly changes the housing mix, as in Portland, there seems to be nowhere else for people to go. Thus, if the region maintains the program over the long run, area residents will presumably have to adjust their housing desires to what the market will supply.

How this shift in the housing supply will affect the Portland region and its residents over the long run is not clear. The effects of the shift in Boulder are much more clear. A 1992 City of Boulder newsletter entitled *Research Perspectives,* carried this headline, "Growth masks out-migration of young families; in-migration of established families."[81] The city's analysis of census and other data shows substantial net out-migration for age cohorts 0–4, 5–9, 17–24, 45–54, and 55–64. There was a small out-migration for the 65–74 age group and substantial in-migration among senior citizens (75–84, 85+) and college-age students (17–24). The Boulder location of the main campus of the University of Colorado explains the latter figure. The only other young age group that showed net in-migration was the 10–16 age group. In contrast, Boulder County outside the city showed net in-migration in all age groups except 17–24, which had substantial out-migration, and 55–64, which showed out-migration of one percent.[82] One commentator, writing in the mid-1980s, commented cheerfully that "the construction and sale of less expensive attached houses in Boulder . . . mitigated the effect of the price increase of detached homes on the housing market overall,"[83] although he tempered his enthusiasm for his own findings somewhat in this comment. "Of course, while Boulder homebuyers paid less, they also received less."[84]

Boulder's own research report explained some of the trends, "[T]he profile of net out-migration among younger children and net in-migration among older children may be explained by families with young children leaving the city to find more affordable housing in the rest of the county. . . . As parents age and earn more, because both parents can work more easily when their children are older and because older parents tend to earn more than younger parents, they can better afford housing in the city of Boulder." That is probably a correct demographic analysis, but it ignores the impact of the legislated shift in the housing market.

A discussion at a governing body meeting in Boulder in early 1992 illustrated the issue better, and in very human terms:

Boulder City Councilman Bob Greenlee says his daughter and her husband can't afford to live in Boulder; they are trying to buy a house in Louisville. Representatives of the Fire and Police Departments said it's hard for their employees to feel committed to their work, because their homes are elsewhere. . . .

But Deputy Mayor Matthew Applebaum responded, there are lots of townhouses and condominiums and apartments available in the city. They *choose* to go to Louisville or Lafayette or Broomfield and live in a house with a garage and a big yard. I like living in a house myself; it would be hard to go back to an apartment, but there is a choice."[85]

The exchange was reminiscent of the title of an early critique of the Ramapo program, *Controlling Urban Growth—But for Whom?*[86] Other census data, not used by the city in its own analysis, confirms the trend of families moving away from Boulder and into surrounding communities.

As Tables 10-5 and 10-6 clearly show, household size has shrunk more rapidly in Boulder than in the rest of Boulder County and much of that shrinkage can be

Table 10-5
Persons per Household, Boulder and Surrounding Communities, 1970–2000

Place	1970	1980	1990	2000
Boulder	2.84	2.40	2.18	2.20
Lafayette	3.03	2.62	2.69	2.62
Longmont	3.04	2.75	2.61	2.64
Louisville	2.99	2.59	2.68	2.61
Boulder County	3.04	2.63	2.45	2.47
Colorado	3.08	2.65	2.51	2.53

Sources: Raw data from Bureau of the Census, 2000, *American Fact Finder, Quick Tables*, www. census.gov; Bureau of the Census, 1991, *Census of Population and Housing: Summary Population and Housing Characteristics*, Part 6, Table 18; Bureau of the Census, 1982, *Summary Characteristics by Governmental Units and Standard Metropolitan Statistical Areas*, Part 6, Table 2; Bureau of the Census, 1972, *City and County Data Book*, Table B-2; Bureau of the Census, 1972, *Census of Population, Vol. 1, Characteristics of the Population*, Part 7, Table 14, 16 (state) and 32 (Louisville only); percentage computations for some years by author.

Table 10-6
Percentage of Population under 18, Boulder and Surrounding Communities, 1970–2000

Place	1970	1980	1990	2000
Boulder	27.5	17.4	15.1	14.8
Lafayette	36.0	28.2	31.6	27.5
Longmont	37.3	30.7	28.5	27.9
Louisville	34.1	26.6	30.7	28.7
Boulder County	23.4	24.9	23.0	22.9
Colorado	35.2	28.0	26.1	25.6

Sources: Raw data from Bureau of the Census, 2000, *American Fact Finder, Quick Tables*, www. census.gov; Bureau of the Census, 1991, *Census of Population and Housing: Summary Population and Housing Characteristics*, Part 6, Table 18; Bureau of the Census, 1982, *Summary Characteristics by Governmental Units and Standard Metropolitan Statistical Areas*, Part 6, Table 2; Bureau of the Census, 1972, *City and County Data Book*, Table B-2; Bureau of the Census, 1972, *Census of Population, Vol. 1, Characteristics of the Population*, Part 7, Table 14, 16 (state) and 32 (Louisville only); percentage computations for some years by author.

Table 10-7
Percentage of Population under 18, Petaluma and Area, 1970–2000

Place	1970	1980	1990	2000
Petaluma	37.6	29.3	25.8	26.2
Santa Rosa	30.2	24.8	23.8	24.3
Sonoma County	33.2	30.4	24.7	24.5
California	33.4	27.0	26.1	28.3

Sources: Raw data from Bureau of the Census, 2000, *American Fact Finder, Quick Tables,* www.census.gov; Bureau of the Census, 1991, *Census of Population and Housing: Summary Population and Housing Characteristics,* Part 6, Table 18; Bureau of the Census, 1982, *Summary Characteristics by Governmental Units and Standard Metropolitan Statistical Areas,* Part 6, Table 2; Bureau of the Census, 1972, *City and County Data Book,* Table B-2; Bureau of the Census, 1972, *Census of Population, Vol. 1, Characteristics of the Population,* Part 7, Table 14, 16 (state) and 32 (Louisville only); percentage computations for some years by author.

traced to the reduction in the number of families with children. It is all arguably attributable to the shift in the housing market achieved by Boulder. Those demographic changes are entirely consistent with the city's own analysis, quoted above, and with the anecdotal exchange at the Boulder council meeting.

Not all growth management programs appear to have had such a significant effect on housing opportunities for families. As Tables 10-7 and 10-8 show, the

Table 10-8
Percentage of Population under 18, Livermore and Alameda County, 1970–2000

Place	1970	1980	1990	2000
Livermore	41.2	33.0	27.2	28.1
Alameda County	31.2	25.1	23.7	24.6
California	33.4	27.0	26.1	28.3

Sources: Raw data from Bureau of the Census, 2000, *American Fact Finder, Quick Tables,* www.census.gov; Bureau of the Census, 1991, *Census of Population and Housing: Summary Population and Housing Characteristics,* Part 6, Table 18; Bureau of the Census, 1982, *Summary Characteristics by Governmental Units and Standard Metropolitan Statistical Areas,* Part 6, Table 2; Bureau of the Census, 1972, City and County Data Book, Table B-2; Bureau of the Census, 1972, *Census of Population, Vol. 1, Characteristics of the Population,* Part 7, Table 14, 16 (state); percentage computations for some years by author.

percentage of persons under 18 years of age in Petaluma and Livermore fell much more quickly than the county figures after the initial adoption of the growth management programs in those communities. Unlike Boulder, however, both communities have stayed above the county means in the percentage of persons under the age of 18, suggesting that they remain significant factors in the family home market.

Analysis and Conclusion

The same types of programs that affect housing cost are, by definition, likely to limit the opportunities for affordable housing in the community. However, the effects of growth management systems in different communities show two different types of exclusion. Some programs, such as the one in Petaluma, tend to reinforce patterns of exclusionary zoning, protecting opportunities for single-family homes on larger lots but increasing overall cost in the housing market, thus adversely affecting those seeking more affordable housing. In contrast, the Boulder program appears to have made the traditional single-family home for a family with children under 18 years of age relatively scarce in the community, a scarcity reflected in significantly reduced household size and significant reductions in the percentage of the population under 18. The regional program in Portland expressly attempts to reduce the portion of the market consisting of single-family detached homes and to increase the portion of multi-family units. The two programs have quite different social implications.

CONCLUSION

Many growth management programs have affected both housing costs and housing opportunities. While the costs related to unnecessary delay are relatively small and also relatively easy to limit or to eliminate, the other impacts are more complex. Programs that constrain the housing or land market clearly increase housing costs and change the mix of housing opportunities available in the community.

Dowall suggested a complex scheme of managing the land market as a cure. Under his proposal, local planners would ensure that, as growth controls limited opportunities in one sub-market in the community, other public actions would open comparable opportunities in other sub-markets.[87] He used a hypothetical community with a demand for 600 housing units over the next year to explain his model. One defect with the model was that he proposed that the community guarantee a surplus of only 100 units above projected demand. That was essentially a 14-month market. With the wild vagaries of the real estate market in many communities, that entire supply could be consumed in a few short months. One relevant example comes from Westminster, which issued more building permits the first quarter of 1977 than it had issued in the entire previous year.[88] Even if the supply were adequate to last for a year, the relative scarcity of the immediately developable lots would surely result in an immediate windfall to the owners of those properties and a probable increase in resulting housing prices.[89] The Portland approach, in which the urban growth boundary contained an initial 20-year supply of developable land, seems more rational. Nevertheless, there is merit to Dowall's monitoring system. Regardless of the actual total supply, it is worth ensuring that reductions in one area are offset by increases in other areas.

In concluding this chapter, it is important to remember that any growth management program can increase delay costs of housing by adding more steps to the process, but that only some types of programs tend to increase costs by constricting land or housing supply. A simpler approach than Dowall's land-monitoring system seems to be to minimize the use of those techniques that have the greatest impact on the market. The next chapter addresses that subject in more depth and in a broader context.

NOTES

1. See generally, Advisory Commission on Regulatory Barriers to Affordable Housing, "'Not in My Backyard': Removing Barriers to Affordable Housing"; Council on Development Choices for the 80s, "Interim Report," Evelina T. Loke, ed., *Homeownership: The American Dream Adrift* (Chicago, Ill.: U.S. League of Savings Associations, 1982), Task Force on Housing Costs, "Final Report," (Washington, D.C.: U.S. Department of Housing and Urban Development, 1978).

2. Advisory Commission on Regulatory Barriers to Affordable Housing, "'Not in My Backyard': Removing Barriers to Affordable Housing." See also other references cited throughout this chapter.

3. But see Anthony Downs, "The Advisory Commission on Regulatory Barriers to Affordable Housing: Its Behavior and Accomplishments," *Housing Policy Debate* 2 (1991): 1107–14.

4. See, for example, Paul B. Downing and Thomas S. McCaleb, "The Economics of Development Exactions," in *Development Exactions*, eds. James E. Frank and Robert M. Rhodes (Chicago, Ill.: Planners Press, 1987); Larry D. Singell and Jane H. Lillydahl, "An Empirical Examination of the Effect of Impact Fees on the Housing Market," *Land Economics* 66 (1990).

5. For some interesting examples, see H. Ward Jandl, John A. Burns, and Michael Auer, *Yesterday's Houses of Tomorrow: Innovative American Homes, 1850 to 1950* (Washington, D.C.: Preservation Press, 1991).

6. Richard F. Babcock, Fred P. Bosselman, and American Society of Planning Officials, *Exclusionary Zoning: Land Use Regulation and Housing in the 1970s* (New York: Praeger, 1973); Richard P. Fishman, *Housing for All Under Law: New Directions in Housing, Land Use and Planning Law: A Report of the American Bar Association Advisory Commission on Housing and Urban Growth* (Cambridge, Mass.: Ballinger Publishing Company, 1978).

7. Advisory Commission on Regulatory Barriers to Affordable Housing, "'Not in My Backyard': Removing Barriers to Affordable Housing."

8. Ibid., 2–12.

9. Bosselman, Feurer, and Siemon, *The Permit Explosion: Coordination of the Proliferation.*

10. Advisory Commission on Regulatory Barriers to Affordable Housing, "'Not in My Backyard': Removing Barriers to Affordable Housing," 2–13.
11. Rice Center for Community Design & Research, "Technical Report: The Delay Costs of Government Regulation in the Houston Housing Market" (Houston, Tex.: Rice University, 1978).
12. Ibid., 97.
13. Stephen R. Seidel and Rutgers University Center for Urban Policy Research, *Housing Costs & Government Regulations: Confronting the Regulatory Maze* (New Brunswick, N.J.: Center for Urban Policy Research, 1978).
14. Ibid.
15. Ibid., 321.
16. James R. Lincoln, Jr., Dean C. Coddington, and John R. Penberthy, "An Analysis of the Impact of State and Local Government Intervention on the Home Building Process in Colorado," (Denver, Colo.: Bickert, Browne, Coddington & Associates, Inc., 1976).
17. James Duncan and Associates Inc. and Kelly, "Adequate Public Facilities Study for Montgomery County, Maryland."
18. Gawf, Petaluma, "Residential Growth Management System User's Guide." The issue is discussed in James Duncan and Associates Inc. and Kelly, "Adequate Public Facilities Study for Montgomery County, Maryland," 27, 39.
19. Section 50-35, Montgomery County Code (1991).
20. Advisory Commission on Regulatory Barriers to Affordable Housing, "'Not in My Backyard': Removing Barriers to Affordable Housing."
21. Ibid., ch. 2, 1–4.
22. United States Bureau of the Census, *Quick Tables* ([cited).
23. Charles Mackay, *Extraordinary Popular Delusions and the Madness of Crowds* (Boston, Mass.: L.C. Page, 1956).
24. Edward L. Glaeser and Joseph Gyourko, "Affordable Housing and the Housing Market: The Impact of Building Restrictions on Housing Affordability," *Federal Reserve Board of New York Economic Policy Review* (2003).
25. Michael Elliott, "The Impact of Growth Control Regulations on Housing Prices in California," *Journal of the American Real Estate and Urban Economics Association* 9 (1981).
26. Glaeser and Gyourko, "Affordable Housing and the Housing Market: The Impact of Building Restrictions on Housing Affordability," 35. The author's conclusion that there is not a housing affordability "crisis" somewhat exceeds their brief; it is an implicit but clear assumption in their study that, if housing prices are close to or below the costs of construction, then housing is affordable; that, of course, ignores the question of whether most or all families can afford housing that is newly constructed.
27. Jeremy R. Groves and Eric Helland, "Zoning and the Distribution of Location Rents: An Empirical Analysis of Harris County, Texas," *Land Economics* 78, no. 1 (2002).
28. Elliott, "The Impact of Growth Control Regulations on Housing Prices in California."
29. Singell and Lillydahl, "An Empirical Examination of the Effect of Impact Fees on the Housing Market."
30. Fischel, *Do Growth Controls Matter? A Review of Empirical Evidence on the Effectiveness and Efficiency of Local Government Land Use Regulation*, 53.
31. William A. Fischel, *The Economics of Zoning Laws: A Property Rights Approach to American Land Use Controls* (Baltimore, Md.: John Hopkins University Press, 1985).

32. Seymour I. Schwartz, David E. Hansen, and Richard Green, "The Effect of Growth Control on the Production of Moderate-Priced Housing," *Land Economics* 60 (1984).
33. Ibid., 232–33.
34. David Braybrooke and Charles Edward Lindblom, *A Strategy of Decision: Policy Evaluation as a Social Process* (New York: Free Press of Glencoe, 1963).
35. J. Thomas Black and James E. Hoben, "Land Price Inflation and Affordable Housing," *Urban Geography* 5 (1985).
36. Ibid., 30–31.
37. Research Division. Urban Land Institute and Gruen Gruen & Associates, "Effects of Regulation on Housing Costs: Two Case Studies," in *ULI Research Reports*, ed. Donald E. Priest (Washington, D.C.: Urban Land Institute, 1977).
38. Knaap, "The Price Effects of an Urban Growth Boundary: A Test for the Effects of Timing"; Knaap, "The Price Effects of Urban Growth Boundaries in Metropolitan Portland, Oregon."
39. Knaap, "The Price Effects of an Urban Growth Boundary: A Test for the Effects of Timing," 20.
40. Ibid., 44.
41. John D. Landis, "Land Regulation and the Price of New Housing," *Journal of the American Planning Association* 52 (1986).
42. Ibid., 130.
43. Ibid., 16–18.
44. Gleeson, "Effects of an Urban Growth Management System on Land Values."
45. Knaap, "The Price Effects of an Urban Growth Boundary: A Test for the Effects of Timing."
46. Gleeson, "Effects of an Urban Growth Management System on Land Values," 359, tbl. 3.
47. Ibid., 359–60.
48. Knaap, "The Price Effects of an Urban Growth Boundary: A Test for the Effects of Timing."
49. Schwartz, Hansen, and Green, "The Effect of Growth Control on the Production of Moderate-Priced Housing."
50. Ibid., 112.
51. Ibid.
52. Landis, "Do Growth Controls Work? A New Assessment."
53. Paul L. Niebanck, "Growth Controls and the Production of Inequality," in *Understanding Growth Management: Critical Issues and a Research Agenda*, eds. David J. Brower, David R. Godschalk, and Douglas R. Porter (Washington, D.C.: Urban Land Institute, 1989), 115.
54. Landis, "Do Growth Controls Work? A New Assessment."
55. Ibid., 21.
56. Ibid., 24.
57. Ibid., 28.
58. William A. Fischel, "Comment on Anthony Downs' 'The Advisory Commission on Regulatory Barriers to Affordable Housing: Its Behavior and Accomplishments,'" *Housing Policy Debate* 2 (1991): 1,145.
59. Landis, "Do Growth Controls Work? A New Assessment," 28.
60. Henry O. Pollakowski and Susan M. Wachter, "The Effects of Land Use Constraints on Housing Prices," *Land Economics* 66 (1990).

61. Ibid.
62. W. Patrick Beaton, "The Impact of Regional Land Use Controls on Property Value: The Case of the New Jersey Pinelands," *Land Economics* 67 (1991).
63. Ketcham and Siegel, "Managing Growth to Promote Affordable Housing: Revisiting Oregon's Goal 10," 68.
64. Beaton, "The Impact of Regional Land Use Controls on Property Value: The Case of the New Jersey Pinelands."
65. Ketcham and Siegel, "Managing Growth to Promote Affordable Housing: Revisiting Oregon's Goal 10," 44, tbl. 5.
66. See Schwartz, Hansen, and Green, "The Effect of Growth Control on the Production of Moderate-Priced Housing," and Table 10-3 and discussion with it.
67. Ibid.
68. Seymour I. Schwartz, Peter M. Zorn, and David E. Hansen, "Research Design Issues and Pitfalls in Growth Control Studies," *Land Economics* 62 (1986).
69. Fischel, *Do Growth Controls Matter? A Review of Empirical Evidence on the Effectiveness and Efficiency of Local Government Land Use Regulation*, 28.
70. Singell and Lillydahl, "An Empirical Examination of the Effect of Impact Fees on the Housing Market."
71. Ibid., 73.
72. Babcock, Bosselman, and American Society of Planning Officials, *Exclusionary Zoning: Land Use Regulation and Housing in the 1970s;* Dowall, *The Suburban Squeeze: Land Conversion and Regulation in the San Francisco Bay Area;* Anthony Downs, *Opening up the Suburbs: An Urban Strategy for America* (New Haven, Conn.: Yale University Press, 1973); Robert C. Ellickson, "Suburban Growth Controls: An Economic and Legal Analysis," *Yale Law Journal* (1977); Niebanck, "Conclusion: The Second Generation of Growth Management."
73. See discussion of principles in Brian W. Blaesser et al., "The Amicus Brief of the American Planning Association in *Wayne Britton V. Town of Chester*," *Washington University Journal of Urban and Contemporary Law* 40 (1991); Fischman, *Housing for All Under Law: New Directions in Housing, Land Use and Planning Law*; Herbert M. Franklin, David Falk, and Arthur J. Levin, *In-Zoning: A Guide for Policy-Makers on Inclusionary Land Use Programs, Based on an Evaluation of Policy-Relevant Research Funded by the National Science Foundation* (Washington, D.C.: Potomac Institute, 1974); Kelly, ed., *Zoning and Land Use Controls*, vol. 1, ch. 3.
74. Ketcham and Siegel, "Managing Growth to Promote Affordable Housing: Revisiting Oregon's Goal 10," 24–25.
75. United States Bureau of the Census, "1990 Census of Population and Housing: Summary of Population and Housing Characteristics."
76. United States Bureau of the Census, *Detailed Tables* (U.S. Department of Commerce, 2000 [cited November 2003]); available from http://factfinder.census.gov/.
77. Thomas I Miller, "Must Growth Restrictions Eliminate Moderate-Priced Housing?" *Journal of the American Planning Association* 52 (1986).
78. Downs, "The Advisory Commission on Regulatory Barriers to Affordable Housing: Its Behavior and Accomplishments," 1,101.
79. Downs, *Opening Up the Suburbs: An Urban Strategy for America.*
80. Real Estate Research Corp., "The Costs of Sprawl: Environmental and Economic Costs of Alternative Residential Development Patterns at the Urban Fringe."
81. "Growth Masks Out-Migration of Young Families: In-Migration of Established Families."

82. Ibid., 2, 3.
83. Miller, "Must Growth Restrictions Eliminate Moderate-Priced Housing?" 325.
84. Ibid.
85. "Housing Costs, Elitism Come Under Fire," *Boulder Daily Camera*, February 2, 1992.
86. Herbert M. Franklin, *Controlling Urban Growth—but for Whom?* (Washington, D.C.: The Urban Institute, 1973).
87. Dowall, "An Examination of Population-Growth-Managing Communities." See also Gerrit J. Knaap, ed., *Land Market Monitoring for Smart Urban Growth*. Cambridge, Mass., 2001.
88. Westminster, "[Untitled Working Documents on Growth Management] A, B, C and D."
89. See generally, Fischel, *The Economics of Zoning Laws: A Property Rights Approach to American Land Use Controls.*

CHAPTER 11

Is Growth Management a Good Idea?

Is growth management a good idea? That question is more complex than it might appear. The answer depends on one's goals and the constituency with which one is concerned. The answer depends also on the planning and governmental structure for the growth management program and on the type of growth management program being considered.

From the perspective of the community involved, to manage growth is generally a good idea, particularly if the alternative is *not* to manage growth. However, managing growth effectively is much more complex than just adopting some sort of point system that allows X hundred dwelling units per year or that permits only developments that earn more than Y points on an arbitrary scale and denies approval to all others. Furthermore, if by "managing" growth a particular community means "limiting" growth—either directly or indirectly—that is not a particularly good idea, at least from a state or regional perspective. The successful effort of one community to limit its growth rate while the region of which it is a part continues to grow simply shifts regional growth to other communities. The problem, however, is worse than that. In *Cities without Suburbs,* David Rusk explains how regions containing cities with suburbs are, by a number of measures, worse off than similar regions containing cities without suburbs.[1]

Montgomery County, Maryland, has managed growth for nearly three decades. It has done so through a comprehensive program involving development rights purchases, planned and managed capital investments and sophisticated adequate public facilities requirements. All of those pieces relate to each other and to the county's annual growth policy, which provides the planning basis for the programs. The Montgomery County program has served it well.

Montgomery County recognized from the beginning that it should absorb growth to the extent of its current ability to do so. Westminster, Colorado, has quintupled in population since 1970, growing from 19,512 then to 100,940 in 2000,[2] with a growth management program in place for 23 of those 30 years. It has effectively absorbed large population increases with its growth management system in effect, using the program in part to keep a balance between the community's actual capacities and the demands placed on them. It has also used the opportunity of growth to improve the quality of life in the community. Like Montgomery County, Westminster continued to accept rapid growth as its region grew rapidly.

In contrast, Petaluma and Boulder have attempted to limit, rather than to manage, growth and clearly contributed to a shifting of growth within their regions. Furthermore, the burden of that shift has not been evenly spread across the socioeconomic spectrum. Boulder has clearly diverted to nearby communities a disproportionate number of families with children. The Davis, California, program has had the effect of increasing costs at the bottom end of the housing market in a "trickle-up effect" through which homes that were once "lower cost" have become affordable only to those with higher incomes.

Even under their growth management programs, Westminster and Montgomery County accepted an increased rate of growth over the short-term in order to meet regional demand. In contrast, Boulder, Petaluma, and several of the other communities used as examples in this book attempted to limit growth in a way that was not necessarily related to the community's ability to absorb growth.

The adoption of such programs sometimes represents an over-reaction to a short-term trend that will not continue. The two-year growth rate of ten percent per year that led to the adoption of the Petaluma program has never been approached again—by Petaluma or by the county or nearby Santa Rosa, neither of which has a growth management program (see Table 11-1). Although Boulder has been successful in holding its growth rate below its stated goal of two percent per year, the county has grown more rapidly and the smaller communities around Boulder have had to absorb the difference (see Table 11-2).

Petaluma's controlled growth rate has been only slightly below that of the county, which does not have a growth management system. Boulder has been more successful than Petaluma in diverting development to nearby small communities that have thus endured extremely high rates of growth. However, the overall growth rate in Boulder County over the 1980s was less than the 2 percent per year rate that Boulder residents once determined to be acceptable. Boulder's actual growth rate has fallen far below its maximum of two percent per year. Clearly, the psychological effects of the program on the market and other aspects of the program have contributed to the development shift to other communities.

In short, just adopting a relatively simplistic program does not amount to managing growth. Many growth management programs fit the adage that for every complex problem there is a solution that is fast, easy and wrong. Nevertheless, there are some types of growth management programs that make sense for most communities and some that make sense for some communities or in particular circumstances. The following discussion reviews those.

Table 11-1
Growth in Petaluma, Santa Rosa, and Sonoma County, 1970–2000

Place	Population 1970	1980	1990	2000	Percentage Increase 1970–2000	1990–2000
Petaluma	24,870	33,834	43,184	54,548	119.3	26.3
Santa Rosa	50,006	83,320	113,313	147,595	195.2	30.3
Sonoma County	204,885	299,681	388,222	458,614	123.8	18.1
California	19,957,715	23,667,902	29,760,021	33,871,648	69.7	13.8

Sources: Raw data from Bureau of the Census, 2000, *American Fact Finder, Quick Tables*, www.census.gov; Bureau of the Census, 1991, *Census of Population and Housing: Summary Population and Housing Characteristics*, Part 6, Table 18; Bureau of the Census, 1982, *Summary Characteristics by Governmental Units and Standard Metropolitan Statistical Areas*, Part 6, Table 2; Bureau of the Census, 1972, *City and County Data Book*, Table B-2; Bureau of the Census, 1972, *Census of Population, Vol. 1, Characteristics of the Population*, Part 7, Table 14, 16 (state); percentage computations for some years by author.

Table 11-2
Growth in Boulder and Other Cities in Boulder County

Place	Population 1970	1980	1990	2000	Percentage Increase 1970–2000	1990–2000
Boulder	66,870	76,685	83,312	94,673	41.6	13.6
Lafayette	3,498	8,985	14,548	23,197	563.2	59.5
Longmont	23,209	42,942	51,555	71,093	206.3	37.9
Louisville	2,409	5,593	13,361	18,937	686.1	41.7
Boulder County	131,899	189,625	225,339	291,288	120.8	29.3
Colorado	2,207,765	2,889,964	3,294,394	4,301,261	94.8	30.6

Sources: Raw data from Bureau of the Census, 2000, *American Fact Finder, Quick Tables*, www.census.gov; Bureau of the Census, 1991, *Census of Population and Housing: Summary Population and Housing Characteristics*, Part 6, Table 18; Bureau of the Census, 1982, *Summary Characteristics by Governmental Units and Standard Metropolitan Statistical Areas*, Part 6, Table 2; Bureau of the Census, 1972, *City and County Data Book*, Table B-2; Bureau of the Census, 1972, *Census of Population, Vol. 1, Characteristics of the Population*, Part 7, Table 14, 16 (state) and 32 (Louisville only); percentage computations by author.

PROGRAMS THAT ARE GOOD IDEAS

Comprehensive Planning

Planning for growth is always a good idea. A local comprehensive plan should serve as the basis for making land-use decisions and also for making decisions about capital investments—particularly for those "growth shapers," local roads, water lines and sewer lines.[3] The topic of comprehensive planning underlies many of the principles set out in this book, but it is not treated in any depth here. For an introduction and thorough treatment, with additional references, see *Community Planning: An Introduction to the Comprehensive Plan.*[4]

Regional Planning

Planning for growth on a regional, rather than a local, basis is always a good idea. Identifying priority areas for growth and for preservation is an important part of local planning; that concept formed the original backbone of the Maryland Smart Growth program.[5] Carefully managing infrastructure investments—particularly those for arterial roadways, interceptor sewer lines and major water lines—to reinforce desired patterns of growth is a good idea for any community in any circumstance. Ideally, a community should coordinate that process with other facility-providers like the local school board and the state transportation department.

Growth does follow sewers and highways. That is not just useful information. It is the basis for a critical technique in managing growth. By building a highway and a sewer line through a wetlands, a community can virtually ensure its development or major litigation over a refusal to permit that development. By building the highway and the sewer line elsewhere, the community may not guarantee the preservation of the wetlands, but it can make that preservation much more likely. Most communities have some sort of plans for future growth. Too few use those plans to influence their investments in infrastructure. All communities should base infrastructure investment plans on their comprehensive plans for community growth. Those plans should tell the community where to build new highways and sewer and water lines. Perhaps more important, those plans should indicate where *not* to build new infrastructure. By using infrastructure "growth shapers" as part of a growth management package, a community can significantly influence its future urban form.[6]

Annexation Policy

Using annexation policy as part of a growth management program is always a good idea in those states in which municipalities can expand their boundaries through annexation. A community in such a state should actively annex and plan to serve that territory, and only that territory, that fits the general expansion plans of the community. There may be occasional exceptions where it is important to a community to control a particular location, such as the only interstate highway interchange serving the area. However, the simple desire to "control" large areas of land does not justify annexation beyond the reasonable growth needs of the community. The most important thing for community officials to remember about annexation as it relates to growth management is that annexation power—particularly the power to refuse to annex—is one of the more effective devices in the growth management toolbox. Annexation increases the likelihood of development. A refusal to annex limits the likelihood of development, although that limitation is less effective in areas where other municipalities or other entities of government are attractive alternative service providers.

Adequate Public Facilities Standards

Adopting adequate public facilities standards is almost always a good idea, at least for some facilities. Economically, adequate public facilities requirements appear to reinforce market patterns that naturally establish higher values for property with public services than for property without them. The concept works most easily for facilities for which capacities can be objectively defined by engineers or other analysts—systems like water and sewer systems. Although establishing an adequate public facilities requirement in a community that did not previously have such a requirement may cause a short-term increase in the cash price of a home, it is simply shifting the cost from a social one to a cash one. If there were no such requirement, new residents (or old ones) would pay the cost of that lack in a reduced quality of life. That reduced quality of life might be measured in greater distances from fewer parks, in overcrowded classrooms or in longer-than-normal traffic delays. Living under those conditions is clearly a cost. Furthermore, it is a cost that most communities are unwilling to tolerate over the long run. Thus, it is likely that a community will eventually cure such a cost by building facilities, thus converting the cost to a cash one at a later date.

There is clear value in adequate public facilities standards for the linear and objectively measurable systems of sewer and water lines and for stormwater systems. Overloading those systems causes negative impacts on some part of the community, although often not on the most recent users, who essentially pushed the system past its limit. Because of consumer pressure, federal and state law, as well as a desire to maintain reasonable fire insurance ratings, local governments will have to cure such overloads. It is almost always cheaper—and always better—to address such a problem before it occurs.

Adequate public facilities standards for roads, however, are more troublesome. There is considerable evidence and considerable logic to support the proposition that congestion serves as a form of transportation demand management (sometimes called TDM). Thus, maintaining traffic flow at optimal levels at all times may simply discourage people from engaging in such commendable behaviors as car-pooling, using public transportation or simply shifting their commuting times away from peak hours. One approach to that issue is to establish minimum level-of-service standards at one level for most of the day and to allow a lower level of service during the local peak hours. It is also worth considering the long-standing

Montgomery County concept of accepting lower levels of service on the roads near transit stations, recognizing both that travel-to-transit stations increases traffic at peak hours in such areas, and that persons caught in traffic near a transit station may decide to leave their cars and commute by rail.

Establishing adequate public facility standards for schools and fire protection, however, is problematic at best. School administrators typically take the position that they will provide educational opportunities for whatever number of students show up. They often deal with space shortages by moving in portable classrooms for temporary use at an otherwise overcrowded school. The Montgomery County system deals with the capacity of clusters of schools, thus recognizing that some crowding problems can be addressed through adjustments in attendance boundaries. Even that flexibility, however, does not entirely address the issue. An elementary school may be designed to hold 525 students, with 25 students in each of three sections for six grade levels, and up to 50 students at a time in half-day kindergarten. If students are evenly distributed among grade levels at all times, when individual grade levels are full, the school will also be full. But what happens in the year that the school has 82 third graders but only 65 second graders. Technically it is not full, but it needs another classroom for a fourth section of third grade and it does not have that. Such issues must, as a practical matter, be addressed with portable classrooms or other temporary fixes. But what if the school district has had the same portable classrooms at the same school for a decade? Is that not an indication that the school is in fact overcrowded and thus beyond its reasonable level-of-service? Certainly these complex issues can be addressed in a policy, but the resulting policy is likely to be complex to adopt and more complex to administer.

Adequate public facility standards for such non-lumpy services as libraries and police are usually not relevant. Libraries and police departments typically receive increased tax revenues from new development and can use those revenues to buy more cars and books and to hire more personnel. Although at some point the central police station or the main library may become overcrowded, that is a long-term capital issue for the community, not an issue that can be traced directly to particular growth decisions.

Falling somewhere in between the two categories are fire and emergency medical services. Almost everyone would agree that all parts of a community should have access to an established, minimum level of service. Defining such a level is not simple, however. Most well-managed communities with professional fire departments can make fire responses within 6 to 8 minutes to virtually any location in the city. That meets one generally accepted minimum level of service. Ideally, however, a full response may involve trucks and engines from as many as three stations within 10 minutes; in many communities, there are significant areas for which that standard cannot be met. It is likely to remain a planning standard for many fire departments, but is it a reasonable minimum level-of-service? Probably not.

The issue of emergency medical response is even more complex. Communities have, in increasing numbers, assigned their EMT responsibilities to fire departments and required EMT or paramedic training for firefighters. That concept makes good use of trained professionals who are already on call and already part of an emergency response system. The response, however, comes from fire stations—and most have been located on the principle that a response time of 6 to 8 minutes is perfectly satisfactory for a fire. For a heart attack or a stroke, a response time of 2 to 3 minutes is a typical planning goal. Yet that goal is unachievable for large parts of most communities that depend on fire departments for emergency medical response. Should the community ignore that significant problem? It certainly cannot set a level-of-service that large parts of the existing community will not meet.

Whether adequate public facilities requirements reduce sprawl depends entirely on where public facilities are available. If a community has extended major public services several miles out of town to serve an airport or an industrial park, adequate public facilities may be available all along that route, thus encouraging a form of linear sprawl. In many metropolitan areas, the availability of public services from nearby communities may limit the influence of one community's policy on regional urban development. However, Brooklyn Park, Minnesota, has demonstrated that even within a major metropolitan area, a community can use a combination of adequate public facilities standards and careful planning of infrastructure extensions to shape urban form.

Developers often argue that the standard established for "adequacy" of facilities in a community may be excessive. A community may require streets to be 32 feet wide, when studies suggest that 26 would be adequate. A community may require eight acres of park land for every 1,000 projected residents in new areas, although it has survived for years with only five acres of park land for every 1,000 residents in the rest of the community. Obviously, the increased requirements increase costs. There is considerable merit in the Florida concurrency approach, under which a community must spend its own money to bring existing facilities up to the same standards that the community establishes for developers to provide in new developments. That brings a healthy sense of balance to the decision-making process, because few communities have sufficient surplus funds in the 90s to build oversized facilities with their own money.

It is important that a community that establishes adequate public facilities requirements also continues to expand its infrastructure network as its population grows. If a community requires that all new development have access to infrastructure and at the same time stops building infrastructure, it will effectively stop growth at the level that its present capacity can serve. If used in that way, an adequate public facilities requirement can become a tool of exclusion. However, that would represent an abuse of the technique, not a logical consequence of its normal implementation.

Urban Service Area Boundaries

Urban service area boundaries are always a good idea if they are rationally drawn, based on the actual service capabilities of the provider. The boundaries

introduce predictability into the land market, by delineating clearly where
services will be available. They also serve as a guide for decisions by local
elected officials and public works administrators who are often asked to accommodate special needs with utilities extensions. Lexington, Kentucky, and the
Twin Cities both represent long-term success stories in using this management
technique, which is classified in Chapter 3 as a form of "phased growth."

PROGRAMS THAT MAY BE GOOD IDEAS

Regional Urban Growth Boundaries

A regional urban growth boundary is probably a good idea where the institutional framework to implement it exists. Such a framework clearly exists in
Hawaii and appears to exist around the metropolitan areas in Oregon. The key to
making a regional urban growth boundary work is some sort of regional planning. In Hawaii, the "regional" planning is actually statewide. In Oregon, there is
state-mandated regional planning.

Neither the Oregon system nor the Hawaii one has totally resolved the issue of
the permanency of the boundaries. There appears to be an excessive number of
individual changes to the boundaries in Hawaii. That creates the appearance of a
highly political system, whether it actually is or not. On the other hand, the net
change in the total urbanized area is quite small. Metropolitan Portland has
established a far more rigid boundary as the outer boundary of the region. However, it is probably too rigid. In the unlikely event that the region's growth projections are accurate (few long-range planning projections are), the region will
run out of land before the target year because of "underzoning" (zoning for less
than planned development) and "underbuilding" (building at a lower intensity
than the maximum allowed by zoning). Ideally, there would have been no "underzoning" or "underbuilding." However, for planners to expect that all land
would develop at exactly the planned levels seems like a naive expectation. The
land shortage resulting from the under-calculation of actual land needs may result in excessive market prices for scarce land in later years of the program, as
well as in an eventual physical shortage of land for housing and other uses. Presumably, state, regional and local officials will cooperate to ensure that such a
scenario does not play out. However, there is no mechanism in place to ensure
that it does not. A more flexible boundary would serve the region better. On the
other hand, as the Knaap study demonstrated, if the boundary is too flexible, no
one will take it seriously and it will accomplish little.[7]

The Oregon experience also illustrates the difficulty of establishing long-term
boundaries. Despite the long-time commitment to the protection of the environment in Oregon, planners in the Portland region apparently included steep slopes
and other sensitive lands in their computation of the development capacity within
the original boundaries. Clearly, such lands should have been omitted. One can
second-guess the work of the planners who made the calculations. On the other

hand, perfect planning and perfect foresight are unlikely to exist and, where they do, the political process may reject them. Thus, a different planning process would probably have avoided that planning error but created others. A system of regional planning must provide a modest amount of flexibility both to address defects in the original process and, more importantly, to respond to changing demographic trends. It must, however, be sufficiently permanent to be taken seriously. That is a delicate but perhaps not impossible balance to achieve.

Minimum Density Standards

The minimum density requirement used in the Portland region seems like a logical corollary of growth management. To the extent that one of the goals of growth management is to reduce sprawl and to ensure the efficient use of land, requiring that land that is developed be optimally developed makes a good deal of sense. With an urban growth boundary, based on projected densities of population, some sort of requirement to ensure that development actually occurs at such densities is essential; traditional zoning will not do that, because the zoning system is designed to ensure that development take place at *not more than* the planned densities. Both theoretical work and practical experience suggest that it is still possible to provide a complete range of housing types at the average minimum densities prescribed in the Portland region, which are in the range of eight dwelling units per acre. In other words, if Portland had simply established minimum densities rather than targets for specific types of smaller dwelling units, the market would have been capable of providing a full range of housing types while achieving the density goal.

If planners and public officials in a region want to make development more compact, they should consider such a minimum density requirement. There is no evidence that other types of growth management programs make development more compact. As Table 11-3 shows, Petaluma and Boulder have achieved relatively high densities, with significant increases in the 1990s, although both declined in the 1980s. It is interesting to note that the density of pro-growth Santa Rosa substantially exceeded that of Petaluma in 1990 and that it has fallen below Petaluma only because of an addition of more than 20 percent to its territory; over the long term, it may show higher densities and greater efficiency of population growth than its neighbor. Note that small city density is necessarily lumpy, because annexations of territory tend to occur in relatively large chunks, followed by some years of filling the annexed territory.

In addition to saving land through more efficient use of land that is developed, minimum density requirements produce fiscal benefits. One thing that is clear from the fiscal impact studies is that it is cheaper to serve development at higher densities. Those savings alone may not be great enough to justify such a program, but they are a nice additional benefit of a minimum density standard. In considering a minimum density program, it would be worth examining a New Zealander's hypothesis that, from a fiscal-impact perspective, there may be a sort of optimal density for a particular community.[8]

Table 11-3
Area and Density Changes in Selected Communities (densities in persons per square mile; areas in square miles)

Place	1970 Area	1970 Density	1980 Area	1980 Density	1990 Area	1990 Density	2000 Area	2000 Density
Boulder	13.0	5143	19.5	3933	22.6	3687	24.37	3884
Livermore	11.9	3168	13.2	3663	19.6	2895	23.92	3066
Petaluma	7.5	3316	9.2	3678	12.3	3511	13.8	3953
Longmont	7.9	2938	9.8	4382	13.1	3935	21.8	3262
Santa Rosa	19.9	2513	26.6	3132	33.7	4773	40.13	3678

Table Sources: Raw data from Bureau of the Census, 2000, *American Fact Finder, Quick Tables,* www.census.gov; Bureau of the Census, 1991, *Census of Population and Housing: Summary Population and Housing Characteristics,* Part 6, Table 18; Bureau of the Census, 1982, *Summary Characteristics by Governmental Units and Standard Metropolitan Statistical Areas,* Part 6, Table 2; Bureau of the Census, 1972, *City and County Data Book,* Table B-2; Bureau of the Census, 1972, *Census of Population, Vol. 1, Characteristics of the Population,* Part 7, Table 14, 16 (state) and 32 (Louisville only); percentage computations by author.

A minimum density program will work best with some form of regional planning. In Portland, the urban growth boundary represents a major element of the regional plan. Consumers have no convenient alternative locations that are not subject to the rules. To mandate a density greater than what the market suggests that consumers want in a single community within a metropolitan area may simply drive growth from that community to others nearby. Thus, to be effective, such a requirement probably should be mandated throughout the region in which growth is likely to occur. However, because the evidence cited in Chapter 7 suggests that it is possible to provide a full range of housing types even at relatively high densities, this effect may not occur. There is no experience from which to draw a conclusion about the effects of a minimum density program in a single community.

Buying Open Space

Buying land to preserve it is generally a good idea. Boulder's greenbelt will be green long after the growth management programs in many other communities have been forgotten. Land acquisition is expensive, but the expense is really a long-term investment. In Boulder's case, the land amounts to a local growth boundary, which, as the next section suggests, is probably not a good idea.

Although it creates a greenbelt, which is a popular idea in planning, it has also created leapfrog sprawl, which is an extremely unpopular idea in planning. Thus, there can be too much of a good thing or unintended negative consequences of a perfectly logical act. Nevertheless, most public land acquisition programs do not have such negative consequences. All communities concerned about their urban form, about preserving environmentally-sensitive lands and about managing growth in general should seriously consider land acquisition as one of the tools to use. There is evidence that requiring the preservation of private open space in cluster developments adds value to the neighboring residential property.[9] Randall Arendt is a fervent advocate for such development patterns,[10] but the concept builds on the much older legacy of William H. Whyte.[11]

Limits on Premature Subdivision of Urbanizable Lands

One concept that appears to be largely untested is any serious effort to prohibit the premature subdivision of urbanizable land. In every community with a plan for managed growth, there is land that logically should be urbanized (or at least suburbanized) over the next 10 to 20 years but that lacks sewer or water service or both at a particular point in time. The fact that the land can logically be urbanized typically means that it is relatively close to the core population area and that it has good access. Those two factors often produce economic and political pressure to develop the property before it is practical to provide sewer and water service to it. Often, separate local or state officials will issue permits for homes on wells and septic tanks in such locations, often on lots of an acre or a little more. Lawrence and Douglas County, Kansas, have long struggled with this issue,[12] but their use of a five-acre minimum lot size in the unserved parts of the Urban Growth Areas has not been effective and was being reexamined as this book went to press.

Clearly, land that will become urban or suburban ought to be developed at a reasonable density—something on the order of three or four dwelling units per acre. If it develops prematurely at one unit per acre, the land-resource impacts are significant. Land consumption varies directly with housing demand, based on lot size. If there is demand for 500 new houses and they each go on one-acre lots, 500 or more (allowing for roads) acres are used for development and lost to other uses. If those same houses are built on lots of 12,000 square feet—quite generous compared to many suburban lots—the result is a net density (after allowing for roads) of about three units per acre, meaning that the same number of homes requires about 170 acres. The difference between the two scenarios is 330 acres, or more than half a square mile of land. In addition, the inefficient, lower density development may create a barrier to logical urban expansion in the direction of the development and to orderly extension of public services to that area.

Thus, the local government managing growth has many reasons to try to avoid such premature subdivision, which is quite different from the same pattern of development occurring in a rural area that is otherwise quite unlikely to develop. It is difficult, however, to find a balance between the competing claims of the landowner—who may have a reasonable legal and political expectation that the land ought to have some value now—and the local government—which would prefer to see nothing happen to the land for several years. Chris Nelson, in making recommendations on revisions to the Oregon system around Portland, recommended the use of very large lot sizes.[13] Such an approach may or may not work, however. The goal is to see the land used efficiently over the long run. Division into five-acre residential lots will simply not accomplish that; with a home— probably a large one—placed somewhere near the center of such a tract, at most there is likely to be enough land left to divide off two or three additional lots. As a practical matter, for residential resubdivision in marginal areas, it is probably necessary to have tracts of 10 to 20 acres, which would create the equivalent of two to five city blocks when urbanized. That is a very large lot size to require in a suburbanizing area, and one that may draw serious political and legal challenges from landowners. Another possibility is to allow interim, clustered development on a part of a larger parcel, with a requirement that the rest of the property be made subject to a development agreement prohibiting its further development until urban services are available. The land that will remain vacant can be used as the location for septic leaching fields, extended from homes placed on the clustered lots.

There appears to have been little experience with such a system for urbanizable, unserved land—but it is a character of land that exists in most rapidly growing communities. The communities that are most successful at growth management will begin to address this issue.

Note that this is a corollary of maximum lot sizes, but it is one that interjects the timing issue that results from the temporary lack of services.

PROGRAMS THAT ARE DIFFICULT TO JUSTIFY

Rate-of-Growth Programs

For *rate-of-growth programs, most* phased growth programs and local growth-boundary programs, the only possible justifications are self-serving ones of the communities adopting the programs. Clearly such programs are likely to shift growth from one community to another. Viewed from a regional planning perspective, the population shift typically increases commuting costs and shifts the burdens of growth to other communities that may or may not be able to bear them. In the case of Boulder, the shift has been to much smaller communities surrounding it, some of which have had phenomenal percentage growth rates directly related to Boulder's effort to slow its own rate. Such leapfrog development is viewed by some as more pernicious than simple suburban sprawl. Depending on where it occurs, it may consume additional prime farmland or other land that should be preserved. When a boundary is a regional one, such issues can be considered. However, a local government adopting such a boundary has little reason to consider more than its own needs and, perhaps, the impacts on land immediately adjacent to it.

Over the long run, the leapfrog suburbs are likely to lead to demand for additional connecting highways for commuting and other public expenditures. This dispersion of growth makes it more difficult to share such community-wide facilities as libraries and hospitals. On a pure cost-benefit basis, it would appear that the net increase in costs to the region far exceeds any cost savings to the community adopting the program, and cost savings are often one of the major arguments for the adoption of such a program.

Viewed from a social perspective, these same programs limit someone's housing choices. Interestingly, while most exclusionary zoning techniques over the years have tended to exclude apartments and townhouses, it is the single-family home suitable in price and size for a family with young children that appears to be most affected by the exclusionary effects of the Boulder and Portland programs. Portland expressly limits the proportion of such homes. Boulder does not appear to discriminate against that dwelling type specifically, but the demographic patterns indicate that the people who typically live in such homes are moving to surrounding communities. Clearly such economic impacts will fall most heavily on those with the fewest economic choices. Although growth managing communities are not typically the kinds of places likely to house many of the poor, those with market-limiting programs limit the opportunities available to those who may not be "poor" for census purposes but who clearly have less economic flexibility and fewer choices than others.

Montgomery County planners were far-sighted indeed in recognizing nearly two decades ago the appropriate role of growth management. Its *First Annual Growth Report* stated in part, "In this report, the Board does not recommend a specific limit on the total number of people the County might ultimately house or the number that should be 'admitted' each year. The County is not sovereign; people have a right to move; and we are persuaded that such population 'caps' are both unwise and of dubious constitutionality."[14]

Local Urban Growth Boundaries

From a local perspective, an urban growth boundary may serve its real purposes. If what Boulder wanted was a firm urban edge and a community surrounded by a greenbelt, it got exactly what it sought. If what it wanted was to stop sprawl, it simply traded leapfrog sprawl for the continuous sprawl that it probably precluded. That may or may not be a good trade in design terms, but it is a bad trade in fiscal terms. Although Boulder may save money by not serving the leapfrog development, some combination of governmental entities will incur increased costs over the long-run to establish and expand free-standing infrastructure systems or long line extensions from Boulder. Either of those alternatives is more expensive than simply serving additional development adjacent to an existing community, as the evidence cited in Chapter 9 clearly shows.

Other Growth Phasing Programs

Rate-of-growth programs and phased-growth programs are typically presented as methods of balancing the capacities of and demands on public facilities. That is a somewhat specious defense of the programs. It is most unlikely that the capacity of all public services in a particular community would expand at the rate necessary to absorb an additional 500 dwelling units or 2 percent population increase each year. The real purpose of establishing such limits appears to be to control a rate of growth that is "too fast." In the case of Petaluma, where the actual growth rate exceeded 10 percent per year for a short time, such concerns are understandable. Should Boulder or Petaluma be precluded from limiting their participation in regional growth? From a regional or statewide perspective it is difficult to answer that question affirmatively. From a local perspective, it is also easy to understand the development of support among citizens for limiting growth, even if the only result is to shift the problem to other communities. This reflects the self-serving nature of many growth management programs.

Communities often implement phased growth systems as an additional stage in the development review process, thus increasing development costs attributable to regulatory overhead. As the experience with San Jose and other communities indicates, a growth phasing system may adversely affect housing costs by distorting the land market (see generally Chapter 10). A phased growth program need not have that effect, if it provides for large enough "phases," but some programs have had that effect.

A comprehensive program such as that of Westminster or Montgomery County certainly contains growth-phasing elements that affect the rate of growth. However, those programs are based squarely on the actual capacities of public facilities. Thus, once Westminster overcame its short-term capacity problems, it absorbed growth demand at a far faster rate than nearby Boulder, which had adopted its rate-limiting program. Over the medium-run, the market caused a slowing of growth in Westminster, also. Because some industries may move into town and others close down, mortgage rates fluctuate and consumer confidence rises and falls, demand for housing and other elements of growth are not constant or steady. To the extent that a community through such a program attempts to level the market, it also distorts the market. Some might argue that it is "only" the market and thus not a concern. However, that market represents people's needs/desires for housing. It is those needs and desires that become more expensive to fulfill or take longer to fulfill or that may go unfulfilled. The market is simply a collection of individual players—in this particular market those players are people, many of them representing families and children and others whose causes may seem socially more worthy than the "market" as an abstract economic concept. Although here Westminster and Montgomery County are classified as "comprehensive" programs, they are comprehensive programs clearly based on the capacities of public facilities and they fall squarely under the finding that adequate public facilities standards do a great deal of good and little if any harm to anyone.

A PROGRAM ON WHICH TO RESERVE JUDGMENT

Shifting the Housing Mix

It is difficult to reach a conclusion on the Portland policy of mandating a housing mix quite different from what has traditionally existed in the market. By 2000, more than 25 years after the Oregon program went into effect, the census data showed very little actual change in the housing mix in the city. An adequate policy analysis of the impact of creating a supply-shift in the entire housing supply will require a good deal more data than is available now. The published data indicating that the program has held housing costs down and made housing more affordable is misleading for the same reason that many of the comparisons in *The Costs of Sprawl* were misleading—they attempt to compare two entirely different types of housing. New housing in Portland includes a far greater percentage of apartments, townhouses and condominiums than the market produced before adoption of the program. Such units are generally less costly than single-family detached homes. Thus, comparing current "average" costs of a dwelling unit with previous "average" costs is meaningless. None of the Portland studies do what Niebanck did in California, which was to analyze the price trends of a particular type of home. Without that data, it is impossible to know what the real effects of the Portland program on housing costs may be.

To the extent that the Portland program ensures the availability of more apartments and more smaller dwelling units, it will create great social benefits by expanding the diversity and quantity of housing available to the low end of the housing market. To the extent that it goes beyond that and requires that apartments supplant some single-family homes in the housing supply, it will have significant social impacts. Whether those impacts will be positive, negative or neutral is difficult to evaluate without additional data. Perhaps people who wanted to live in single-family homes will be perfectly content living in apartments or condominiums as they see that more of their neighbors are doing so. However, it is not clear that forcing people with the economic means to afford "the American dream" to live in less than a single-family home will create a net social benefit. It clearly will create resentment among some of those. It is conceivable that it will have the same sort of effect that the Boulder program has had and that some people will actually move outside the Portland region and endure very long commutes in order to enjoy single-family-home living. Only time and a good deal of additional research will tell.

Whether such a requirement is a good idea is a different question. It is important to remember that the Portland program not only mandated higher densities, but it mandated that those densities be achieved with a different housing mix. The goal in Portland centered on increasing the statistical affordability of housing in the region by changing the mix to include more lower-priced products. If the goal of a community were simply to increase the compactness of development without unnecessarily disturbing the housing mix, the community could impose a maximum density requirement without the housing-type targets used in

Portland. If a community wants to conserve land, that is to reduce the total amount of land that a given amount of growth will consume, such a technique will work well.

RELATIONSHIP OF PROGRAMS TO ISSUES

Figure 11.1 provide a summary of how well each technique seems to address the major issues that lead communities to consider adopting growth management programs and how each affects other, typical community goals.

CONCLUSION

Is growth management a good idea? Yes, if it is based on good planning and a solid understanding of the costs and benefits of different growth management techniques. The strongest message of this book is the need for effective local planning as a basis for making any reasonable decisions about managing growth. The second strong message is that some form of regional planning in our nation's metropolitan areas is an important goal and an essential underpinning for equitable growth management. That regional planning must originate with the state, as it has in Hawaii and Oregon.

What is the message, though, for local governments in states without such regional planning? Should they attempt to manage growth? Yes. However, in most cases they will significantly improve the local, regional and social cost-benefit ratio by using a combination of tools rather than one of the relatively simplistic growth management programs. By including adequate public facilities standards in its local controls, a local government encourages development to occur near existing infrastructure. By planning where to locate its infrastructure—extending it voluntarily into areas in which it wishes to target development and avoiding extensions, even ones that would more than pay for themselves, into areas in which it does not want growth—a community can strengthen the importance of its adequate public facilities standards.

A community should annex selectively, accepting eagerly those lands on which it wants future urbanization and avoiding those lands on which it does not. Through zoning and subdivision controls within its boundaries (and, in some states, even beyond those boundaries) a community can encourage appropriate land uses and a quality of development suitable for the circumstances. A community may want to consider reducing the impact of new development on the land supply by including minimum density requirements, as well as maximums, in its zoning ordinances. Some communities may want to follow the examples of those that have dedicated revenue sources to large-scale acquisition of lands to be preserved. Most communities should occasionally use strategic land acquisitions to help to manage urban form and to protect lands or topographic features of particular local significance.

ISSUE/ TECHNIQUE	Adequate Public Facilities	Phased Growth	Urban Growth Boundaries	Rate of Growth	Minimum Density	Targeted Capital Investment	Annexation Policy	Land Acquisitions
PUBLIC SERVICES—COST AND AVILABILITY								
Minimize net costs of providing public services	++	+	+		++	++	++	
Balance public service capacities and demands	+++	++	+	+	+	+++	++	
Limit growth in traffic congestion	+	+	−			++		
URBAN FORM								
Define urban edge		+	++			+	+	++
Limit continuous sprawl		+	++			+	+	
Limit discontinuous (leapfrog) development	++	++	−			++	+	
Encourage more compact development	+	+	+		+++	+	+	
COMMUNITY CHARACTER								
Stop growth								
Maintain semi-rural character								
Establish greenbelt		+					+	++
ENVIRONMENTAL								
Preserve sensitive lands within urban area								++
Preserve sensitive lands near urban area	+		++			++	++	++
Preserve open space generally	+		+					++
HOUSING CHOICE								
Promote affordable housing		−	−	−				
Promote diverse housing opportunities		−	−	−	+			

Figure 11.1   Evaluative checklist of growth management programs.

Note: + indicates positive effects of a particular technique to accomplish a particular purpose: − indicates a negative effect on that public purpose; a blank cell indicates that the effect of the particular technique on that public purpose is typically neutral.

Through this combination of modern and traditional techniques, a community can exert powerful control over the shape of its future growth. Implementing such a system requires a combination of political will and management skill. Managing such a system is more complex than administering one of the simpler growth management programs. Using a complicated package of tools that the average citizen may not fully understand will probably not provide as much press as adopting a program to limit new growth to an annual rate of 2 percent or 500 dwelling units. On the other hand, the evidence demonstrates clearly that such a program works and that it does so without the negative impacts on housing opportunities and regional sprawl that characterize several types of growth management programs.

NOTES

1. David Rusk, *Cities without Suburbs*, 2nd ed., *Woodrow Wilson Center Special Studies* (Washington, D.C., U.S.A. Baltimore, Md.: Woodrow Wilson Center Press; Distributed by Johns Hopkins University Press, 1995).
2. Colorado State Demographer, *Colorado Historical Census* [Website] (Colorado Department of Local Affairs, December 10, 2002 2003 [cited November 2003]); available from http://www.dola.colorado.gov/demog/history/allhist.cfm.
3. Kelly and Becker, *Community Planning: An Introduction to the Comprehensive Plan*, chps. 12–13.
4. Ibid.
5. Maryland Governor's Office of Smart Growth, *Smart Growth* (cited).
6. Kelly and Becker, *Community Planning: An Introduction to the Comprehensive Plan*, chps. 12–13.
7. Knaap, "The Price Effects of Urban Growth Boundaries in Metropolitan Portland, Oregon."
8. Dekel, "Housing Density: A Neglected Dimension of Fiscal Impact Analysis."
9. Irwin, "The Effects of Open Space on Residential Property Values."
10. Randall Arendt, *Conservation Design for Subdivisions* (Washington, D.C.: Island Press, 1996); Randall Arendt, *Rural by Design* (Chicago, Ill.: APA Planners Press, 1994).
11. Whyte, *Securing Open Spaces for Urban America: Conservation Easements*.
12. Lawrence-Douglas County Metropolitan Planning Commission, *Horizon 2020: The Comprehensive Plan for the City of Lawrence and Unincorporated Douglas County*, rev. ed. Lawrence: 1998.
13. Nelson, "Oregon's Urban Growth Boundary Policy as a Landmark Planning Tool," 38.
14. Montgomery County Planning Board, "First Annual Growth Policy Report: Framework for Action," 6.

Bibliography

Abbott, Carl, Deborah A. Howe, and Sy Adler. *Planning the Oregon Way: A Twenty-Year Evaluation.* Corvallis, Ore.: Oregon State University Press, 1994.

Abe, Mary Morgan. "Urban Growth Management: Trends, Issues and Responsibilities." Ph.D. diss., Claremont Graduate School, 1977.

Advisory Commission on Regulatory Barriers to Affordable Housing. "'Not in My Back-yard': Removing Barriers to Affordable Housing." Washington, D.C.: U.S. Department of Housing and Urban Development, 1991.

Alexander, Ernest R., K. David Reed, and Peter Murphy. "Density Measures and Their Relation to Urban Form." Madison, Wis.: Center for Architecture and Urban Planning Research, University of Wisconsin, 1988.

Alonso, William. *Location and Land Use: Toward a General Theory of Land Rent.* Cambridge, Mass.: Harvard University Press, 1964.

Ambrose, Stephen E. *Nothing Like It in the World: The Men Who Build the Transcontinental Railroad 1863–1869.* New York: Simon & Schuster, 2000.

American Law Institute. *A Model Land Development Code, with Commentary by Alison Dunham, Chief Reporter.* Washington, D.C.: American Law Institute, 1975.

Arampatzis, G., C.T. Kiranoudis, P. Scaloubacas, and D. Assimacopoulos. "A GIS-Based Decision Support System for Planning Urban Transportation Policies." *European Journal of Operations Research* 152, no. 2 (2004): 465–76.

Arendt, Randall. *Conservation Design for Subdivisions.* Washington, D.C.: Island Press, 1996.
———. *Rural by Design.* Chicago, Ill.: APA Planners Press, 1994.

Audirac, Ivonne, Anne H. Shermyen, and Marc T. Smith. "Ideal Urban Form and Visions of the Good Life: Florida's Growth Management Dilemma." *Journal of the American Planning Association* 56 (1990): 470–82.

Babcock, Richard F. *The Zoning Game: Municipal Practices and Policies.* Madison, Wis.: University of Wisconsin Press, 1966.

Babcock, Richard F., Charles L.Siemon, and Lincoln Institute of Land Policy. *The Zoning Game Revisited.* Cambridge, Mass.: Lincoln Institute of Land Policy, 1985.

Baerwald, Thomas J. "The Site Selection Process of Suburban Residential Builders." *Urban Geography* 2 (1981): 339–57.

Barnett, Jonathan. *The Fractured Metropolis: Improving the New City, Restoring the Old City, Reshaping the Region.* 1st ed. New York: IconEds., HarperCollins, 1995.

Bassett, Edward M., Katherine McNamara, and Russell Sage Foundation. *Zoning: The Laws, Administration, and Court Decisions During the First Twenty Years.* New York: Russell Sage Foundation, 1936.

Beaton W. Patrick. "The Impact of Reginal Land Use Controls on Property Value: The Case of the New Jersey Pinelands." *Land Economics* 67 (1991): 173–94.

Binkley, Clark. *Interceptor Sewers and Urban Sprawl.* Lexington, Mass.: Lexington Books, 1975.

Black J. Thomas, and James E. Hoben. "Land Price Inflation and Affordable Housing." *Urban Geography* 5 (1985): 27–47.

Boggs, H. Glenn, and Robert C. Apgar. "Concurrency and Growth Management: A Lawyer's Primer." *Journal of Land Use and Environmental Law* 7 (1991): 1–27.

Bosselman, Fred P., David L. Callies, and Council on Environmental Quality (U.S.). *The Quiet Revolution in Land Use Control.* Washington, D.C.: For sale by the Supt. of Docs., U.S. Government Printing Office, 1972.

Bosselman, Fred P., Duane A. Feurer, and Charles L. Siemon. *The Permit Explosion: Coordination of the Proliferation, Management & Control of Growth Series.* Washington, D.C.: Urban Land Institute, 1976.

Boulder, City of, Planning and Development Services Department, and Boulder County Land Use Department. "Boulder Valley Comprehensive Plan." 2001.

Bowyer, Robert A. "Capital Improvement Programs: Linking Budgeting and Planning." In *Planning Advisory Service*, 53. Chicago, Ill.: American Planning Association, 1993.

Brand, Daniel. "Research Needs for Analyzing the Impacts of Transportation Options on Urban Form and the Environment." In *Transportation, Urban Form and the Environment.* Washington, D.C.: Transportation Research Board, 1991.

Braybrooke, David, and Charles Edward Lindblom. *A Strategy of Decision: Policy Evaluation as a Social Process.* New York: Free Press of Glencoe, 1963.

Breen, Eleanor, Frank Costa, and William S. Hendon. "Annexation: An Economic Analysis: Whether a Small Village or Town Should Annex Adjacent Land Is a Cost/Revenue Problem." *American Journal of Economics and Sociology* 45, no. 2 (1986): 159–72.

Brower, David J. *Urban Growth Management through Development Timing.* New York: Praeger, 1976.

Brower, David J., David R. Godschalk and Douglas R. Porter. *Land, Growth & Politics.* Washington, D.C.: Planners Press American Planning Association, 1984.

Brower, David J., David R. Godschalk, and Douglas R. Porter, eds. *Understanding Growth Management: Critical Issues and a Research Agenda.* Washington, D.C.: Urban Land Institute, 1989.

Burchell, Robert W. "Fiscal Impact Analysis: State of the Art and State of the Practice." In *Financing Growth: Who Benefits? Who Pays? And How Much?*, edited by Susan G. Robinson. Washington, D.C.: Government Finance Research Center, 1990.

Burchell, Robert W., and David Listokin. *The Fiscal Impact Handbook: Estimating Local Costs and Revenues of Land Development.* New Brunswick, N.J.: Center for Urban Policy Research, 1978.

Burchell, Robert W., and Sanan Mukherji. "Conventional Development Versus the Costs of Sprawl." *American Journal of Public Health* 93, no. 9 (2003): 1,534–40.

Burrows, Lawrence B. *Growth Management: Issues, Techniques, and Policy Implications.* New Brunswick, N.J.: Center for Urban Policy Research, Rutgers University, 1977.

Callies, David L. "Dealing with Scarcity: Land Use and Planning." In *Politics and Public Policy in Hawaii*, edited by Zachary A. Smith and Richard C. Pratt. Albany, N.Y.: State University of New York Press, 1992.

———. *Regulating Paradise: Land Use Controls in Hawaii*. Honolulu, Hawaii: University of Hawaii Press, 1984.

Callies, David L., Nancy C. Neuffer, and Carlito Caliboso. "Ballot Box Zoning: Initiative, Referendum and the Law." *Washington University Journal of Urban and Contemporary Law* 39 (1991): 53–98.

Canty, Donald, Urban America (Organization), and National Committee on Urban Growth Policy. *The New City*. New York: Published for Urban America Inc., 1969.

Carson, John Michael, Goldie W. Rivkin, and Malcolm D.Rivkin. *Community Growth and Water Resources Policy*. New York: Praeger, 1973.

Caves, Roger W. *Land Use Planning: The Ballot Box Revolution, Sage Library of Social Research; V. 187*. Newbury Park, Calif.: Sage Publications, 1992.

Cervero, Robert. "Jobs-Housing Balance and Regional Mobility." *Journal of the American Planning Association* 55 (1989): 136–50.

Chinitz, Benjamin. "Growth Management: Good for the Town, Bad for the Nation?" *Journal of the American Planning Association* 56 (1990): 3–8.

Clawson, Marion. *Suburban Land Conversion in the United States: An Economic and Governmental Process*. Baltimore, Md.: Published for Resources for the Future by the Johns Hopkins Press, 1971.

Coe, Charles K. "Costs and Benefits of Municipal Annexation." *State and Local Government Review* 15 (1983): 44–47.

Commission on Population Growth and the American Future. "Population and the American Future." Washington, D.C.: Commission on Population Growth and the American Future, 1972.

Council of State Governments. "State Growth Management." Washington, D.C.: U.S. Department of Housing and Urban Development, 1976.

Council on Development Choices for the 80s. "Interim Report." Washington, D.C.: U.S. Department of Housing and Urban Development, 1980.

Daniels, Tom. *When City and Country Collide: Managing Growth on the Urban Fringe*. Washington, D.C.: Island Press, 1999.

DeGrove, John, ed. *Balanced Growth: A Planning Guide for Local Government*. Washington: International City Management Association, 1991.

de Haven-Smith, Lance. *Controlling Florida's Development*. Wakefield, N.H.: Hollowbrook Publishing, 1991.

Dekel, Gabriel P. "Housing Density: A Neglected Dimension of Fiscal Impact Analysis." *Urban Studies* 32, no. 6 (1995): 935–51.

de la Barra Tomas. *Integrated Land Use and Transport Modelling: Decision Chains and Hierarchies*. Edited by Leslie Martin and Lionel March, *Cambridge Urban and Architectural Series*. Cambridge, UK: Cambridge University Press, 1989.

Dowall, David E. "An Examination of Population-Growth-Managing Communities." *Policy Studies Journal* 9 (1980): 414–26.

———. *The Suburban Squeeze: Land Conversion and Regulation in the San Francisco Bay Area, California Series in Urban Development; [3]*. Berkeley, Calif.: University of California Press, 1984.

Downs, Anthony. "The Advisory Commission on Regulatory Barriers to Affordable Housing: Its Behavior and Accomplishments." *Housing Policy Debate* 2 (1991): 1,095–137.

―――. *New Visions for Metropolitan America.* Washington, D.C., and Cambridge, Mass.: Brookings Institution; Lincoln Institute of Land Policy, 1994.

―――. *Opening Up the Suburbs: An Urban Strategy for America.* New Haven, Conn.: Yale University Press, 1973.

―――. "The Real Problem with Suburban Anti-Growth Policies." *The Brookings Review* (1988).

Dubbink, David. "I'll Have My Town Medium Rural, Please." *Journal of the American Planning Association* 50 (1984): 406–18.

Dubbink, David [Theodore]. "Cosmopolitan Villages: Growth Management Planning and the Vision of Small Town Society." University of California, Los Angeles, 1983.

Easley V., Gail. "Staying Inside the Lines: Urban Growth Boundaries." In *Planning Advisory Service*, 30. Chicago: American Planning Association, 1992.

Ellickson, Robert C. "Suburban Growth Controls: An Economic and Legal Analysis." *Yale Law Journal* (1977): 86: 385.

Elliott, Michael. "The Impact of Growth Control Regulations on Housing Prices in California." *Journal of the American Real Estate and Urban Economics Association* 9 (1981): 115–33.

Environmental Impact Center Incorporated. "Secondary Impacts of Transportation and Wastewater Investments: Research Results." Washington, D.C.: Council on Environmental Quality, 1975.

Fagin, Henry. "Regulating the Timing of Urban Development." *Law and Contemporary Problems* 20, no. 2 (1955): 298–304.

Finkler, Earl. "Nongrowth as a Planning Alternative: A Preliminary Examination of an Emerging Issue." In *Planning Advisory Service*. Chicago, Ill.: American Society of Planning Officials, 1972.

―――. "Nongrowth: A Review of the Literature." In *Planning Advisory Service*. Chicago, Ill.: American Society of Planning Officials, 1973.

Finkler, Earl, and David Lee Peterson. *Nongrowth Planning Strategies: The Developing Power of Towns, Cities, and Regions.* New York: Praeger, 1974.

Fischel, William A. "Comment on Anthony Downs' "The Advisory Commission on Regulatory Barriers to Affordable Housing: Its Behavior and Accomplishments." *Housing Policy Debate* 2 (1991): 1139–60.

―――. *Do Growth Controls Matter? A Review of Empirical Evidence on the Effectiveness and Efficiency of Local Government Land Use Regulation.* Cambridge, Mass.: Lincoln Institute of Land Policy, 1990.

―――. *The Economics of Zoning Laws: A Property Rights Approach to American Land Use Controls.* Baltimore, Md.: John Hopkins University Press, 1985.

Fischel, William A., and Lincoln Institute of Land Policy. *Do Growth Controls Matter?: A Review of Empirical Evidence on the Effectiveness and Efficiency of Local Government Land Use Regulation.* Cambridge, Mass.: Lincoln Institute of Land Policy, 1989.

Fishman, Richard P. *Housing for All Under Law: New Directions in Housing, Land Use and Planning Law—A Report of the American Bar Association Advisory Commission on Housing and Urban Growth.* Cambridge, Mass.: Ballinger Publishing Company, 1978.

Florida Department of Community Affairs. "Techniques for Discouraging Sprawl." In *Balance Growth: A Planning Guide for Local Government*, edited by John Melvin DeGrove, 36–41. Washington, D.C.: International City Management Association, 1991.

Frank, James E. *The Costs of Alternative Development Patterns: A Review of the Literature.* Washington, D.C.: Urban Land Institute, 1989.

Frank, James E., and Robert M. Rhodes, eds. *Development Exactions.* Chicago, Ill.: Planners Press, 1987.

Franklin, Herbert M. *Controlling Urban Growth—but for Whom?* Washington, D.C.: The Urban Institute, 1973.

Freilich, Robert H., and Michael M. Schultz. *Model Subdivision Regulations: Planning and Law—A Complete Ordinance and Annotated Guide to Planning Practice and Legal Requirements.* 2nd ed. Chicago, Ill.: Planners Press, 1995.

Frug, Gerald E. *City Making: Building Communities without Building Walls.* Princeton, N.J.: Princeton University Press, 1999.

Fuguitt, Glenn V., Paul R. Voss, and J.C. Doherty. *Growth and Change in Rural America.* 7 vols. Vol. 7, *Management and Control of Growth.* Washington, D.C.: Urban Land Institute, 1979.

Fulton, William. "The Second Revolution in Land Use Planning." In *Balanced Growth: A Planning Guide for Local Government,* edited by John Melvin DeGrove, 116–24. Washington, D.C.: International City Management Association, 1991.

Fulton, William, and Ted Mondale. "Managing Metropolitan Growth: Reflections on the Twin Cities Experience." In *Case Study.* Washington, D.C.: Brookings Institution, 2003.

Garreau, Joel. *Edge City: Life on the New Frontier.* 1st ed. New York: Doubleday, 1991.

Gilmore, J. S., and Mary K. Duff. *Boom Town Growth Management: A Case Study of Rock Springs—Green River, Wyoming.* Boulder, Colo.: Westview Press, 1975.

Glaeser, Edward L., and Joseph Gyourko. "Affordable Housing and the Housing Market: The Impact of Building Restrictions on Housing Affordability." *Federal Reserve Board of New York Economic Policy Review* (2003): 21–39.

Gleeson, Michael E. "Effects of an Urban Growth Management System on Land Values." *Land Economics* 55 (1979): 350–65.

Gleeson, Michael E., Ian Traquair Ball, Stephen P. Chinn, Robert C. Einsweiler, Robert H. Freilich, and Patric Meagher. *Urban Growth Management Systems. Planning Advisory Service.* RPT. No. 309–10, Chicago, Ill.: American Society of Planning Officials, 1975.

Glickfeld, Madelyn, and Ned Levine. *Regional Growth—Local Reaction: The Enactment and Effects of Local Growth Control and Management Measures in California.* Cambridge, Mass.: Lincoln Institute of Land Policy, 1992.

Godschalk, David R. *Constitutional Issues of Growth Management.* Rev. ed. Washington, D.C.: Planners Press, 1979.

Goldberg, Michael A., and Daniel D. Ulinder. "Residents Developer Behavior 1975: Additional Empirical Findings." *Land Economics* 52 (1976): 363–70.

Gonzalez, Rodolfo A., and Stephen L. Mehay. "Municipal Annexation and Local Monopoly Power." *Public Choice* 57 (1987): 245–55.

Greenberg, Douglas Andrew. "Growth and Conflict at the Surburban Fringe: The Case of the Livermore-Amador Valley." Ph.D. diss., University of California, 1986.

Grogan, Paul S., and Tony Proscio. *Comeback Cities: A Blueprint for Urban Neighborhood Revival.* Boulder, Colo.: Westview Press, 2000.

Groves, Jeremy R., and Eric Helland. "Zoning and the Distribution of Location Rents: An Empirical Analysis of Harris County, Texas." *Land Economics* 78, no. 1 (2002): 28–44.

Hanson, Mark E. "Automobile Subsidies and Land Use: Estimates and Policy Responses." *Journal of the American Planning Association* 58 (1991): 60–71.

Healy, Robert G., John S. Rosenberg, and Resources for the Future. *Land Use and the States*. 2d ed. Baltimore, Md.: Published for Resources for the Future by the Johns Hopkins University Press, 1979.

Heeter, David, and American Society of Planning Officials. *Toward a More Effective Land Use Guidance System: A Summary and Analysis of Five Major Reports*. Chicago, Ill.: American Society of Planning Officials, 1969.

Hepner, Geroge F. "An Analysis of Residential Developer Location Factors in a Fast Growth Urban Region." *Urban Geography* 4 (1983): 355–63.

Howard, Ebenezer, and Frederic James Osborn. *Garden Cities of Tomorrow*. Cambridge, Mass.: M.I.T. Press, 1965.

Howe, Deborah A., and William A. Rabiega. "Beyond Strips and Centers: The Ideal Commercial Form." *Journal of the American Planning Association* 58 (1992): 213–19.

Hudnut, William H., and Urban Land Institute. *Cities on the Rebound: A Vision for Urban America*. Washington, D.C.: The Urban Land Institute, 1998.

Hughes, James W. *New Dimensions of Urban Planning: Growth Controls, New Dimensions of Urban Planning Series, vol. 1*. New Brunswick: Center for Urban Policy Research, Rutgers—The State University of New Jersey, 1974.

Innes, Judith. "Group Processes and the Social Construction of Growth Management: The Cases of Florida, Vermont and New Jersey." In *Institute of Urban and Regional Development Working Paper Series*. Berkeley, Calif.: Institute of Urban and Regional Development, 1991.

———. "Implementing State Growth Management in the U.S.: Strategies for Coordination." In *Institute of Urban and Regional Development Working Paper Series*. Berkeley, Calif.: Institute of Urban and Regional Development, 1991.

International City Management Association, and Smart Growth Network. "Getting to Smart Growth II: 100 More Policies For." Washington, D.C.: Smart Growth Network/ International City Management Association, 2003.

Irwin, Elena G. "The Effects of Open Space on Residential Property Values." *Land Economics* 78, no. 4 (2002): 465–80.

James Duncan and Associates Inc., and Eric Damian Kelly. "Adequate Public Facilities Study for Montgomery County, Maryland." Austin, Tex.: James Duncan and Associates, Inc., 1991.

———. "Technical Appendix to Adequate Public Facilities Study for Montgomery County, Maryland." Austin, Tex.: James Duncan and Associates Inc., 1991.

James Duncan and Associates Inc., Van Horn-Gray Associates Inc., Ivey Bennet Harris and Walls, and Wade-Trim Inc. "The Search for Efficient Urban Growth Patterns: A Study of the Fiscal Impacts of Development in Florida." Tallahassee, Fla.: Florida Department of Community Affairs, 1989.

———. "The Search for Efficient Urban Growth Patterns: Technical Appendices." Tallahassee, Fla.: Florida Department of Community Affairs, 1989.

Jandl, H. Ward, John A. Burns, and Michael Auer. *Yesterday's Houses of Tomorrow: Innovative American Homes, 1850 to 1950*. Washington, D.C.: Preservation Press, 1991.

Johnson, Arthur T. "Intergovernmental Influences on Local Land Use Decisions." Washington, D.C.: National League of Cities, 1989.

Johnson, Denny, Patricia E. Salkin, and Jason Jordan. "State of the States: A Survey of State Planning Reforms and Smart Growth Measures in Order to Manage Growth and

Development." Edited by Denny Johnson, 150. Chicago, Ill.: American Planning Association, 2002.

Jones, E. Terrence. *The Metropolitan Chase: Politics and Policies in Urban America.* Upper Saddle River, N.J.: Prentice-Hall, 2003.

"The Journey to Work: Relation Between Employment and Residence." In *Planning Advisory Service.* Chicago, Ill.: American Society of Planning Officials, 1951.

Kaiser, Edward John, David R. Godschalk, and F. Stuart Chapin. *Urban Land Use Planning.* 4th ed. Urbana, Ill.: University of Illinois Press, 1995.

Katz, Bruce. *Reflections on Regionalism.* Bruce Katz, Editor; Foreword by Al Gore. Washington, D.C.: Brookings Institution Press, 2000.

Kelly, Eric D. *Planning, Growth, and Public Facilities: A Primer for Local Officials, Planning Advisory Service Report No. 447.* Chicago, Ill.: American Planning Association, Planning Advisory Service, 1993.

Kelly, Eric Damian, and Barbara Becker. *Community Planning: An Introduction to the Comprehensive Plan.* Washington, D.C.: Island Press, 2000.

Kelly, Eric Damian. "Piping Growth, the Law, Equity and Economics of Sewer & Water Connection Policies." *Land Use Law & Zoning Digest* 36, no. 7 (1984): 3–7.

———. "Planning v. Democracy." *Land Use Law & Zoning Digest* 38, no. 7 (1986): 3–6.

———, ed. *Zoning and Land Use Controls.* Supplemented to date. ed. 10 vols. New York: Matthew Bender & Company, 2003.

Kendig, Lane, and Susan Connor. *Performance Zoning.* Washington, D.C.: Planners Press American Planning Association, 1980.

Ketcham, Paul, and Scot Siegel. "Managing Growth to Promote Affordable Housing: Revisiting Oregon's Goal 10." Portland, Ore.: 1000 Friends of Oregon, 1991.

Knaap, G.J., Arthur C. Nelson, and Lincoln Institute of Land Policy. *The Regulated Landscape: Lessons on State Land Use Planning from Oregon.* Cambridge, Mass.: Lincoln Institute of Land Policy, 1992.

Knaap, Gerrit. "The Price Effects of Urban Growth Boundaries in Metropolitan Portland, Oregon." *Land Economics* 61 (1985): 26–35.

Knaap, Gerrit J., Ed. 2001. *Land Market Monitoring for Smart Urban Growth.* Cambridge: Lincoln Inst. of Land Policy.

Krasnowiecki, Jan. "Model Land Use and Development Planning Code." In *Final Report: Legislative Recommendations*, edited by Maryland. Planning and Zoning Law Study Commission, 53–122. Baltimore, Md.: Colony Press, 1969.

Kunstler, James Howard. *The Geography of Nowhere: The Rise and Decline of America's Man-Made Landscape.* New York: Simon & Schuster, 1993.

Land Use Planning Committee, ed. *Planning and Zoning for Better Resource Use.* Ankeny, Iowa: Soil Conservation Society of America, 1971.

Landis, John D. "Do Growth Controls Work? A New Assessment." In *Institute of Urban and Regional Development Working Paper.* Berkeley, Calif.: Institute of Urban and Regional Development, 1991.

———. "Land Regulation and the Price of New Housing." *Journal of the American Planning Association* 52 (1986): 9–21.

Le Gates, Richard T., and Sean Nikas. "Growth Control through Residential Tempo Controls in the San Francisco Bay Area." In *San Francisco State University Public Research Institute Working Paper Series.* San Francisco, 1989.

Leach, James. "A Homebuilder Looks at Boulder's Growth Controls." In *Growth Management: Keeping on Target?* Edited by Douglas R. Porter. Washington, D.C.: Urban Land Institute, 1986.

Lewis, Sylvia. "The Town That Said No to Sprawl." In *Balanced Growth: A Planning Guide for Local Government.* Edited by John Melvin DeGrove. Washington, D.C.: International City Management Association, 1990.

Loke, Evelina T., ed. *Homeownership: The American Dream Adrift.* Chicago, Ill.: U.S. League of Savings Associations, 1982.

Lucas, Therese E. "The Direct Costs of Growth: A Comparison of Changes in Local Government Expenditure in Growth and Non-Growth Counties in Colorado." Denver, Colo.: Colorado Land Use Commission, 1974.

Mackay, Charles. *Extraordinary Popular Delusions and the Madness of Crowds.* Boston, Mass.: L.C. Page, 1956: reprint of the 1852 ed.; originally published 1841 under title *Memoirs of Extraordinary Popular Delusions.*

Mandelker, Daniel R. *The Zoning Dilemma: A Legal Strategy for Urban Change.* Indianapolis, Ind.: Bobbs-Merrill, 1971.

Maryland Planning and Zoning Law Study Commission. "Legislative Recommendations: Final Report." Baltimore, Md.: Colony Press, Inc., 1969.

Maryland. Department of Housing and Community Development. *Smart Codes.* Maryland Department of Housing and Community Development, 2003 [cited November 2003]. Available from www.dhcd.state.md.us/smartcodes/index.asp.

Maryland Governor's Office of Smart Growth. *The Maryland Tool Box.* Maryland. Office of the Governor, 2003 [cited November 2003]. Available from www.smartgrowth.state.md.us/tool%20box.pdf.

———. *Smart Growth.* Maryland Office of the Governor, 2003 [cited November 2003]. Available from www.smartgrowth.state.md.us/.

McHarg, Ian L. *Design with Nature.* 25th anniversary ed. New York: J. Wiley, 1994.

Meadows, Donella H., and Club of Rome. *The Limits to Growth: A Report for the Club of Rome's Project on the Predicament of Mankind.* New York: Universe Books, 1972.

Meck, Stuart. "Growing Smart Users Guide." Chicago, Ill.: American Planning Association, 2002.

———, ed. *Growing Smart Legislative Guidebook: Model Statutes for Planning and the Management of Change.* Chicago, Ill.: American Planning Association, 2002.

Mill, John Stuart. *On Liberty.* 1986 trade paperback ed. Buffalo, N.Y.: Prometheus Books, 1859.

Miller, Thomas I. "Must Growth Restrictions Eliminate Moderate-Priced Housing?" *Journal of the American Planning Association* 52 (1986): 319–25.

Moe, Richard, and Carter Wilkie. *Changing Places: Rebuilding Community in the Age of Sprawl.* 1st ed. New York: Henry Holt & Co., 1997.

Montgomery County Planning Board. "Annual Growth Policy for Montgomery County, 2003." Silver Spring, Md.: Maryland National Capital Park and Planning Commission, 2002.

———. "First Annual Growth Policy Report: Framework for Action." Silver Spring, Md.: Maryland-National Capital Park and Planning Commission, 1974.

Mukherjee, Avijit, Eugene R. Russell, and E. Dean Landman. "Building a Travel Demand Model for a Small City." *Transportation Quarterly* 55, no. 4 (2001): 105–21.

Muller, Thomas. *Fiscal Impacts of Land Development: A Critique of Methods and Review of Issues.* Washington, D.C.: The Urban Institute, 1975.

Mumphrey, Anthony J. Jr., John Wildgen, and Louise Williams. "Annexation and Incorporation: Alternative Strategies for Municipal Development." New Orleans: University of New Orleans College of Urban & Public Affairs, 1990.

Myers, Dowell. "The Ecology of 'Quality of Life' and Urban Growth." In *Understanding Growth Management: Critical Issues and a Research Agenda.* Edited by David J. Brower, David R. Godschalk, and Douglas R. Porter. Washington, D.C.: Urban Land Institute, 1989.

Myers, Phyllis. "So Goes Vermont." Washington, D.C.: The Conservation Foundation, 1974.

———. "Zoning Hawaii." *Environmental Comment,* July 1976, 17–20.

"National Agricultural Lands Study: Final Report." Washington, D.C.: National Agricultural Lands Study, 1981.

National Association of Home Builders. *Smart Growth Policy* National Association of Home Builders, June 13, 2003 [cited 2003 November]. Available from www.nahb.org/generic.aspx?sectionID=636&genericContentID=3519.

Nelson, Arthur C. "Oregon's Urban Growth Boundary Policy as a Landmark Planning Tool." In *Planning the Oregon Way: A Twenty-Year Evaluation.* Edited by Carl Abbott, Deborah A. Howe, and Sy Adler. Corvallis: Oregon State University Press, 1994, 2548.

———. *System Development Charges for Water, Wastewater, and Stormwater Facilities.* Boca Raton, Fla.: CRC Press, 1995.

Nelson, Arthur C., and American Planning Association. *Development Impact Fees: Policy Rationale, Practice, Theory, and Issues.* Chicago, Ill.: Planners Press, American Planning Association, 1988.

Nelson, Arthur C., and James B. Duncan. *Growth Management Principles and Practices.* Chicago, Ill., and Washington, D.C.: Planners Press, American Planning Association, 1995.

New Jersey County and Municipal Government Study Commission. "Housing & Suburbs: Fiscal & Social Impact of Multifamily Development." Trenton, N.J.: County and Municipal Government Study Commission, 1974.

Newman, Peter, and Jeffrey R. Kenworthy. *Cities and Automobile Dependence: A Sourcebook.* Aldershot, England, and Brookfield, Vt.: Gower Technical, 1989.

Nicholas, James C. "Growth Management and Smart Growth in Florida." *Wake Forest Law Review* 35, no. 3 (2000): 645–71.

Niebanck, Paul L. "Conclusion: The Second Generation of Growth Management." In *Growth Management: Keeping on Target?* Edited by Douglas R. Porter. Washington, D.C.: Urban Land Institute, 1986.

———. "Growth Controls and the Production of Inequality." In *Understanding Growth Management: Critical Issues and a Research Agenda.* Edited by David J. Brower, David R. Godschalk, and Douglas R. Porter. Washington, D.C.: Urban Land Institute, 1989.

Ohls, James C., and David Pines. "Discontinuous Urban Development and Economic Efficiency." *Land Economics* 51 (1975): 224–34.

Orfield, Myron. *Metropolitics: A Regional Agenda for Community and Stability.* Washington, D.C., and Cambridge, Mass.: Brookings Institution Press; Lincoln Institute of Land Policy, 1997.

Peiser, Richard B. "Density and Urban Sprawl." *Land Economics* 65 (1989): 193–204.

———. "Does It Pay to Plan Suburban Growth." *Journal of the American Planning Association* 50 (1984): 419–33.

Pelham, Thomas G. "Adequate Public Facilities Requirements: Reflections on Florida's Concurrency System for Managing Growth." *Florida State University Law Review* 19, no. 4 (1992): 973–1052.

Peterson, Craig A., and Clare McCarthy. "Farmland Preservation by Purchase of Development Rights: The Long Island Experiment." *De Paul Law Review* 26 (1977): 447–91.

Pierce, Lawrence W. Chip, and Kenneth L Rust. "Government Enterprises." In *Local Government Finance: Concepts and Practices*, edited by John E Petersen and Dennis R Strachota. Washington, D.C.: Government Finance Officers Association, 1991.

Pivo, Gary. "The Net of Mixed Beads: Suburban Office Development in Six Metropolitan Regions." *Journal of the American Planning Association* 56 (1990): 457–69.

Pivo, Gary, Robert Small, and Charles R. Wolfe. "Rural Cluster Zoning: Survey and Guidelines." *Land Use Law & Zonnig Digest* 42, no. 9 (1990): 3–10.

Pollakowski, Henry O., and Susan M. Wachter. "The Effects of Land Use Constraints on Housing Prices." *Land Economics* 66 (1990): 315–24.

Popper, Frank. *The Politics of Land Use Reform*. Madison, Wis.: University of Wisconsin Press, 1981.

Porter, Douglas R. *Growth Management: Keeping on Target?, Lincoln Institute Monograph; #86-1*. Washington, D.C.: The Urban Land Institute, in association with Lincoln Institute of Land Policy, 1986.

―――. "Regional Governance of Metropolitan Form: The Missing Link in Relating Land Use and Transportation." In *Transportation, Urban Form and the Environment: Proceedings of a Conference*. Washington: Transportation Research Board, 1991, 63–80.

Rahenkamp, John. "Boroughing Isn't Boring." *Pennsylvania Planner* 46 (1991): 1.

Rahenkamp, Sachs, Wells & Associates, and American Society of Planning Officials. "Innovative Zoning: A Digest of the Literature." Washington, D.C.: U.S. Department of Housing and Urban Development, 1977.

―――. "Innovative Zoning: A Local Official's Guidebook." Washington, D.C.: U.S. Department of Housing and Urban Development, 1977.

Real Estate Research Corp. "The Costs of Sprawl: Environmental and Economic Costs of Alternative Residential Development Patterns at the Urban Fringe." Washington, D.C.: U.S. Council on Environmental Quality, 1974.

Research Division. Urban Land Institute, and Gruen Gruen + Associates. "Effects of Regulation on Housing Costs: Two Case Studies." In *ULI Research Reports*. Edited by Donald E. Priest. Washington, D.C.: Urban Land Institute, 1977.

Rice Center for Community Design & Research. "Technical Report: The Delay Costs of Government Regulation in the Houston Housing Market." Houston, Tex.: Rice University, 1978.

Robinson, Susan G., ed. *Financing Growth: Who Benefits? Who Pays? And How Much?* Washington, D.C.: Government Finance Research Center, 1990.

Rosenbaum, Nelson. *Land Use and the Legislatures*. Washington, D.C.: Urban Institute, 1976.

Rothblatt, Donald N., and Andrew Sancton. *Metropolitan Governance: American/Canadian Intergovernmental Perspectives, North American Federalism Project; V. 1*. Berkeley, Calif.: Institute of Governmental Studies Press, University of California, 1993.

Rusk, David. *Cities without Suburbs.* 2nd ed, *Woodrow Wilson Center Special Studies.* Washington, D.C., and Baltimore, Md.: Woodrow Wilson Center Press; Distributed by Johns Hopkins University Press, 1995.

————. *Inside Game/Outside Game: Winning Strategies for Saving Urban America.* Washington, D.C.: Brookings Institution, 1999.

Rust, Edgar. *No Growth: Impacts on Metropolitan Areas.* Lexington, Mass.: Lexington Books, 1975.

Schnidman, Frank, and Jane Silverman. *Management & Control of Growth: Updating the Law.* Five vols. Vol. V. Washington, D.C.: Urban Land Institute, 1980.

Schnidman, Frank, Jane A. Silverman, and Rufus D. Young, Jr., eds. *Management & Control of Growth: Techniques in Application.* Four vols. Vol. 4, *Management & Control of Growth.* Washington, D.C.: Urban Land Institute, 1978.

Schwartz, Seymour I., David E. Hansen, and Richard Green. "The Effect of Growth Control on the Production of Moderate-Priced Housing." *Land Economics* 60 (1984): 110–14.

Schwartz, Seymour I., Peter M. Zorn, and David E. Hansen. "Research Design Issues and Pitfalls in Growth Control Studies." *Land Economics* 62 (1986): 224–33.

Scott, Mel. *American City Planning Since 1890: A History Commemorating the Fiftieth Anniversary of the American Institute of Planners.* Berkeley, Calif.: University of California Press, 1969.

Scott, Randall W., David J. Brower, Dallas D. Miner, and Urban Land Institute. *Management & Control of Growth: Issues, Techniques, Problems, Trends.* Washington, D.C.: Urban Land Institute, 1975.

Seidel, Stephen R., and Rutgers University. Center for Urban Policy Research. *Housing Costs & Government Regulations: Confronting the Regulatory Maze.* New Brunswick, N.J.: Center for Urban Policy Research, 1978.

Sengstock, Frank S. *Annexation: A Solution to the Metropolitan Area Problem.* Reprint of 1960 Edition published by University of Michigan Law School ed. Buffalo, N.Y.: William S. Hein & Co., 1960.

Singell, Larry D., and Jane H. Lillydahl. "An Empirical Examination of the Effect of Impact Fees on the Housing Market." *Land Economics* 66 (1990): 82–92.

Smart Growth Network. *Principles of Smart Growth.* Smart Growth Network, 2003 [cited 2003 November]. Available from www.smartgrowth.org/about/principles/default.asp.

So, Frank, and Judith Getzels, eds. *The Practice of Local Government Planning.* 2nd ed. Washington, D.C.: International City Management Association, 1988.

Speir, Cameron, and Kurt Stephenson. "Does Sprawl Cost Us All? Isolating the Effects of Housing Patterns on Public Water and Sewer Costs." *Journal of the American Planning Association* 68, no. 1 (2002): 56–70.

Spengler, Edwin H. *Land Values in New York in Relation to Transit Facilities.* New York and London: Columbia University Press; P. S. King & Son, Ltd., 1930.

Strong, Ann L. *Land Banking: European Reality, American Prospect, Johns Hopkins Studies in Urban Affairs.* Baltimore, Md.: Johns Hopkins University Press, 1979.

————. *Private Property and the Public Interest: The Brandywine Experience, Johns Hopkins Studies in Urban Affairs.* Baltimore, Md.: Johns Hopkins University Press, 1975.

————. "Vermont's Act 250 and Prime Farmland." Philadelphia, Pa.: Regional Science Research Institute (University of Pennsylvania), 1977.

Szold, Terry S., Armando Carbonell, and Lincoln Institute of Land Policy. *Smart Growth: Form and Consequences.* Cambridge, Mass.: Lincoln Institute of Land Policy, 2002.

Tabors, Richard D., Michael H. Shapiro, and Peter P. Rogers. *Land Use and the Pipe: Planning for Sewerage.* Lexington, Mass.: Lexington Books, 1976.

Task Force on Housing Costs. "Final Report." Washington, D.C.: U.S. Department of Housing and Urban Development, 1978.

Tiebout, Charles M. "A Pure Theory of Local Expenditures." *The Journal of Political Economy* 64 (1956): 416–24.

United States Deptartment of Commerce. Advisory Committee on City Planning and Zoning. *A Standard City Planning Enabling Act by the Advisory Committee on City Planning and Zoning Appointed by Secretary Hoover.* Washington, D.C.: U.S. Government Printing Office, 1928.

————. *A Standard State Zoning Enabling Act under Which Municipalities May Adopt Zoning Regulations.* Rev. ed. Washington, D.C.: Government Printing Office, 1926.

United States General Accounting Office, Staff of the. "Land Use Issues." Washington, D.C.: U.S. General Accounting Office, 1978.

Urban Land Institute. *Smart Growth* Urban Land Institute, 2003 [cited 2003 November]. Available from smartgrowth.net/Home/sg_Home_fst.html.

Urban Systems Research & Engineering, Inc. "The Growth Shapers: The Land Use Impacts of Infrastructure Investments." Washington, D.C.: U.S. Council on Environmental Quality, 1976.

Wakeford, Richard. *American Development Control: Parallels and Paradoxes from an English Perspective.* London: Her Majesty's Stationery Office, 1990.

Walker, Donald V.H. "Boulder Preserves Open Space." In *Growth Management: Techniques in Application.* Edited by Frank Schnidman, Jane Silverman and Rufus D. Young, Jr. Washington, D.C.: Urban Land Institute, 1978, 147–50.

Warner, Sam B., Jr. *Street Car Suburbs: The Process of Growth in Boston, 1870–1900, Publications of the Joint Center for Urban Studies.* Cambridge, Mass.: Harvard University Press, M.I.T. Press , 1962.

Washington State Growth Strategies Commission. "A Growth Strategy for Washington State." Olympia: Washington Department of Community Development, 1990.

Watkins, Andrew R. "Impacts of Land Development Charges." *Land Economics* 75, no. 3 (1999): 415–24.

Weitz, J. "CPL Bibliography 355/356/357: From Quiet Revolution to Smart Growth: State Growth Management Programs, 1960 to 1999." *Journal of Planning Literature* 14, no. 2, (1999): 267–338.

Weitz, Jerry. *Sprawl Busting: State Programs to Guide Growth.* Chicago, Ill.: American Planning Association, 1999.

Westminster, City of. "Growth Management Plan: Phase II Report." Westminster, Colo.: City of Westminster, 1978.

————. "[Untitled Working Documents on Growth Management] A, B, C and D." Westminster, Colo.: City of Westminster, 1978.

Whyte, William Hollingsworth. *Securing Open Spaces for Urban America: Conservation Easements.* Washington, D.C.: Urban Land Institute, 1959.

————. "Urban Sprawl." In *The Exploding Metropolis.* Edited by the Editors of *Fortune Magazine,* 114–39. New York: Doubleday & Co., 1958.

Williams, Norman. *American Land Planning Law: Cases and Materials*. New Brunswick, N.J.: Center for Urban Policy Research, Rutgers University, 1978.

Williamson, Thad, David Imbroscio, and Gar Alperovitz. *Making a Place for Community: Local Democracy in a Global Era*. New York and London: Routledge, 2002.

Windsor, Duane. "A Critique of *The Costs of Sprawl*." *Journal of the American Planning Association* 45 (1979): 279–92.

Wingo, Lowdon. *Transportation and Urban Land*. New York: AMS Press, 1983.

Witt, John W., and Janis Sammartino. "Facility Financing in the 1990s: The Second Step in Urban Growth Management." *Washington University Journal of Urban and Contemporary Law* 38 (1990): 115–55.

Yaro, Robert. "Growing and Governing Smart: A Case Study of the New York Region." In *Reflections on Regionalism*. Edited by Bruce Katz, 43–77. Washington, D.C.: The Brookings Institution, 2000.

Yokley, E. C. *The Law of Subdivisions*. Charlottesville, Va.: Michie Co., 1963.

York, Marie L. "Boca Raton's Changing Approach." In *Growth Management: Keeping on Target?* Edited by Douglas R. Porter, 45–52. Washington, D.C.: Urban Land Institute, 1986.

Young, Tobias. "Infill Likely as Petaluma Growth Confined." *Press Democrat*, June 13 1999.

Index

Adequate public facilities programs, 21, 44–48, 111–12; effects, 138, 163; evaluation, 223–25; examples, 44–48, 111–12

Adirondack Park, New York, protection of, 160

Advisory Commission on Regulatory Barriers to Affordable Housing, 193–94, 196

Agricultural lands, protection of, 108–10, 111–13. *See also* Sensitive lands

Airports, relationship to location of development, 94

Alonso, William, 83–84

Amador Valley, California, growth in, 140. *See also* Livermore, Pleasanton

American Institute of Planners, 105

American Law Institute (Model Land Development Code), 34–35

American Planning Association, 34, 38–39, 66. *See also* American Society of Planning Officials [predecessor organization]

American Society of Planning Officials, 34–38, 66. *See also* Growing Smart

Annexation of territory: evaluation, 222; relationship to growth management, 77–80, 164

APA. *See* American Planning Association

Arkansas, state law regulating development, 16

ASPO. *See* American Society of Planning Officials

Big Cypress Area, Florida, protection of, 115

Boca Raton, Florida, growth cap in, 38

Boston, built on formerly wet areas, 160; metropolitan area location of development, 81–82

Boulder, Colorado, 1–2; greenbelt, 95–98; (map, Fig. 5.3, 97); housing mix, 108–12 (tbl. 10-4, 209); mountain backdrop, 52, 164–65; population trends, 1–2, 57–58 (tbl. 4-2, 58), 196 (fig. 10.2, 198; tbls. 10-5, 10-6, 211), 220–21 (tbl. 11-2, 221); rate-of-growth program, 1–2, 55–59, 60, 152, 170–71, 220; suit over sewer service outside city, 94, 171; urban growth boundary, 52–53

Boulder County, Colorado, growth trends compared to City of Boulder (tbls. 4-2,

About the Author

Eric Damian Kelly is a land-use attorney and planner who has worked with local governments and planning commissions in many states. He is a specialist in the regulation of signs, sexually oriented businesses, and cell towers. Kelly is a former dean of the College of Architecture and Urban Planning at Ball State University in Muncie, Indiana.